THE FORGOTTEN QUARTERBACK

REMEMBERING THE UNHERALDED HEROES BEHIND CENTER

ALPHA GEEK PUBLISHING

DEDICATED TO MY FAVORITE QB
RYKER ROHALEY

FOREWORD BY CHRIS MILLER

The quarterback is the hardest yet most rewarding position in all of sports. It has given me a great life, rewarding me with many close friends, and has simultaneously cursed me with a lifetime of aches and pains. But I wouldn't trade all the aches for a single day of it. Football isn't just a way of life, it is life for a quarterback. This position takes on a life of its own and consumes you, and you either embrace it and accept the challenge or you will be defeated before you begin. It is all or nothing, and unlike many things in life, you cannot succeed at this position on talent alone without a lifelong plan of sacrifice and dedication.

I was very fortunate to have the opportunity to play in the

FOREWORD BY CHRIS MILLER

NFL and grew up surrounded with support that helped me succeed and chase my dream. Although I suffered many injuries and had to retire before my time was up, I appreciate every second that I got to play at the professional level. I met so many quarterbacks on my journey who were incredible athletes and men, and I'm still friends with many of them. Not all of them got the opportunities that they earned; whether it was due to unfortunate injuries, coaching changes, an overload of talent at the position so that they may have been overlooked, or simply bad luck, I know that had they gotten the chances to prove themselves, they could have been mentioned among the greats of the game.

Players always talk about what they learned from their coaches, and I, too, have had some great teachers. But what isn't discussed nearly enough is what quarterbacks learn from their counterparts. Competition is tough, but bonds and brotherhoods develop when you are in meeting rooms, locker rooms, practices, and even on golf courses with these same couple guys day in and day out. When you compete together, you all learn from each other and pick up skills and traits along the way without even realizing it at the time. I would not have been the quarterback that I was without the help of the other quarterback brothers around me. The fans may not remember all the backup quarterbacks' names, but I remember every single one.

And that is exactly why I love this book that Chris 51 wrote. Finally, a book that pays homage to those quarterbacks behind the scenes who gave their all to win games for their team without the reward of big money or notoriety. This book perfectly describes the sacrifice that so many have made, losing

FOREWORD BY CHRIS MILLER

family time and sacrificing their bodies for years on end, for just a chance at one moment in the sun. This book is for the men who never gave up on their dream.

I was teammates with several players featured in this book. I loved seeing my friends Bill Musgrave, Hugh Millen, Steve Dills, and others acknowledged herein because they deserve it. I miss those guys, and I miss being behind center. I may be done playing a quarterback, but I will never be done being a quarterback.

— Chris Miller

Growing up in Eugene, Oregon, and attending Sheldon High School, where I constantly saw all his trophies in glass cases by the gym, Chris Miller was not just a local hero, but my personal quarterback hero too. Then, when I started this book, he was my one and only choice to write the foreword, and I wouldn't take no for an answer. Not that I had to, because Miller is the most gracious person I know, and he happily wanted to help out. His support was invaluable, and not only in writing the foreword, but also for reaching out to his several friends and colleagues who are featured in this book. Miller is one of a kind.

— Chris 51

Chris Miller was a three-sport star in high school, excelling at baseball, basketball, and football. After rewriting Sheldon High School's gridiron record books in Eugene, Oregon, Chris Miller decided to stay near home and accepted a scholarship from the University of Oregon. Miller had grown up so close to Oregon's Autzen Stadium that he could walk there from his parents' house. The hometown hero quickly became a national hero as he began hunting down the Ducks' records.

Miller was the regular starter by his sophomore year in 1984 and ended his junior season near the top in every Pac-10 passing category, including a division-leading 18 touchdowns. Miller closed out his senior campaign completing

over 60 percent of his passes to establish himself as one of the nation's top quarterbacks and earning several coaches' votes for Heisman Trophy candidacy.

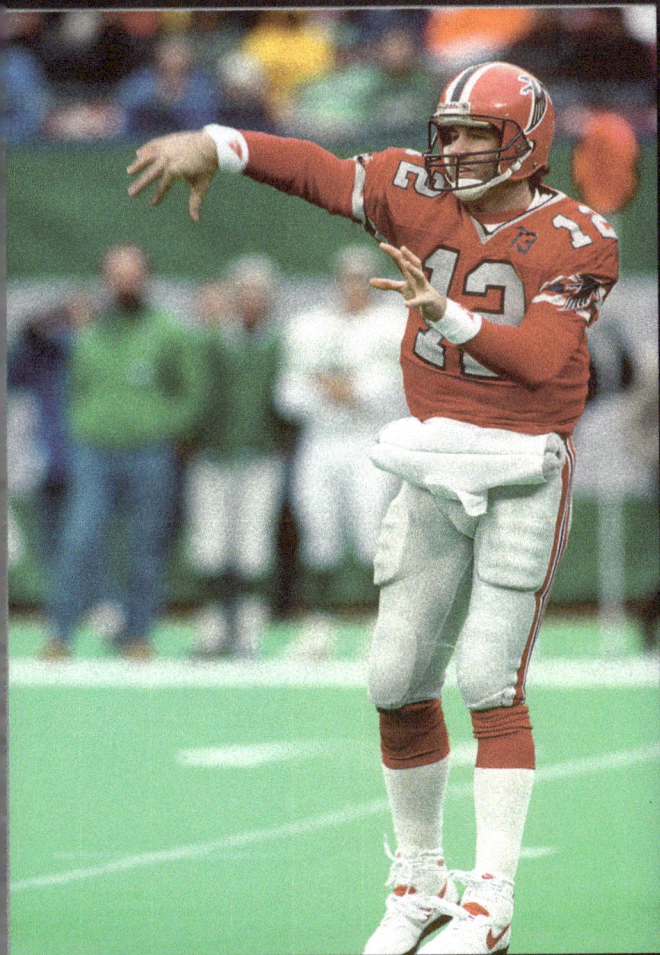

Miller was the Atlanta Falcons' no. 1 pick in the 1987 NFL Draft and the third quarterback chosen, behind Vinny Testaverde and Kelly Stouffer. The NFL strike took hold and severely cut down on Miller's playing time his rookie season, but Miller immediately captured the starting role the following year. He swiftly proved his high draft worth by passing for 2,133 yards and 11 touchdowns. In 1989, only his second full season, Miller already looked a polished veteran, settling himself in among the league elite with his 3,459 yards passing and 16 touchdowns and leading the NFL with a 1.9 percent interception ratio. In 1991 Miller had the best season of his career after passing for over 3,000 yards and 26 touchdowns, earning Pro Bowl honors. He continued with Atlanta for a couple more seasons before signing with the Rams. Even battling through injuries, Miller had a pair of great seasons in St. Louis before forced him to retire at his prime in 1996.

Three years later in 1999, Chris Miller made a comeback with Denver. After leading the Broncos to a pair of wins in his three starts, Miller suffered another concussion and retired for good. His time as a player drew to a close, but the rest of his career had only just begin.

Miller returned home to Oregon in 2001 to begin his coaching career as South Eugene High School's head coach, where he remained until 2006. He retuned to the NFL in 2009, taking a quarterbacks coach position with the Arizona Cardinals, where he trained future Hall of Famer Kurt Warner. Miller returned to Oregon a few years later as West Linn High School's head coach from 2014 to 2019. Miller then accepted the offensive coordinator position

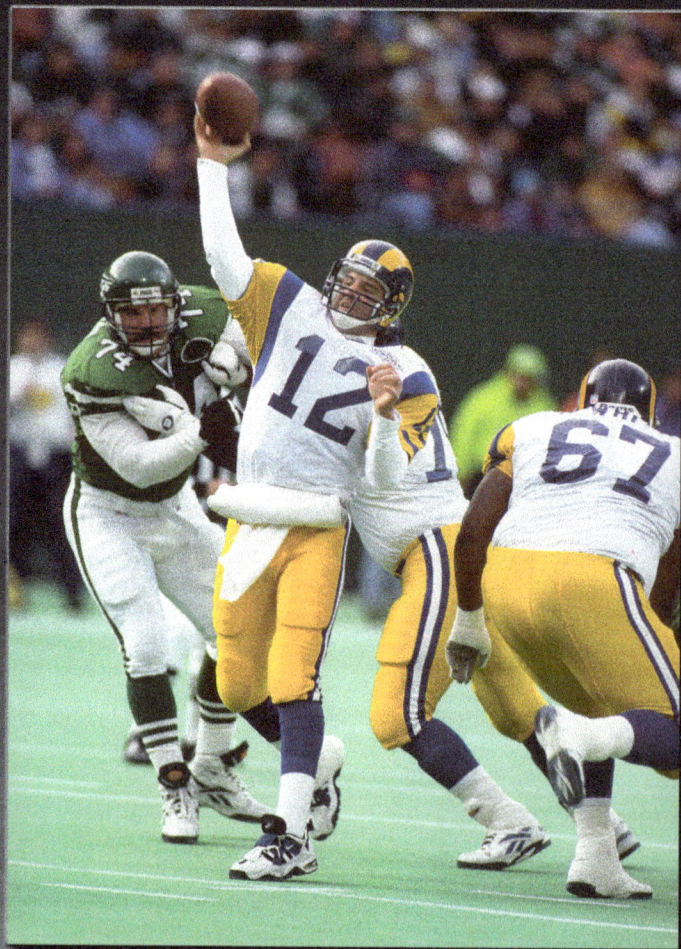

for the Houston Roughnecks of the newly reformed XFL in 2020. Off the field, the University of Oregon inducted Chris Miller into their Sports Hall of Fame in 1999. Five years later, Miller was also inducted into the State of Oregon Sports Hall of Fame in 2004.

Today, Chris Miller trains quarterbacks throughout the state of Oregon, many of which have gone on to become Division I and scholarship players. From middle-school to high-school ages, Miller molds young quarterbacks with the skills needed to become next-level athletes.

I've even been fortunate enough to have Chris Miller close in my own life. My son has been privately trained by many quarterback coaches over the years, but that all stopped once we met Chris Miller. Not only does Miller offer my son greater expertise and developmental skill than any other quarterback coach around, he is also one of the kindest and most positive humans I have ever met.

PREFACE

Stoney Case, Gale Gilbert, Bill Musgrave, Turk Schonert, the Huard brothers —true football legends whose names you may have never heard, whose jerseys you've never seen on a fan. Yet these unknown quarterbacks and hundreds more like them have discreetly helped teams win championships from behind the scenes, on the clipboard, off the bench, and in the practice field trenches. Most of them found no glory or endorsements in professional football; they held no trophies or press conferences, but their contributions remained strong through focus, dedication, and passion for the game. They will never be remembered in the history books, but they will be remembered in this one...

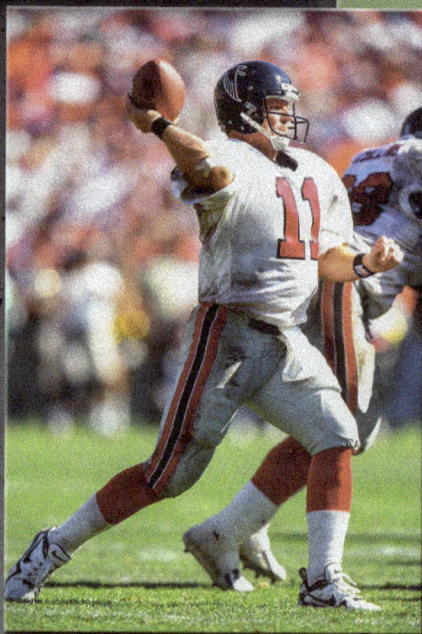

INTRODUCTION

Like it or not, admit it or not, football revolves around the quarterback. Offense relies on the quarterback being a leader of men, having patience and poise in the heat of battle, and practicing regular amnesia when plays go bad. On defense, too, whether it's sacking, disrupting, or intercepting the quarterback, all sights are first and foremost on the man behind or under the center.

Quarterbacks get all the glory and all the blame. It's a precarious position to be in, scrutinized under the microscope of millions of adoring fans that can turn sour at the drop of a ball or a single missed pass. Quarterbacks can rise to the top in an instant and fall into obscurity even quicker. Some never even see the field of play, being relegated to clipboard holding duties no matter how good they were in college. There's only room for one starter on a team, and there are only thirty-two starters in the entire National Football League (NFL)

Some quarterbacks will get only a small taste, a cup of coffee, while others get to enjoy the whole damn plantation. Some are heralded but can't live up to their hype or potential, often called busts. Some are never expected to be more than the guy who warms up the practice team and the end of the bench, yet they become legends when given the opportunity. Other gunslingers are patiently waiting

for just a chance to prove they belong on a roster, and some piss away all their talent with poor life choices.

We all know the legendary quarterbacks, the Hall of Famers and the guys we see on TV every Sunday, Monday, and Thursday night. We see them in commercials, endorsing shoes and sports drinks. We scroll past them on social media, pictured in designer clothes or with their hot model wives. We see legions of fans donning their jerseys and buying autographed memorabilia for man caves. We all know those quarterbacks, and whether we love or hate them, we will never forget them. This book is not about those guys. Those guys don't need any more books.

This book is about the forgotten quarterbacks. Let's pay tribute to the best of the rest, the quarterbacks that only die-hard fans remember from their favorite teams. That guy who came in for one game to bring his team from behind and led them to victory, or the guy who got to start the last couple games of a season and played so poorly he was never seen

or heard from again. This book is for the quarterback you got an autograph from as a kid, which made a much longer lasting impression on you than he ever made playing in the league. Let's be here for the third stringers and undrafted free agents that defied all odds to get into an NFL game under center. Let's be here to remember the athletes that were forgotten by time but not by us. Let's pay homage to the less than 2 percent of college players that make an NFL roster, and the even smaller number that will start at quarterback for an NFL team. Let's not forget that most of these guys worked just as hard as their counterparts to make it to the top but came up a little short on talent or opportunity. This doesn't diminish what they accomplished to become pro athletes.

Some quarterbacks arrived with a big reputation yet exited without celebration. Some guys attended colleges that no one has ever heard of or are even defunct now. Some came from other leagues and manifested their own destinies through sheer determination and relentlessness, while others just got damn lucky being in the right place at the right time.

This encyclopedia of estranged passers will not discriminate. It will pay tribute to the underappreciated and unknown guys who once led their high school or college teams to victory and were good enough to become a paid professional at the utmost level of excellence in the game. Quarterbacks featured in this book may not have been among the all-time best, but at one time they were the best on some level. They outshined thousands of others vying for the pinnacle of play and glory, and that is always very important to remember.

This book will not execute slanderous plays on why some quarterbacks didn'tbask in the shining light of the NFL sun. A quarterback's skills, contributions, and attributes will not be diminished just because they didn't set records or have their own jerseys hanging in the team store. Too many unheralded quarterbacks have helped superstar passers become legends without receiving the acknowledgments they deserve. Too many sideline quarterbacks have saved teams and careers in emergency situations but were cut the next season. Too many gave a huge portion of their youth to the game that gave them crumbs of gratitude in return. Too many backup quarterbacks have taken the back seat for too long, and we are going to give them their moment in the spotlight and their rightful place in the history books, or at least in this book.

HOW THIS BOOK PLAYS

Players are listed alphabetically and in no order of importance or accomplishment. As you read along, you will see names that are highlighted in red. These names are highlighted to show when the subject player crosses paths with another quarterback featured in this book. You will be amazed at how many origin stories intertwine and unfold into a new story together. Some players replaced another in college and broke the previous quarterback's school records, only to later back him up in the NFL. Other quarterbacks were competing for the same Heisman or Johnny Unitas trophy and met at the award ceremony, only to come off their respective benches and face off again years later in an NFL game. As these biographies and stories unfold, you will discover a carousel of quarterbacks who just refused to give up or give in and, through commonality, became a community.

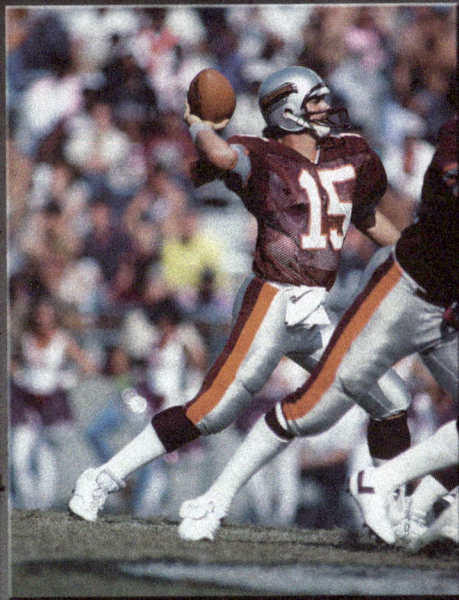

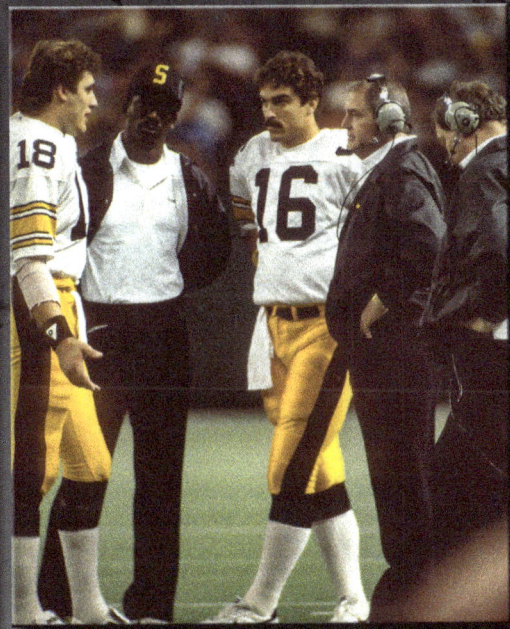

QUARTERBACKS
A - Z

ADAMS, TONY

Tony Adams is part of a fraternity of rare quarterbacks who have played and started in three different professional football leagues: the WFL (World Football League), NFL, and CFL (Canadian Football League).

Adams began his collegiate career at the University of Texas where he threw 13 touchdown passes, leading the freshman team to a perfect 5–0 record. He then moved to Utah State University where he was the starting quarterback for three years, playing in all thirty-three of the Aggies games. Adams amassed over 6,000 passing yards and threw 52 touchdowns. As a senior he set a National Collegiate Athletic Association (NCAA) record with 561 passing yards and 5 touchdowns (TDs) versus their rival, Utah State. Adams finished his college career with an impressive 124.9 quarterback rating, and Utah State immediately retired his number 11 jersey in 1972.

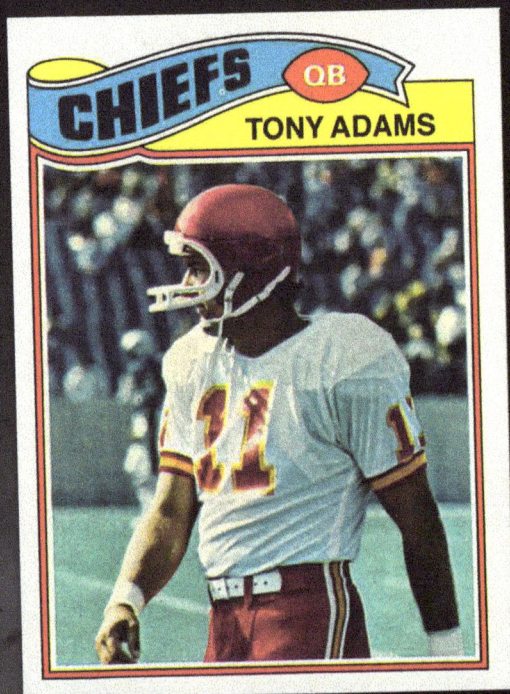

CHIEFS
QB
TONY ADAMS

Although drafted in the 14th round (343rd overall) of San Diego's 1973 NFL Draft, Adams never actually played for the Chargers. His first professional season came a year later with the Southern California Sun of the World Football League (WFL). In his debut pro season, Adams completed 276 of 510 passes for 3,905 yards and 23 touchdowns, leading the league in passing and earning him an All-WFL selection as a rookie. After winning the 1974 Western Division crown and leading the Suns to the playoffs, Adams won a shared MVP title.

In 1975 Adams moved back to the NFL and began a four-year stint with the Kansas City Chiefs. He appeared in fifty games, starting seven. With the Chiefs, he accounted for 2,126 yards, 9 TDs, and 22 interceptions.

After being released by the Chiefs, Adams looked north and joined the Toronto Argonauts of the CFL. From 1979 to 1980, Adams played in twenty games, throwing for 3,231 yards with 13 TDs and 24 interceptions.

Years later, when his career was all but finished, Adams was called on to lead the Minnesota Vikings as a replacement player during the 1987 NFL strike. Adams, then thirty-seven years old, hadn't seen playing time in seven years, yet he started all three games of the players' strike, finishing his final campaign with 607 yards and 3 touchdowns.

ADKINS, SAM

Sam Adkins has the distinction of being the only member of the Seahawks to ever wear the number 12.

Sam Adkins attended Wichita State University and started for three years (1974–76). He threw for 3,822 yards, third most in school history, and his 336 career completions set a school record that stood for nearly a decade. Adkins was one of only four Shockers quarterbacks to rush for over 100 yards in a game—a feat he accomplished twice—and his incredible passing accuracy produced the lowest interception ratio in school history. Adkins was inducted into the Wichita State Hall of Fame in 1995.

A 10th round selection

A

(254th player selected overall) of the Seattle Seahawks in 1977, Adkins made the roster but saw action in only one game his rookie season and no field time at all in 1978. In 1979 he finally got a chance to use his arm, attempting 3 passes. Adkins saw the most playing time of his career in 1980; playing in four games, he completed 10 of 23 passes for 136 yards. But with the emergence of Jim Zorn's flashy playing, the next couple years saw very limited time on the field for Adkins. After missing the 1983 season due to hand surgery, he decided to hang up his cleats. During his tenure, Adkins played in eleven games and completed 17 of 39 passes for 232 yards and 2 touchdowns.

In 1984 the number 12 was retired in honor of the Seahawks fans. Adkins stayed close to Seattle, working as a host for Seahawks postgame shows and as a color commentator for University of Washington football broadcasts on the radio, even becoming a cult fan favorite and fixture in the community.

ARCHER, DAVID

When he was an NFL rookie, David Archer was the youngest starting quarterback in the league and became one of only four players in professional football history to pass for over 6,000 yards in a season. He would become a league MVP, title game MVP, and a college hall of fame inductee, and yet no colleges had offered him a scholarship out of high school. He went undrafted to the NFL. Nobody wanted David Archer. He had to go out and prove his worth time and again.

Upon graduating Soda Springs High School in Idaho, Archer didn't get a scholarship offer. He decided to play at Snow Community College in Utah, where he finished his second season as the fourth best passer in the country and received JUCO (junior college) All-American honors. After that, coaches took notice and the scholarship offers started flying in. He was heavily recruited by Iowa State University, LSU, Texas, New Mexico and UTEP. When LSU and Texas both informed Archer that they wanted to redshirt him his first year, he chose Iowa State, who wanted him to compete for the starting job right out of the gate.

Archer won the starting job, but it was a major adjustment going from one of the nation's top passing junior colleges to an I-formation option offense. He struggled some at first, but what he learned from the transition led to an amazing senior season.

FALCONS

QUARTERBACK
DAVE ARCHER

A

In 1983 Archer set ISU school records and led the Big 8 with 234 pass completions, 402 pass attempts, and 18 touchdowns. During that year, he passed for a school-record 346 yards against no. 1 ranked Nebraska. His 2,639 yards passing and 2,698 yards total offense are still among the best ever at Iowa State.

Even after his stellar senior season, nobody in the NFL wanted Archer, and he went undrafted in 1984. The Denver Gold of the new United States Football League (USFL) selected him in a late round, but Archer wanted to play with the best and knew he could. He would have to prove himself yet again at the next level. Archer signed a free agent deal with the Atlanta Falcons and made their third-string quarterback spot behind starter Steve Bartkowski and backup Mike Moroski. He saw time in two games, completing 11 of 18 passes for 181 yards. The next season, Archer moved up a spot on the depth chart, and when Bartkowski went down with an injury in week five, Archer got the call to start the remaining eleven games of the season. Archer finished 1985 with 1,992 yards passing and 347 yards rushing—good enough to be considered for the starting role the next season. In 1986 Archer beat out Turk Schonert and was named the season's starter.

Archer began 1986 on a hot streak with a 5–1–1 record and was named the National Football Conference (NFC) Player of the Month for September. He was

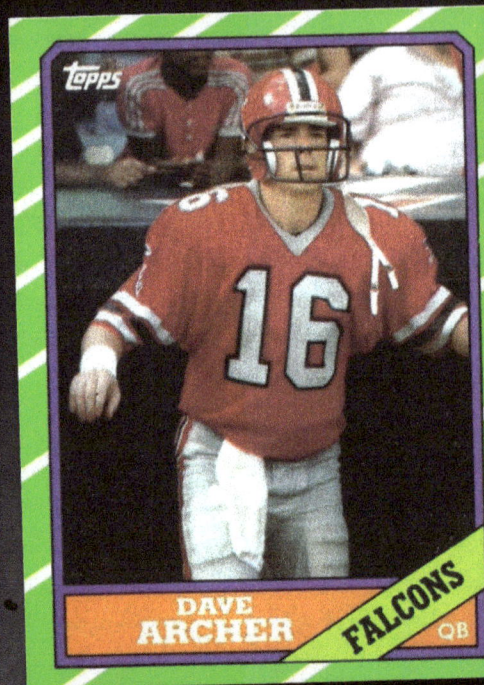

twenty-four years old and the youngest starting quarterback in the NFL. Everything was going great for Archer, and through eleven games, he had 2,007 yards passing with 10 touchdowns and 298 yards rushing. Everything was going great until he separated his shoulder in week ten and was out for the rest of the season. By the time Archer was fully healed in 1987, he had lost his starting job to Scott Campbell and rookie Chris Miller.

Archer was released in 1988 and signed with the Washington Redskins as third string, behind Doug Williams and Mark Rypien. Archer only saw playing time in one game and threw 2 incomplete passes. In 1989 Archer moved to the other coast and signed with the San Diego Chargers as a backup for Jim McMahon and Billy Joe Tolliver. Archer saw limited action and completed 5 of 12 passes for 62 yards and an interception (INT). He was released the following year and never played another down in the league. The NFL may have been done with Archer, but at thirty years old, Archer was not yet done with professional football.

In 1992 Archer signed with the Sacramento Surge of the new World League of American Football (WLAF). Through his incredible playing, he led the Surge to an 8–2 record. In those ten games, Archer completed 61.2 percent of his passes for 2,964 yards (an NFL Europe record) with 23 TDs and only 7 INTs. The Surge won the World Bowl, and Archer was subsequently named MVP of both the game and the entire league. Archer stayed in Sacramento in 1993 but with a different team.

The Surge departed, but the Canadian Football League expanded, and the Sacramento Gold Miners were their first American franchise. The Gold Miners signed Archer, and what happened next would not only become historic in the

A

CFL, but make history in all of professional football.

Archer set Canadian and world records for his rookie season in the CFL. He completed 403 of 701 passes for an absurd 6,023 yards. He is one of only four players to ever accomplish that feat. Doug Flutie was one of the other players who reached the 6,000-yard prominence, doing it the same year and in the same league as Archer, though with the Calgary Stampeders, and his 6,092 yards beat out Archer's total for the CFL leader by only 69 yards. Archer also threw 35 touchdowns, good for third best in the league.

Archer stayed one more season in Sacramento, passing for 3,340 yards and 21 touchdowns. In 1995 he signed with the San Antonio Texans of the CFL and, with 4,471 yards and 30 TDs, helped lead the Texans to the second round of the playoffs. Archer signed with the Ottawa Rough Riders in 1996 and passed for 3,977 yards with 23 touchdowns. After retiring in 1997 and becoming a CFL television analyst, Archer came back to the CFL for one more season in 1998 with the Edmonton Eskimos. He threw for 2,860 yards and 11 TDs and led his team to the Western Finals in the playoffs.

Archer passed for 4,337 yards with 18 TDs in the NFL, 2,964 yards with 23 TDs in the WLAF, and 20,671 yards with 120 TDs in the CFL. Not bad for a quarterback who wasn't offered a scholarship out of high school or drafted to the NFL.

Archer has been broadcasting for the Atlanta Falcons for over twenty years.

AVELLINI, BOB

With more DUIs (6) than rushing TDs (5), Bob Avellini has had his problems off the field. But that doesn't diminish his talent and accomplishments on the turf, and that's what we are here to focus on.

The Long Island native Avellini was a three-sport star in high school, lettering in football, basketball, and baseball.

Avellini started for the University of Maryland from 1972 to 1974, finishing first in the Atlantic Coast Conference (ACC) in virtually every passing category in 1972 and 1974. In his senior season, Avellini placed third in the NCAA with a 60.2 completion percentage and second for his 135.5 quarterback rating. Along with his teammate, future Hall of Famer Randy White, Avellini led Maryland to the Liberty Bowl against Tennessee in 1974. He finished his collegiate career with a 126.3 quarterback rating.

Avellini was drafted in the 6th round (135th overall) by the Chicago Bears in 1975. He started four games in his rookie season and every game the next two seasons. Achieving 2,004 yards passing and 11 touchdowns, 1977 would prove to be the best season of Avellini's professional career.

A

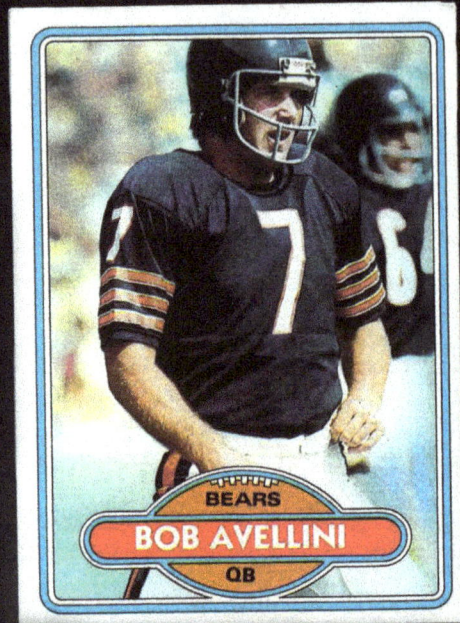

BEARS

BOB AVELLINI

QB

Against the Cowboys in the postseason, he threw the Bears' first TD pass in a playoff game since 1946. Avellini lost the starting quarterback job to Mike Phipps at the end of the 1978 season, and he would then watch his playing time steadily decline shortly after, eventually seeing no field action in 1980. Avellini bounced between second- and third-string quarterback positions behind Phipps, Vince Evans, and Jim McMahon until 1984, when McMahon suffered an injury. Coach Mike Ditka chose the veteran Avellini to start a road game against the Packers even though he had only started five games in the last five years. The decision paid off, though, and Avellini and the Bears won the game. The next week, Avellini got the nod again, this time against the Seahawks. After losing to Seattle 38–9, Ditka cut Avellini, ending his tenure with the Bears just one year before they would win the Super Bowl with one of the most famous and inspiring teams in NFL history.

Avellini caught on with the New York Jets for the rest of 1984 but saw no time on the field and was cut at the end of the year. After a year's hiatus, Avellini made a brief comeback with the Dallas Cowboys in 1986, starting in three pre-season games, but was cut before the regular season started. Avellini finished his decade-long professional career with 560 completions for 7,111 yards with 33 touchdowns and 69 interceptions.

In 2014 Avellini was sentenced to eighteen months in prison after his sixth DUI-related arrest. He is now actively involved in several Chicago area charities and is a fixture in the sports community on television and radio shows.

BARKER, JAY

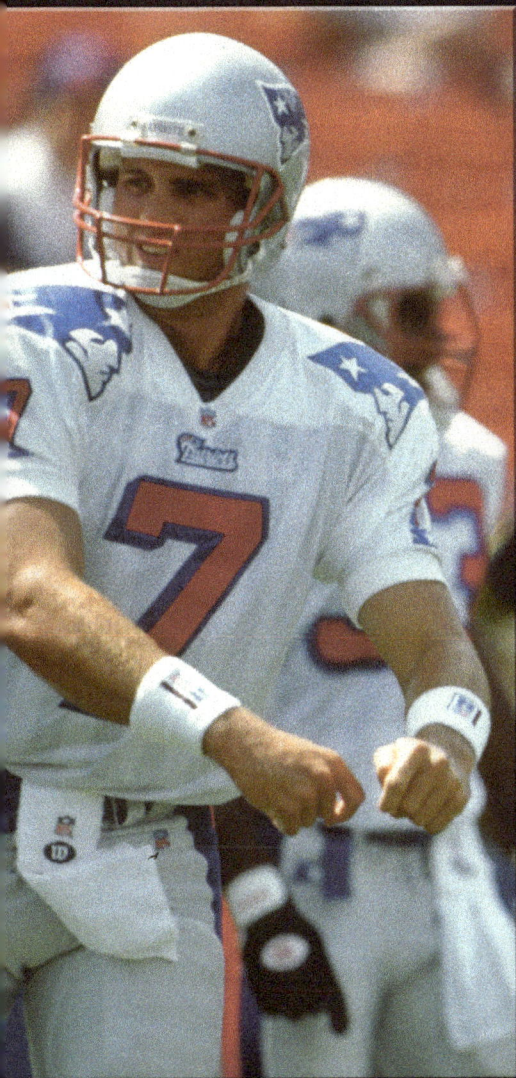

Jay Barker enrolled at the University of Alabama and was starting by his sophomore year (1992). Under legendary coach Gene Stallings, the sophomore Barker helped lead the Crimson Tide to a perfect 13–0 record and a no. 1 overall ranking. Even though Barker only passed for 18 yards in the Sugar Bowl, that was all he needed because Alabama defeated the Miami Hurricanes on 267 yards rushing and a 34–13 win. Barker recorded the win against Gino Toretta, a Heisman Trophy winner.

As a senior in 1994, Barker almost duplicated his sophomore outcome, leading Alabama to a 12–1 record, losing only to Florida by one point in the Southeastern Conference (SEC) Championship game. Barker and company defeated Ohio State 24–17 in the Florida Citrus Bowl and finished the season ranked at no. 5 in the nation. Barker threw 14 TDs that year, compared to only 5 interceptions, ending the year in the NCAA's top five with a 151.7 quarterback rating. He finished fifth in Heisman Trophy voting, won the illustrious Johnny Unitas Golden Arm Award, and was awarded the 1994 SEC Player of the Year.

B

Barker led the Crimson Tide to a 35–2–1 record as the starter during his career at Alabama, tallying 5,689 yards and 26 touchdowns while attending.

Barker was selected in the 5th round (160th overall) of the 1995 NFL Draft by the Green Bay Packers, though he did not make the team out of preseason and was released. He later signed on with the Patriots but was waived at final cuts when Scott Zolak and Tom Tupa beat him out for Drew Bledsoe's backups. The following season, he spent time with the Carolina Panthers organization but never saw any playing time during the regular season.

In 1998 Barker joined the Toronto Argonauts of the Canadian Football League. For the next three seasons, he would be a mainstay in Toronto, playing in forty-six games. He completed 269 passes for 3,433 yards and 11 touchdowns in the CFL.

Barker left Canada to join the new startup XFL in 2001. As a backup for the Birmingham Bolts, Barker started two games mid-season for an injured Casey Weldon. Barker completed 6 of 37 passes for 425 yards, and his 1-to-5 ratio of TDs to INTs would have been much worse had his only touchdown not been for a record 92 yards. Barker then suffered a concussion and cervical strain that ended his season and his entire career.

Barker became an on-air personality for WJOX in Birmingham shortly after his playing days and has since become an analyst for ESPN Radio.

BENJAMIN, GUY

Imagine the quarterbacking knowledge Guy Benjamin possessed after playing alongside Joe Montana, Bob Griese, and Archie Manning.

A Los Angeles native, Benjamin stayed in California after high school to attend Stanford University. As a senior in 1977, he was coached by the legendary Bill Walsh and helped lead the Cardinals to victory over LSU in the Sun Bowl. Benjamin topped the Pac-8 with a nation-leading 208 pass completions out of 330 pass attempts for 2,521 yards and 19 TDs. Benjamin shared Pac-8 Player of the Year honors with Washington's Warren Moon. That season, Benjamin also won both the Sammy Baugh Trophy for top passer in college football and the W. J. Voit Memorial Trophy for outstanding college players on the Pacific coast. Benjamin finished his Cardinal career with 5,946 yards and 45 touchdowns, completing over 60 percent of all his passes.

The Miami Dolphins took Benjamin in the 2nd round in the 1978 draft. He backed up future Hall of Famer Bob Griese and Don Strock for two

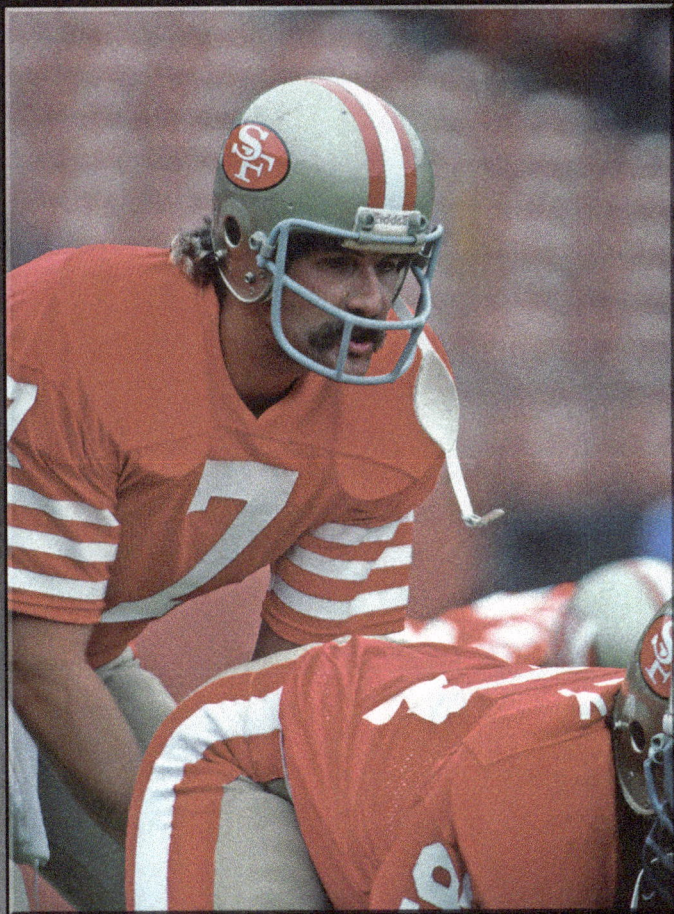

seasons before moving on to New Orleans where he learned behind another legendary quarterback, Archie Manning. He only saw action in two games, completing 7 of 17 passes for 28 yards.

Benjamin was reunited with his old college coach Bill Walsh in San Francisco in 1981, where he backed up another Hall of Famer, Joe Montana, and earned a ring for Super Bowl XVI. Benjamin spent a couple more seasons with the 49ers and retired in 1984 after having hand surgery.

Benjamin attempted only 68 passes in his pro career, completing 39 of them. He had only 3 touchdowns and never got to start an NFL game. But being stuck behind such enormous talent didn't minimize his own expertise; his position would expand it exponentially. Benjamin would go on to share his experiences and education with younger players for decades to come.

Soon after retirement from playing, Benjamin became offensive coordinator for the University of Hawaii. Moving on to more professional leagues later, he coached the Hawaii Hammerheads of the Indoor Professional Football League (IPFL) to the league championship in 1999, the team's only season. He went on to become head coach for the IPFL's Portland Prowlers then returned to Hawaii where he coached the Hawaiian Islanders of the Arena Football League's AF2(AFL's minor league).

BORYLA, MIKE

The son of a former NBA player and coach, Mike Boryla was also a multisport superstar in high school, which ultimately led to him earning a spot on the Stanford Cardinal football team.

Stanford University produced some legendary quarterbacks, and Mike Boryla was among those greats. As a junior in 1972, he led Pac-8 quarterbacks in nearly every passing category. Boryla resumed his dominance as a senior in 1973 and was first-team All-Pacific-8 and the team's MVP, even throwing for 5 touchdowns in a single game against Washington State. Boryla finished his collegiate career with over 4,000 yards passing, 31 touchdowns, and a 113.1 passer rating.

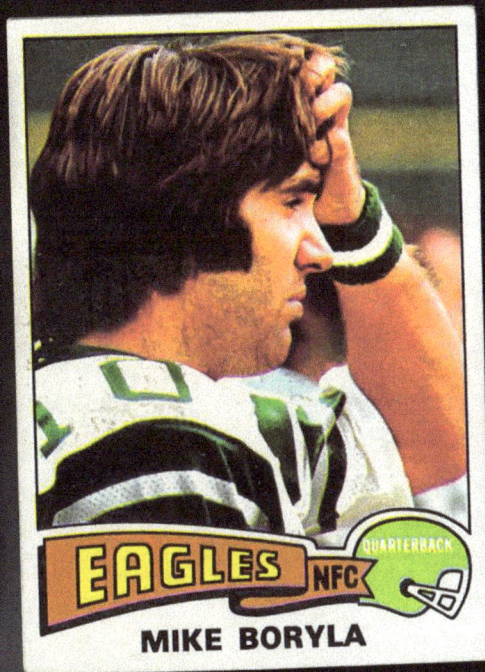

MIKE BORYLA

Boryla was drafted in the 4th round (87th overall) by the Cincinnati Bengals but was immediately traded to the Eagles for 1st and 6th draft picks after he threatened to defect to the new World Football League if he wasn't traded.

Though Boryla only saw action in four games during his 1974 rookie campaign, replacing starter Roman Gabriel for the last three, he won all of them and threw 5 touchdowns in the process. After his successful mop-up job in 1974, he earned the starting position in 1975. Benched early for much of the season, Boryla got another chance late in the year and didn't disappoint. He threw for 3 touchdowns against the 49ers in his first game back as the starter. Boryla finished the season with 996 yards, 9 touchdowns, and 12 interceptions in seven games, hardly Pro Bowl numbers.

The twenty-four-year-old was getting ready to start law school at NYU at the season's end, going as far as buying his books and scheduling classes, when he got a call from the Eagles General Manager who told him he was selected to the Pro Bowl. Boryla had to drop out of law school and head to the Superdome in New Orleans.

The league MVP, Minnesota's Fran Tarkenton, was slated to play in the Pro Bowl but had a sore arm. The Cowboys' Roger Staubach also declined, citing sore ribs fresh off his Super Bowl loss to the Steelers. The NFL then asked Archie Manning and Steve Bartkowski to play in the game, both declining due to sore arms from the grueling season. So, the NFL asked for Boryla to back up St. Louis Cardinals starter Jim Hart.

An unlikely hero, Boryla entered the Pro Bowl with only 5 minutes, 39 seconds remaining in the fourth quarter, his team trailing 9–20. He then threw two touchdown passes to lead the NFC to a 23–20 comeback victory.

Boryla saw even more playing time in 1976 but was sidelined all of 1977 with a knee injury. He returned in 1978 with the Tampa Bay Buccaneers, competing with Mike Huff as the backup to newly drafted Doug Williams. Boryla made the roster but only got to start one game, going 2 for 5 with 15 yards.

Over his career, Boryla passed for 2,838 yards and 20 TDs. He walked away from the game in 1979 to again pursue his dream of becoming a lawyer.

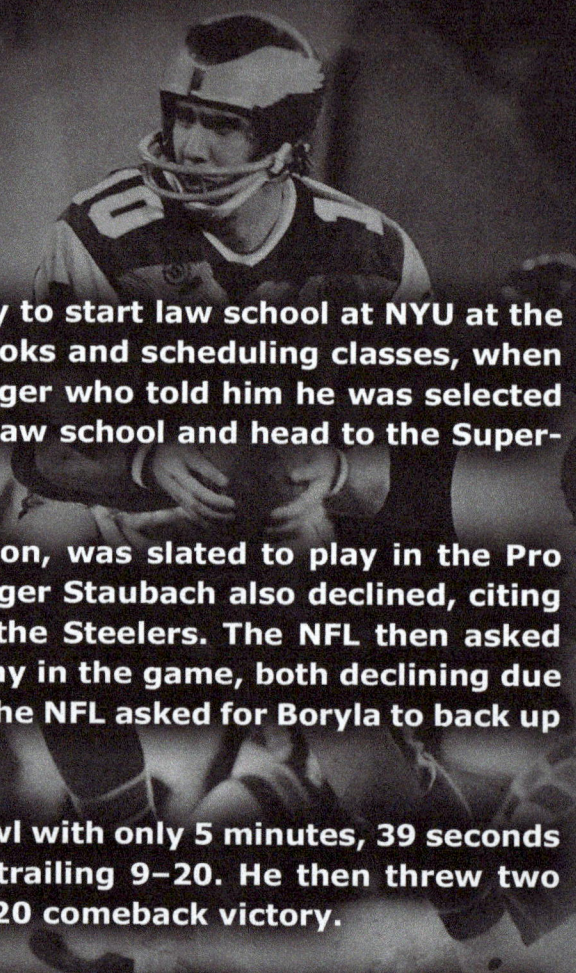

BRENNAN, COLT

Colt Brennan was the most talented, record-setting, and prolific college quarterback to ever get drafted in the NFL and never play a down on the pro field. His story is one of tragedy, triumph, and more tragedy.

Brennan started his high school career at Mater Dei (California) as a backup. The guy in front of him was named Matt Leinart, who went on to star at USC and get drafted to the NFL. After Leinart graduated, Brennan not only excelled in football but helped Mater Dei's basketball team advance to the league championship.

Brennan attended the University of Colorado and spent the 2002 season as a redshirt freshman. In early 2004 he was arrested on felony burglary and trespassing charges, but the court vacated the guilty verdict due to a lack of evidence, and Brennan passed a court-ordered polygraph test. Regardless of the legal outcome, he was kicked off the team and expelled.

B

With few options left and a damaged reputation, Brennan then transferred to Saddleback College in 2004. Amassing 2,532 yards passing and 24 total touchdowns, he helped bring the school to a 9–4 record and a conference championship. Brennan was offered a scholarship from Syracuse, but it was rescinded due to the felony on his record.

New University of Hawaii head coach June Jones was hunting for gunslinging quarterbacks for the new pro-style offense that he was bringing with him to the school, and he offered Brennan a chance to walk on at Hawaii. In his first start (2005), Brennan threw for 347 yards and 3 TDs against Idaho. After that, it was the Colt show. He tied or broke eleven school offensive records in his first season and led the NCAA with 4,301 passing yards, 35 touchdowns, and 4,455 total yards. He had a 515-yard, 7-TD performance against New Mexico, four 400-yard games, and nine 300-yard games.

If 2005 didn't prove he was becoming a college football legend, then 2006 solidified his status when he set the NCAA on fire to become one of college football's all-time greatest quarterbacks. He led his Rainbow Warriors to a 10–3 record and 41–24 whipping of Arizona State in the Hawaii Bowl, a game in which he threw 5 TDs, bringing his season total to 58 and breaking David Klingler's NCAA record of 53. Brennan led the entire nation in several categories, including an incredible 72.6 completion percentage, 5,549 yards, 58 TDs, and 186 rating, while shattering school records along the way. He finished sixth in Heisman Trophy voting, was an O'Brien Award finalist, and was awarded Western Athletic Conference (WAC) Offensive Player of the Year, first team All-WAC, and the Sammy Baugh Trophy for best passer in the nation. He also set an NCAA record for most points responsible for (in a season) with 384.

B

Brennan declined the NFL draft to return to Hawaii for his senior season in 2007. He entered the year as the Heisman Trophy front-runner, and once again proved why he was a legend in the making. He led the Warriors to a perfect 12–0 regular season and an appearance at the Sugar Bowl. After throwing 5 TDs against no. 17 Boise State on November 23, 2007, Brennan broke the NCAA Division I-A record for career touchdown passes. He finished the season with his second consecutive first-team All-WAC and WAC Offensive Player of the Year honors.

But the Sugar Bowl was not kind to Brennan, and behind his 3 interceptions, Hawaii lost to Georgia 41–10 before a national audience. Brennan was pressured throughout the whole game by the Bulldogs' D-line, and interceptions cost him the NCAA record for all-time top quarterback rating, dropping his stock in the upcoming draft. Even then, he finished second in Heisman voting. Despite tearing the labrum in his right hip during practice leading up to the game, Brennan still managed to play in the 2008 Senior Bowl.

After his 4,343-yard, 38-TD senior season, Brennan finished his college career with 14,193 yards, 131 touchdowns, and 42 interceptions. He had set thirty-one career NCAA records, including for most 400-yard games (20), a .704 completion percentage, and 373.5 passing yards per game.

After his Sugar Bowl performance and hip surgery, Brennan's draft stock would slip all the way to the 6th round. He was selected 186th overall in the 2008 NFL Draft by the Washington Redskins and signed a four-year, $1.8 million rookie contract. Brennan first saw action at the Hall of Fame game in preseason against the Colts. Completing 9 of 10 passes for 123 yards and 2 TDs,

B

he led the Redskins to victory and looked impressive. Two weeks later against the Jets in preseason, he continued his success, connecting on 4 of 5 passes for 79 yards and throwing the game-winning touchdown. Brennan led all rookie quarterbacks in preseason with 3 TD passes, 411 yards, and a 109.9 quarterback rating. However, with Jason Campbell starting every game, Brennan didn't see the field during the regular season. In 2009 Brennan suffered another hip injury and a torn hamstring, so he was placed on injured reserve, missing the entire season. 2010 came along and so did quarterback John Beck, who the Redskins traded for, and Brennan subsequently became expendable, so he was released.

The hits continued to pile up for Brennan in 2010. He was the passenger in a car accident that left him with broken ribs, a broken collar bone, and a traumatic brain injury. The brain injury, which was later discovered to have caused stage one (or higher) chronic traumatic encephalopathy (CTE), created a permanent change in Brennan's personality and emotions. He began drinking and using drugs to cope. Brennan was arrested several times over the next decade for DUIs and charges related to alcohol and drugs. He was in and out of therapy and treatment programs all while still trying to fulfill his football dream.

Three years into his career and yet to play a regular season game, Brennan kept pushing forward and was signed by the Oakland Raiders in 2010, only to be released in preseason. In 2011 Brennan continued the football fight and signed with the Hartford Colonials of the United Football League, but another twist of fate saw the Colonials franchise fold, and Brennan was out of a job. Brennan got a chance up north and signed with the Saskatchewan Roughriders of the Canadian Football League in 2012 but was cut before the season started.

B

Giving professional football one more shot in 2013, Brennan signed with the Los Angles Kiss of the Arena Football League, but he was cut after complications arose from his prior brain injury.

Remarkably, Brennan managed to get sober in 2021 despite his brain injury worsening. However, on May 10, 2021, he was found unconscious in a hotel room. Brennan relapsed and died by accidental overdose. Fentanyl, methamphetamine, amphetamine, and ethanol were all found in his system. Brennan was taken to the hospital, where he was comatose and put on a ventilator. It quickly became clear that the damage was irreversible, and he was allowed to die.

Needing more answers about their beloved son, Colt's parents donated his brain to Boston University's CTE Center to determine whether he had been suffering from the disease. Examinations found atrophy in his frontal cortex, brain stem, and other regions, revealing that Colt did indeed suffer from CTE, which would have affected his emotions, addictions, personality, impulses, and coping mechanisms.

Colt Brennen never played a down in a regular season game of professional football at any level. He was only thirty-seven years old when he died.

BROCK, DIETER

Legend has it that Brock could throw the ball 93 yards in the air and 55 yards across the field from down on one knee. He was appropriately nicknamed the Birmingham Rifle.

After making only 19 pass attempts with the Auburn Tigers in 1971, Ralph "Dieter" Brock transferred to Jacksonville State University where he quickly claimed his place in their record books. In 1973 he passed for 1,293 yards and 17 touchdowns and led the Gulf South Conference in many quarterback categories.

The Birmingham, Alabama, native signed a one-year deal with the Winnipeg Blue Bombers of the Canadian Football League (CFL) in 1975. After Brock spent his first season as a barely used backup, he began his assault on the league's record books. He won back-to-back CFL Most Outstanding Player awards in 1980 and 1981 and didn't stop there.

B

Brock broke the league's single season passing yardage record with 4,796 yards in 1981. In 1983 Brock was traded to the Hamilton Tiger-Cats and ended up facing his previous team, the Blue Bombers, in the Championship Grey Cup game of 1984. Hamilton and Brock lost the game, and the Grey Cup title was about the only accomplishment that eluded Brock's illustrious, decade-long CFL career.

Brock's powerful arm grew a reputation of its own during his CFL days, with some even touting it as greater than John Elway's. To help achieve this, he would tape pellets to practice balls, weighing them down to build arm strength.

Brock's reputation eventually spread south, and he was signed to a four-year deal by the LA Rams in 1985, becoming the NFL's oldest rookie so far. Brock then set a record for longest winning streak for a rookie by defeating his first seven opponents. The Rams took a skid after that but made it to the NFC Championship game, where they suffered a loss to the Bears. That would be Brock's final game, as he suffered an injury the following preseason and developed chronic back problems.

Although Brock's NFL career lasted only one season, he went 11–4 as a starter, throwing for 2,658 yards and 16 touchdowns and leading his team to within one game of the Super Bowl.

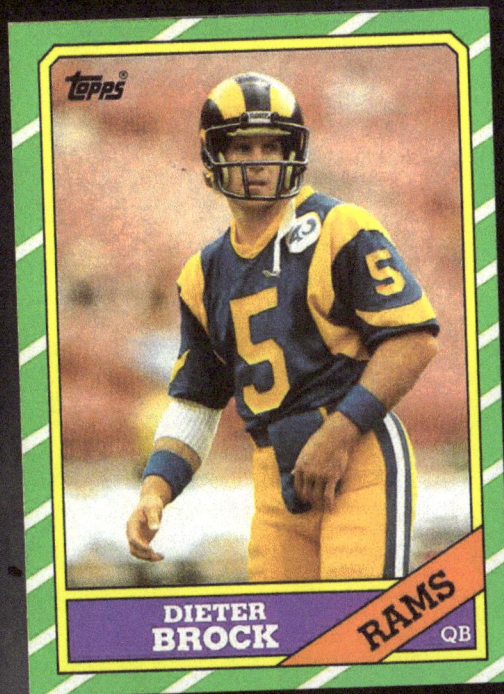

B

Brock amassed 34,830 yards and threw 210 touchdowns in the CFL. He completed 2,602 of 4,535 passes, good for a 57.4 percent completion ratio. Brock tallied thirty-seven 300-yard games in his career, more than any other pro quarterback at the time. Over the course of his last five seasons, Brock threw for over 20,000 yards, which was also more than any quarterback in any pro football league.

Although he never saw the field again as a player, Brock would visit the turf every week for many years as a coach in the CFL. In 1990 Brock was inducted into the Canadian Football League Hall of Fame, and in 2016 he was inducted into the Blue Bombers stadium Ring of Honor.

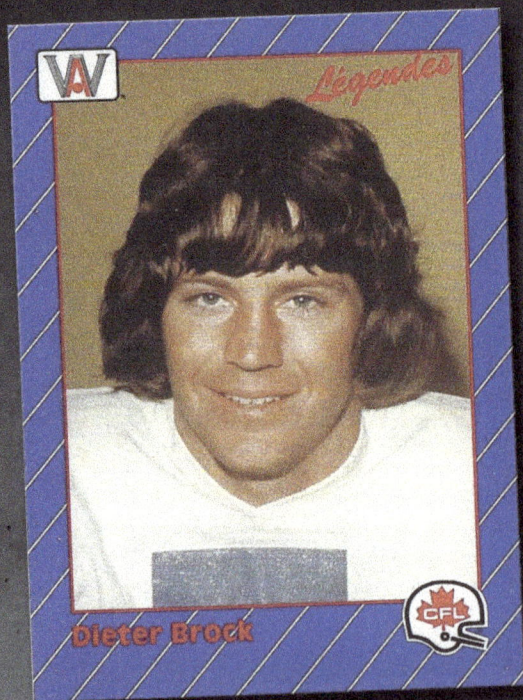

Dieter Brock

BROHM, BRIAN

Brohm was a football legend long before leading Louisville to three bowl games and playing in the NFL.

In high school he led his Trinity Shamrocks to the 4-A state title in 2001, 2002, and 2003 and was the MVP of all three games. In 2002, his junior season, he threw for 552 yards and 7 TDs in the championship game. While captaining his team to a perfect 15–0 record that year, Brohm threw 47 touchdown passes and only one interception, landing him on the cover of Sports Illustrated. In his senior year, Brohm was award- ed the USA Today Offensive Player of the Year, Kentucky Mr. Football, and Kentucky Gatorade Player of the Year.

Brohm also led the school's basketball team to its first Re- gional title. In base- ball, he advanced his team to a state runner-up finish, earning him the MVP title, and he

B was subsequently drafted by the Colorado Rockies in the 49th round of the 2004 MLB Draft.

With all his football awards, finishes, and honors, the offers came rolling in. Brohm turned down scholarships from Notre Dame, Alabama, Tennessee, and others to stay and play in his hometown of Louisville.

Despite not starting a single game, Brohm was named Conference USA Freshman of the Year in 2004 and helped lead his Cardinals to the Liberty Bowl and finish the season with a no. 6 ranking. In 2005 Brohm started at quarterback at Louisville like his brother Jeff and father Oscar before him. Brohm passed for 2,883 yards, 19 TDs, and only 5 interceptions before going down with a knee injury in the Gator Bowl game. However, he was still named the Big East Offensive Player of the Year.

In 2006 Brohm improved yet again, despite missing two games with a thumb injury. He still managed to pass for 3,049 yards, 16 TDs, and only 5 interceptions with a 159.1 passer rating. Brohm led his Cardinals to the Orange Bowl and Louisville's first ever Bowl Championship Series (BCS) victory, earning him MVP honors. He was projected to be a 1st round pick in the NFL draft—some even said the top pick—but Brohm decided to remain at Louisville for his senior season.

In 2007 Brohm had his first complete, injury-free season and made the most of it, completing 308 of 473 passes for over 4,000 yards and 30 touchdowns. He finished his college career completing 780 passes for 10,775 yards with 71 touchdowns. His lifetime 158.3 quarterback rating is number one of all-time in

B

the Big East conference.

Brohm was drafted in the 2nd round (56th overall) by the Green Bay Packers in 2008, but he wound up the third quarterback on the depth chart, behind Aaron Rodgers and the Packers' 7th round pick, Matt Flynn. He was waived before the first game then signed to the practice squad for the remainder of the year and into the following season.

The Buffalo Bills signed Brohm off the Packers practice squad in November 2009 after the Bills waived Gibran Hamdan. Brohm got his first NFL start a month later against the Falcons, a losing game but one in which Brohm threw a pass to Terrell Owens, giving the receiver his one thousandth career reception. In 2010 Brohm competed with Ryan Fitzpatrick as the backup to Trent Edwards. When Edwards was released, Fitzpatrick became the starter and Brohm was able to start the final game of the season against the Jets. In the two NFL seasons in which he saw playing time, Brohm started two games, losing both. He completed 27 of 52 passes for 252 yards with no touchdowns and 5 interceptions.

In 2011 Brohm headed to the United Football League (UFL) to play for the Las Vegas Locomotives under coach Jim Fassel. Brohm completed 10 of 19 passes for 111 yards and 2 touchdowns, helping his team to reach the championship game. Later that year, Brohm tried out for the Detroit Lions but didn't make the team. Early in 2012 he tried out for the New Orleans Saints, throwing to Randy Moss in a highly publicized workout, and later tried out for the 49ers. Brohm returned to the Locomotives of the UFL in 2012 and completed an

B

80-yard touchdown on his first pass of the season.

In 2013 Brohm moved north to the Canadian Football League. He signed with the Hamilton Tiger-Cats but spent the entire season on the injured list and saw no action. In 2014 Brohm was traded to the Winnipeg Blue Bombers for a draft pick. He would remain with the Bombers for the next two seasons, garnering 907 yards on 90 completions, throwing 1 TD and 4 picks.

In 2016 Brian was reunited with his brothers, Greg and Jeff, who were coaching at Western Kentucky when he was named their quarterback's coach. In 2017 Jeff Brohm was hired as Purdue's head coach and in turn hired Brian as an assistant coach. The two brothers would eventually return home to coach at the University of Louisville, a fitting landing for Brian Brohm's storied football path.

BULL, SCOTT

Bull was ahead of his time. At 6'5" and 211 pounds, he was a monster for a quarterback at the time. He ran just as hard as he threw and was known as one of the hardest-running quarterbacks of his era, fitting for the power of his namesake.

As a senior at Arkansas, Bull threw for almost as many yards as he ran, passing for 533 yards and rushing for another 570. Bull's 1,000-plus yards of total offense and 11 total touchdowns culminated in the Razorbacks' 31–10 victory over the Georgia Bulldogs in the 1976 Cotton Bowl. Bull was also a pitcher on the Arkansas baseball team.

Drafted in the 6th round of the 1976 NFL Draft by the San Francisco 49ers, Bull saw two starts during his rookie campaign on a quarterback staff with Marty Domres and Jim Plunkett. He led the 49ers to victory in both starts, throwing for 2 TDs and rushing for 2 more. In 1977 starter Jim Plunkett remained healthy the entire year, so Bull's playing time diminished, and he attempted only 24 passes. In 1978 the 49ers released Plunkett and signed rookie Steve DeBerg, and Bull saw five starts to DeBerg's eleven. In his starts, Bull would direct the 49ers to a 1–4 record, throwing just 1 TD and 11 interceptions. Bull injured his knee in the final game of the 1978 season and would spend the 1979 season on injured reserve before retiring.

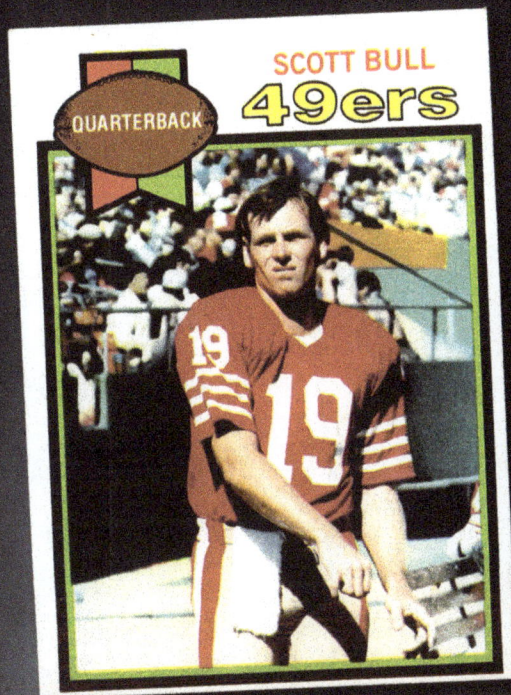

SCOTT BULL
49ers
QUARTERBACK
19

CARANO, GLENN

If football didn't work out for Glenn Carano, he could have always joined his small family business, which owns the pioneering conglomerate Eldorado, Silver Legacy, and several other casino hotels in Reno, Nevada, and around the country.

From the moment Carano started playing football, he had talent and talented people around him. His Pop Warner coach was none other than former NFL quarterback Eddie LeBaron. After his senior year of high school in Reno, Nevada, Carano earned All-American honors and a scholarship to UNLV.

Carano became the starter as a true freshman and never relinquished that role. In his sophomore year, Carano helped UNLV to a no. 2 ranking in Division II. With Carano at the helm, along with senior running back Mike Thomas who would become the 1975 NFL Rookie of the Year with the Redskins, the Rebels had their only undefeated season in school history and a bowl game appearance.

Carano passed for 2,029 yards with 13 touchdowns as a junior and 2,024 yards with another 13 TDs as a senior. Playing beside his favorite receiver, his twin brother Gene, Carano led UNLV to the Division II Midwest Regional and a no. 7 national ranking.

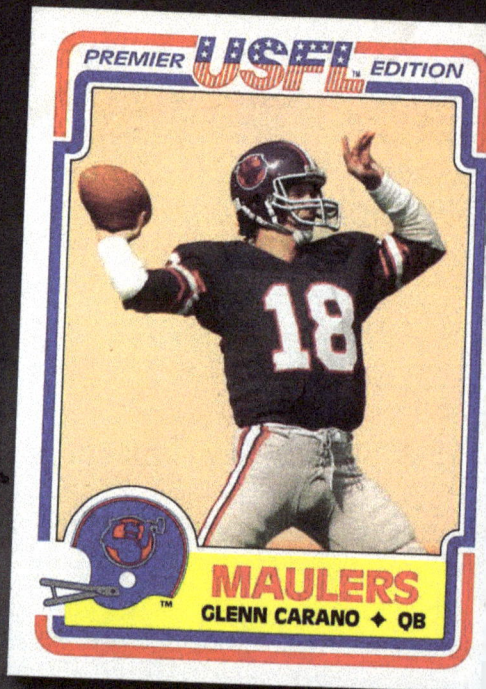

Carano finished at UNLV holding virtually every passing record, including 337 pass completions, 636 pass attempts, 5,095 passing yards, 37 TDs, and 19 rushing touchdowns.

Carano was selected by the Dallas Cowboys in the 2nd round of the 1977 NFL Draft. He beat out fellow rookie Steve DeBerg to secure the third-string slot on the roster behind Roger Staubach and Danny White. Placed behind a future Hall of Famer—and perhaps even the most popular quarterback in the country—and his very competent backup, Carano didn't see much playing time in his first few years. From 1977 to 1980 he only attempted 12 passes in 8 games of relief work, but of his 5 completions, 2 went for TDs.

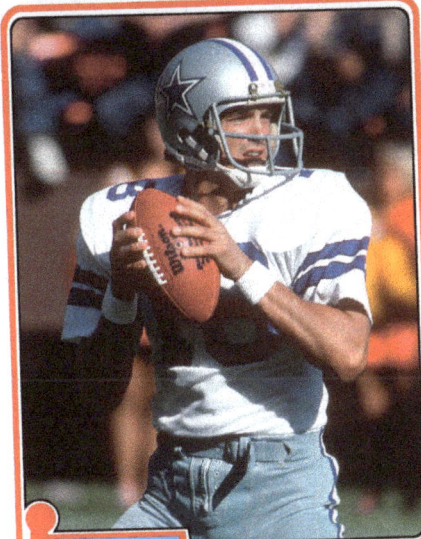

COWBOYS
QB
GLENN CARANO

In 1980 Staubach retired, leaving Danny White as the starter and Carano as the primary backup. In 1981 Carano replaced the injured White on Thanksgiving Day and led the Cowboys to a come-from-behind win over the Bears. The next week, he got his first start and again brought the Cowboys to victory, this time in a 37–13 trouncing of the Colts. It would be the only start of Carano's career. Oddly enough, the Colts' quarterback, David Humm, was also making his first and only NFL start. The duo became the only pair of "one and done" quarterbacks in NFL history to ever face off, and the anomaly became the subject of an NFL Films piece. Even stranger was the fact that Carano and Humm had been friends since high school, both having played high school football in Nevada. They remained friends until Humm's death in 2018.

With the addition of Gary Hogeboom to the Cowboys in 1982, Carano was returned to third string on the quarterback depth chart and would not throw another pass in the NFL. After finishing his tenure with the Cowboys in 1983, Carano moved on to the new USFL league for a second chance at his first love.

With the newly formed Pittsburgh Maulers in 1984, Carano got one last opportunity to shine. He surpassed his NFL career passing total of 304 yards and 3 TDs very quickly, ending his USFL season with 2,368 yards passing and 13 TDs. Carano retired before the next season.

Although he was an unheralded backup for most of his NFL career, Carano was an important part of five NFC Championships and two Super Bowls, walking away with a ring from Super Bowl XII. In 1989 he was inducted into the UNLV Athletics Hall of Fame, and in 2015 Carano was inducted into the Southern Nevada Sports Hall of Fame.

After football, Carano returned home to Reno where he is currently the GM for his family's company, continuing their legacy of running the top casinos in the city. He is heavily involved in the community and has held such positions as member of the Board of Directors for the Boys & Girls Club of Truckee Meadows, Commissioner with the Nevada Athletic Commission, member of the Board of Directors for the Airport Authority of Washoe County, member of the Partners In Education with Sparks High School and Wooster High School, board member with the Reno-Sparks Convention and Visitors Authority, and more.

CARLSON, CODY

Not many career backup quarterbacks earn a nickname or command respect with their abilities, but "Commander" Cody Carlson was no average backup quarterback.

At San Antonio Churchill High School, Carlson led his team to a 31–5 record in his three years as quarterback. As a senior, Carlson's 2,270 yards passing earned him All-District, All-City, and All-State honors.

Carlson enrolled at Baylor University and wasted no time in establishing himself. As a freshman in 1983 he passed for 1,617 yards with 12 touchdowns and led the Bears to the Bluebonnet Bowl. Carlson split playing time with Tom Muecke during his sophomore and junior seasons and helped lead Baylor to another Bowl game in 1985. He was named MVP of the Liberty Bowl after his victory over LSU. As a senior in 1986, and with the departure

C

of Muecke, Carlson started every game, passing for 2,284 yards with 10 TDs and an added 356 yards rushing with another 3 TDs. He led the Bears to a 9–3 record and a finish at no. 12 in the nation. Carlson competed in his third bowl game in four seasons, defeating Colorado 21–9 in the Bluebonnet Bowl.

Carlson was a two-time All-Southwest Conference selection and set Baylor school career records with 5,411 passing yards, 52 TDs, and 5,835 total offense. He was later honored as the SWC's Outstanding Player of the 1980s.

Carlson was selected in the 3rd round (64th overall) of the 1987 NFL Draft by the Houston Oilers. As a rookie, Carlson found himself at third-string behind starter Warren Moon and backup Brent Pease, but by his second season, he moved up to the primary backup. With Moon injured, Carlson started five games in 1988, winning three of them. He passed for 775 yards with 4 TDs and rushed for another. Moon was healthy all of 1990, so Carlson only got into six games for mop-up relief and started one, then it was back to limited relief work behind a healthy Moon in 1991.

Warren Moon suffered another injury in 1992, which allowed Carlson six starts in eleven games. This would be his most productive year in the NFL, and he completed over 65 percent of his passes for 1,710 yards with 9 TDs and 11 INTs. He brought the Oilers to a 4–2 record during his starts and showed the poise of a veteran quarterback, commanding respect in the league. Several players were quoted as saying that Carlson could easily be starting for teams in the league.

Carlson had two more starts in 1993, and when Moon departed in 1994, Carlson was finally named the Oilers' starting quarterback. Unfortunately, he kicked off the year with a 1–4 record then suffered a season-ending injury. He never played in the NFL again.

Carlson is currently a business development specialist in healthcare and has represented healthcare clients before the Texas State Legislature. A father of three, Carlson has also been a communications coordinator at a children's hospital, an author, and is a respected community leader.

CODY CARLSON

CARMAZZI, GIO

When Carmazzi was drafted in 2000, he did not own a television. He was living in California as a yoga practitioner and farmer that owned five goats. He was selected long before Tom Brady yet never played in an NFL game.

Carmazzi enrolled at Hofstra University in 1996. He became the full-time starter his sophomore year and immediately made a huge impact. Carmazzi rewrote the school record books with 408 pass attempts, 288 completions, 3,554 yards, 27 touchdowns, and a 70.6 completion percentage. He led the Pride to a 9–2 record and the I-AA playoffs, and they finished the year with a no. 14 national ranking.

With 2,751 yards passing and 19 TDs, Carmazzi took Hofstra to an 8–3 record and no. 20 national ranking in 1998. But 1999 was his best finish yet. Carmazzi and company ended the season with a 10–1 record, a playoff berth, and ranked no. 5 in the nation. He passed for 2,651 yards with 21 touchdowns.

Carmazzi finished his college career as

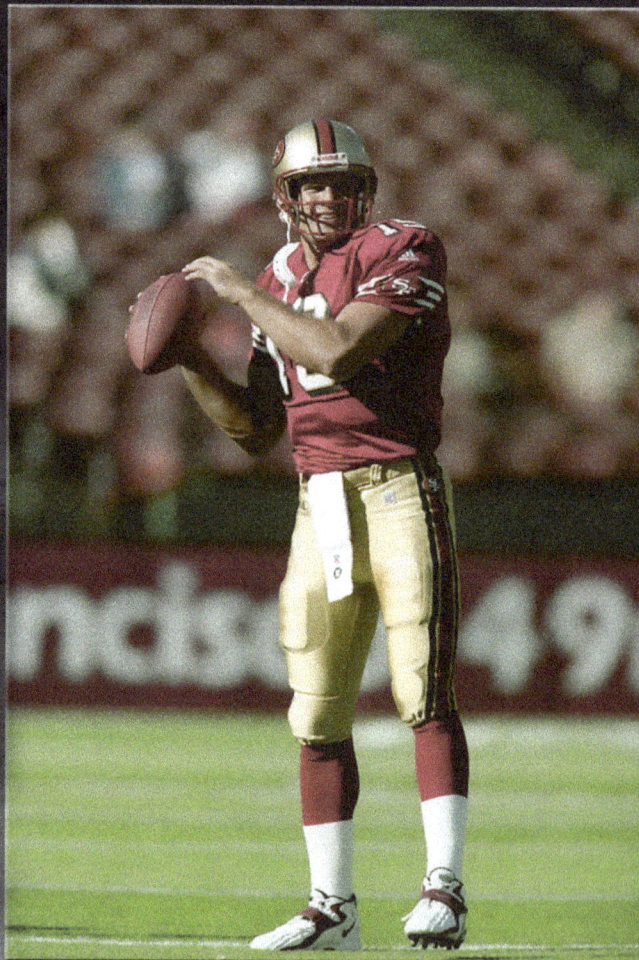

C

Hofstra's all-time leader with 9,371 yards passing, 764 completions, 71 touchdown passes, and over 10,000 yards of total offense. In addition to his passing prowess, Carmazzi also rushed for 1,044 yards and 32 TDs with the Pride.

Carmazzi was selected in the 3rd round (65th overall) of the 2000 NFL Draft by the San Francisco 49ers. He was the second quarterback taken and one of six drafted before Tom Brady. He and Brady faced each other when they were rookies in the 2000 Pro Football Hall of Fame game. Carmazzi only completed 3 of 7 passes for 19 yards, and Brady won the preseason contest 20–0. Carmazzi wouldn't see the field during the season, falling to third on the quarterback depth chart behind starter Jeff Garcia and backup Rick Mirer.

2001 was almost a repeat of Carmazzi's rookie season. As the third quarterback behind Garcia and backup Tim Rattay, Carmazzi didn't see any action and was sent to NFL Europe the next season to work on his game with the Rhein Fire.

With the Fire in 2001, Carmazzi backed up Phil Stambaugh and completed 42 of 71 pass attempts for 448 yards with 4 TDs. He was later released by San Francisco.

After a couple years away from pro ball, Carmazzi gave the game another try. He signed with the BC Lions of the CFL and completed the sole pass he attempted for 12 yards. He signed with the Calgary Stampeders the next season but didn't set foot on the field.

C

Carmazzi was the smartest guy in the 49ers locker room at any given time, but unfortunately he never got the chance to play for that team in a regular-season game. He was a 1996 High School Scholar-Athlete of the Year, a National Football Foundation Scholar-Athlete in 1999, and a Hofstra Hall of Fame inductee in 2011.

Today, Carmazzi has become a devoted yoga practitioner and develops software used by physicians .

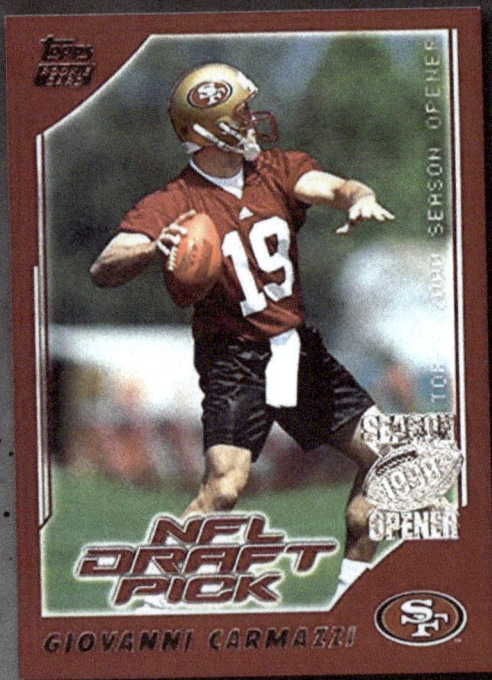

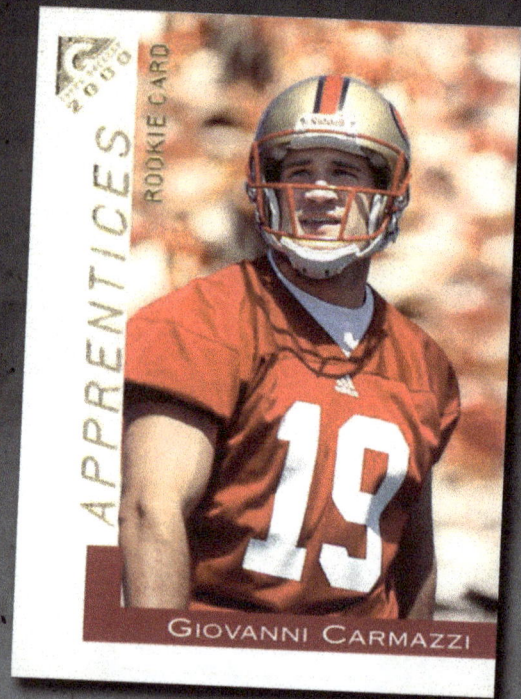

CARTER, VIRGIL

Brigham Young University is known for producing incredible quarterback talent, and that reputation began with Virgil Carter. While at BYU, he set six national, nineteen conference, and twenty-four school records. During his sophomore effort in 1965, Carter led his team to their first conference championship in program history while throwing 20 touchdowns. In 1966 Carter threw for over 2,000 yards with 21 touchdowns passing and another 9 rushing. Totaling 5,125 yards passing, 50 passing TDs, and another 24 rushing touchdowns in his collegiate career, Carter's success strongly influenced BYU adopting a pass-oriented offense.

The Chicago Bears selected Carter in the 6th round of the 1967 NFL/AFL Draft. After two years in the Windy City, during which he started only five games, he was waived. Carter then signed with the Buffalo Bills but was traded to the Cincinnati in the preseason after the Bengals' quarterback went down with an injury. With this new team, Carter enjoyed his finest couple of years as a pro. In 1970 Carter was instrumental in leading his new club to the American Football Conference (AFC) Central Division Championship, thrilling fans with both his powerful arm and scrambling feet. From 1970 to 1971,

C

he started twenty-one games for the Bengals and won eleven of them. In 1971 he led the NFL with a 62.2 completion percentage and had the longest completion of the year at 90 yards. In 1972 Carter split time with highly touted newcomer Ken Anderson, who would eventually take over as the starter. Carter didn't fare better in 1973, when he was sidelined with a broken collar bone and missed the entire year.

With Ken Anderson now the Bengals' star, Carter was traded to the San Diego Chargers in 1974, but Carter opted to sign with the Chicago Fire of the new World Football League. Back In Chicago where he was originally drafted, but now in a different league, Carter shined again. He was the WFL's leading passer in 1974 until another injury sidelined him after week eleven. Even after missing several games, he still finished the

C

season with 2,629 yards passing and 27 touchdowns. The 1974 Fire's aerial offense, led by Virgil Carter, is closely compared to the more recent West Coast offense.

Carter went back to the NFL in 1975 and joined the Chargers, starting in just one game. Then he rejoined his original team, the Bears, in 1976 and saw limited action as a backup. After the 1976 season, he retired.

Carter was a highly intelligent quarterback. He earned a master's degree while playing with the Bears in his early years and taught statistics and mathematics at Xavier University while playing with the Bengals. Carter is credited as one of the founding developers of a football metric called "Expected Points," and his work was later expanded into several aspects of the game's analytics.

CASE, STONEY

When asked in an interview with the Baltimore Sun what his fondest memory of playing in Baltimore was, Stoney Case replied with, "The crabs. Every restaurant I went to in that city, if the owner recognized me, he'd bring out his signature crab dish, that was cool."

At Odessa Permian High School, Stoney Case led the Panthers to a perfect 16–0 record and took the Texas 5A state title in 1989. Case also lettered in high school baseball, playing outfield, first base, and pitcher.

Case was enthusiastically recruited by the University of New Mexico and became a four-year starter at quarterback for the Lobos. His statistics improved year over year, and his yardage and touchdown totals doubled from his

C

freshman season to his senior season. As a senior in 1994, Case threw for 3,117 yards with 22 TDs and 12 interceptions, and he also rushed for another 11 TDs. He was named WAC Player of the Year and led the NCAA with his 33 total TDs and 3,649 combined yards.

Case was the first player in NCAA Division I-A history to throw for over 9,000 career passing yards and 1,000 career rushing yards. His 98 total touchdowns were second in I-A history to BYU's Ty Detmer.

Case was picked by the Arizona Cardinals in the 3rd round of the 1995 NFL Draft, though he was limited to backup duties and only saw playing time in five games from 1995 to 1998.

STONEY CASE

Case made the Baltimore Ravens in 1999 and won his first start, giving head coach Brian Billick his first win with the Ravens. Case won his second start the following week with a 54-yard touchdown pass in overtime. Unfortunately, he lost his next two games and threw a couple of pick-sixes. Case was demoted to backup behind Tony Banks. Case passed for nearly 1,000 yards, a career best, but countered 3 TDs with 8 INTs.

In 2000 Case signed with the Detroit Lions as an unrestricted free agent to

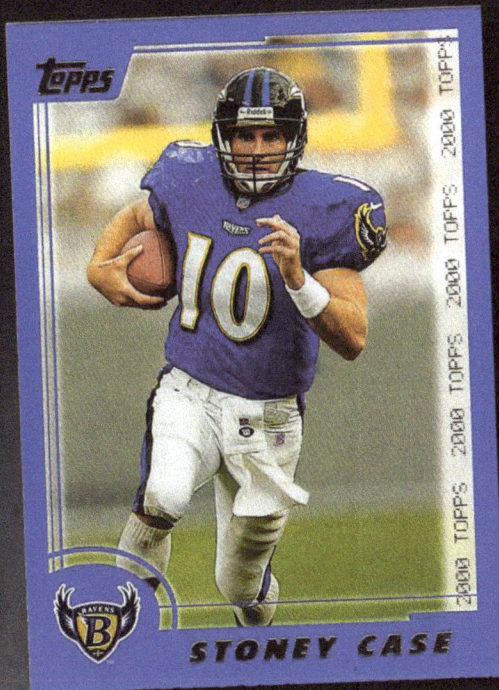

C

back up Charlie Batch. Filling in for the injured Batch, he saw action in five-games and won his only start. He threw for 503 yards, 1 TD, and 4 interceptions.

Major shoulder surgery would end Case's NFL career and, seemingly, his football career in general after his Lions contract expired. However, he managed to rehabilitate and caught on with the Tampa Bay Storm of the Arena Football League in 2005, but Case appeared in only three games, completing 4 of 7 passes for 2 touchdowns. In 2006 Case signed on as a backup quarterback for the San Jose SaberCats. The following season, he returned to Tampa Bay as an AFL free agent and took over as the Storm's starting quarterback four games deep in the season. His return would prove short-lived, however, when he dislocated his shoulder and required season-ending shoulder surgery.

Stoney Case is a quarterback legend. He accomplished things on the field in high school and college that few men have or ever will again, then he had a thirteen-year professional football career.

CAVANAUGH, MATT

Little did Matt Cavanaugh know that when he first stepped into a locker room at the professional level, he wouldn't leave that environment for almost four decades.

In 1976 Cavanaugh led the University of Pittsburgh to an undefeated season, and, along with teammate Tony Dorsett, defeated Georgia 27–3 in the Sugar Bowl and won the National Championship. He received the Sugar Bowl MVP.

As a senior in 1977 Cavanaugh threw for 1,844 yards, which was good for second most in Panthers history. Again, he led his team to a bowl game, and his four touchdown passes defeated Clemson 34–3. Cavanaugh was once again named MVP of his bowl game.

Cavanaugh was picked in the 2nd round of the 1978 NFL Draft by the New England Patriots. He wouldn't see much field time in

C

his first few seasons, but in 1981 Cavanaugh started half of the team's sixteen games, which was the most playing time he would ever see in his career. In 1983 he moved on to San Francisco, where he became Joe Montana's backup and would receive his first Super Bowl ring in 1984. Cavanaugh then signed with Philadelphia in 1986 and remained an Eagle for the next four seasons, starting just two games in that stretch. He landed with the New York Giants in 1990 to back up Jeff Hostetler, just in time to collect his second Super Bowl ring. Cavanaugh would wrap up his thirteen-year pro career after one more season in New York. He appeared in 112 games, starting 19 over the course of his career and finishing with 4,332 yards passing and 28 touchdowns.

1991 may have been his last season as a player, but it was hardly his last season in football. Wasting no time, Cavanaugh returned to his alma mater to become Pitt's chief recruiter and offensive coach from 1992 to 1993. In 1994 he returned to the NFL to start a coaching career that would dwarf his playing career, and Cavanaugh is still coaching the sport thirty years later. He would go on to receive a third Super Bowl ring in 2000 as the offensive coordinator for the Ravens.

Taking into account his National Championship and record-setting college career, his thirteen years as one of the NFL's most reliable backups, and his three-decade coaching career, Matt Cavanaugh epitomizes professional football.

CAVANAUGH'S COACHING HISTORY

- **Pittsburgh (1992–93)**
  Tight ends coach
- **Arizona Cardinals (1994–95)**
  Quarterbacks coach
- **San Francisco 49ers (1996)**
  Quarterbacks coach
- **Chicago Bears (1997–98)**
  Offensive coordinator
- **Baltimore Ravens (1999–2004)**
  Offensive coordinator
- **Pittsburgh Steelers (2005–08)**
  Offensive coordinator
- **New York Jets (2009–12)**
  Quarterbacks coach
- **Chicago Bears (2013–14)**
  Quarterbacks coach
- **Washington Redskins (2015–16)**
  Quarterbacks coach
- **Washington Redskins (2017–18)**
  Offensive coordinator
- **Washington Redskins (2019)**
  Senior offensive assistant
- **New York Jets (2021)**
  Senior offensive assistant

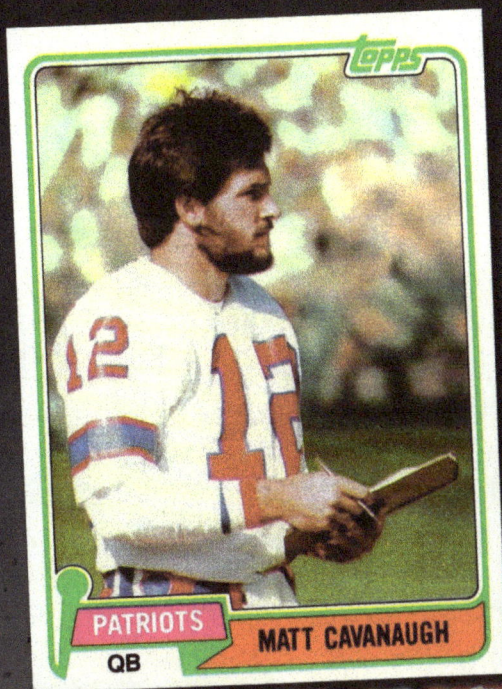

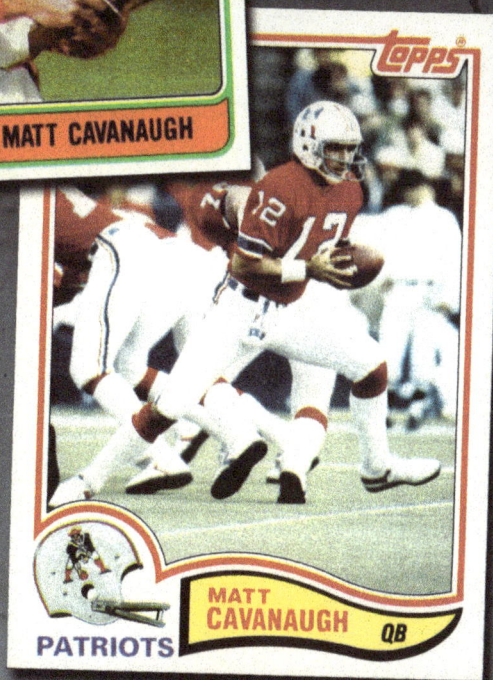

PATRIOTS
QB
MATT CAVANAUGH

MATT
CAVANAUGH QB
PATRIOTS

COOK, CONNOR

Connor Cook got one NFL start. Just one. But with that start, he set an NFL record. Cook became the first quarterback in NFL history to record his first start in a playoff game.

Ranked as the nation's thirteenth best quarterback in high school, Cook was exceptional, but he wasn't the only one from his family to excel in athletics. Connor's father, Chris, was a tight end at Indiana from 1982 to 1984. His mother, Donna, played basketball at Cincinnati, and his older sister, Jackie, was a shooting guard for the Old Dominion University Monarchs.

Cook enrolled at the Michigan State University in 2011 and redshirted his freshman season, then he backed up starter Andrew Maxwell in 2012. Maxwell was benched toward the end of the season, and Cook took the reins as a redshirt freshman, helping to lead the Spartans to a 17–16 victory over TCU at the Buffalo Wild Wings Bowl.

Cook began 2013 as Maxwell's backup again, but after Maxwell struggled in the opening game, Cook replaced him and never looked back. Cook passed for 2,755 yards and 22 TDs, with only 6 interceptions, to snag a 12–1 record and a Bowl game for Michigan State. He passed for 304 yards and 3 touchdowns to defeat Ohio State for the Big 10 Championship, earning the game's MVP honors.

SPARTANS

WEST LOWER
PRICE $150.00   ST:1:E
J   24   48   11
GATE   SEC   ROW   SEAT

GLORIOUS GREEN
AFTER 26-YEAR WAIT, SPARTANS TASTE SWEET VICTORY

SPARTANS
VS
Michigan
Oct. 25, 2014

FOR GAME TIME CALL 517.432.TIME

WEST LOWER
PRICE $150.00   ST:1:E
J   24   48   11
GATE   SEC   ROW   SEAT
Account 6728

7782986815367 4

GAME 5   Michigan

C

Cook then led his Spartans to a 24–20 win over Stanford in the Rose Bowl with a 332-yard, 2-touchdown performance, again earning MVP.

As a junior in 2014, Cook kept shaking up Michigan State's record books. He passed for a conference high of 3,214 yards and 24 TDs, leading his team to an 11–2 record and another bowl game. Michigan State defeated Baylor in the Cotton Bowl that year, 42–41.

In his final season at Michigan State, Cook continued his dominance in the Big 10 from the quarterback position. He led the Spartans to another 11–2 season and yet another bowl game. Cook's performance in the Big 10 Championship game earned him MVP honors once again and another Cotton Bowl appearance. Both his 229 completions and 408 attempts led the division, as did his 24 touchdown passes, and his 3,131 yards were good for second place. Cook threw only 7 interceptions that final season, finishing his collegiate career with just 22, compared to a school-record 71 touchdowns. His career 673 completions in 1,170 attempts for 9,194 yards were all Michigan State records as well.

Cook finished college with a 34–5 record as Michigan State's starting quarterback, which made him the top quarterback in school history. He topped it off by winning the Johnny Unitas Golden Arm Award for the nation's outstanding passers.

Cook was selected in the 4th round (100th overall) by the Oakland Raiders in the 2106 NFL Draft, signing a four-year deal. After preseason, Cook found himself at third on the quarterback depth chart behind starter Derek Carr and reserve Matt McGloin. Late in his rookie season, Cook made his debut on New Year's Day 2017 after Carr had suffered a season-ending injury the game prior and backup McGloin suffered an injury in the first half. Cook threw a 32-strike TD to Amari Cooper for his first NFL touchdown and completed 14 of 21 passes in a losing effort against the Broncos. The following week, Cook started the AFC Wild Card game against the Texans to become the NFL's first rookie quarterback to ever start a playoff game. He completed 18 of 45 passes for 161 yards with 1 TD and 3 interceptions, and the Raiders lost.

Cook returned to third string in 2017 and didn't see any action on the field. He was released after preseason in 2018. The Carolina Panthers picked Cook up and subsequently released him a month later, and the Cincinnati Bengals added Cook to their practice squad for the remainder of the year. He was briefly signed by the Detroit Lions in 2019, but Cook was released before the season began.

Cook was a 1st round draft pick by the Houston Roughnecks of the 2020 XFL Draft, but he lost the starting position to P. J. Walker, who led the league in passing before it ceased operations due to Covid.

Although Connor Cook didn't play in the NFL after his rookie season, he will always have his record-setting college career that got him to the professional level, and nobody will ever take away his record for being the first rookie quarterback to start an NFL game. He earned the chance to play with the best of the best and threw a touchdown pass in regular season and one in post season. Not many athletes can say that.

DEAN, RANDY

How many NFL quarterbacks were also punters and Olympic handball players? The only one was Randy Dean.

Dean quarterbacked Whitefish Bay High School to a co-championship his senior year in 1972 and was selected first-team All-State. He was also a punter and a star basketball player.

Dean played at Northwestern University, but not as a quarterback; he was first recruited as a punter. From 1974 to 1976, he was a punter for all three seasons and a quarterback for his junior and senior years. Northwestern did not have winning records in the 1970s—in fact, they only won three games between 1976 and 1981—but Dean managed to pass for 2,699 yards in the 1975–76 seasons while punting for another 1,166. Dean was also on the Northwestern basketball team and earned the NCAA Top Five Award for athletic and academic excellence.

While Dean was playing two positions in college football and a spot on the college basketball team, he also managed to find the time and energy to play handball. He didn't just play handball leisurely, however. He competed with the nation's best. In 1975 Dean won the USA Team Handball Nationals with the Northwest Suburban YMCA, and the next year, he placed third in the nationals. Playing alongside his twin brother Robert in the 1976 Montreal Olympic

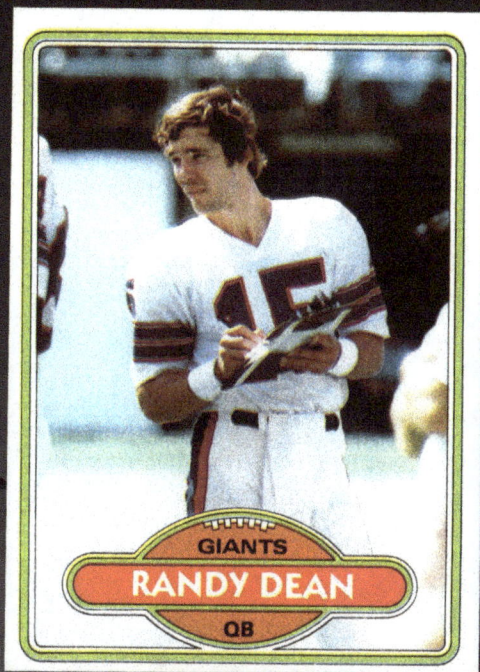

D

Games, Randy was the US team's leading scorer with 24 goals, taking them to eighth place.

Dean was selected in the 5th round of the 1977 NFL Draft by the New York Giants. Playing behind Joe Pisarcik and Jerry Golsteyn, Dean only saw playing time in one game his rookie season. He made two starts in 1978, winning one. That year he completed 19 of 39 passes for 188 yards and threw 1 touchdown. With the addition of Phil Simms, drafted in 1979, Dean didn't see any increase in playing time and started just one game that he lost.

Dean was traded to the Green Bay Packers the following season for a future draft pick. In a crowded quarterback field with Lynn Dickey, David Whitehurst, Bill Troup, and Steve Pisarkeiewiz, Dean was released before the start of the season.

Dean may not have had the longest or most memorable professional football career, but he has the proud distinction of being the only athlete in history to start an NFL game, throw an NFL touchdown, and score 24 goals on the USA's Olympic handball team.

DILS, STEVE

After starring at Fort Vancouver High School in Vancouver, Washington, the Seattle native Dils would stay on the west coast to play for Stanford University.

At Stanford, Dils played under legendary coach Bill Walsh and had one of the most memorable seasons in team history. In 1978 Dils led his Cardinals to a 25–22 victory over Georgia to win the Bluebonnet Bowl and was named the game's MVP. He finished the season with 247 completions of 391 passes for a 63.2 completion percentage, leading the entire nation in all three categories. Dil's 2,943 passing yards and 22 touchdowns also led the nation and earned him the Sammy Baugh Trophy for the top passer in the nation. He finished his college career with an amazing 137.3 passer rating. Dils was inducted into the Stanford Athletics Hall of Fame in 2003.

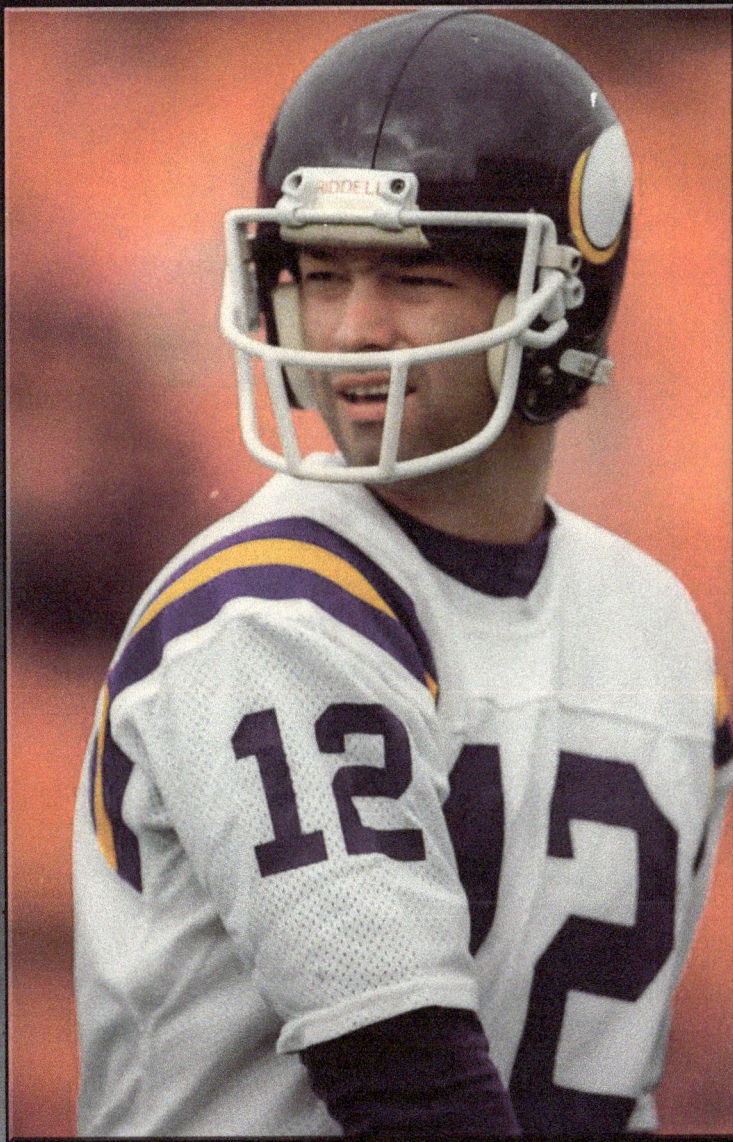

D

When asked about a memory, good or bad, Dils replied:

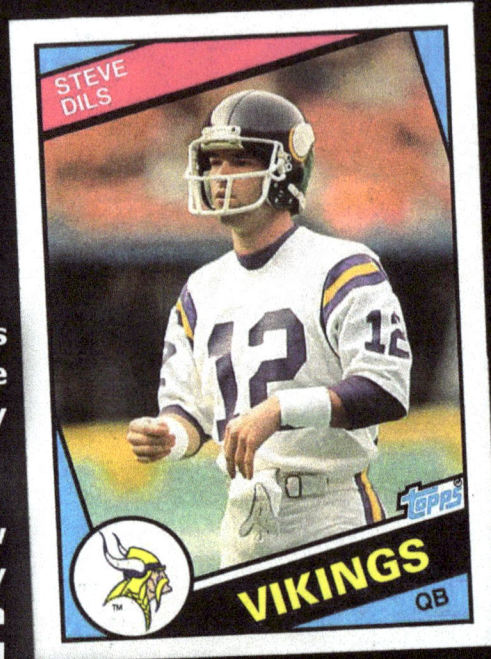

As you would expect, I have a lot of memories that are positive and some that were a little less positive. The one story that is probably most interesting is related to the draft in '79.

So, there is some background you need to know to make the story relevant. Bill Walsh was my coach the last two years at Stanford. I had a successful senior year under his coaching and had gone from being someone who no one knew to the leading passer in the nation.After my senior season, Bill was hiredby the 49ers as their head coach. A week and half before the draft I was at an event with him and he asks me if I have an agent. I said no, I hadn't hired one yet. He said don't, because they were going to draft me, and they would take care of me. Clearly, that was the best news I could get. In the time between that conversation and the draft, he went down to try out James Owens at UCLA as a receiver. The quarterback who showed up to throw to James was Joe Montana. He saw something in that workout that caused him to change his mind about who he would draft as a quarterback. On draft day I was listening to the radio station that would give updates about the draft—no ESPN back then. When they came on and said that the 49ers had drafted quarterback...Joe Montana, I wasn't sure that I had heard it right. It took me a few minutes to process that news. Long story short, I was very disappointed at the time, but they clearly made the right decision as Joe was the best quarterback of our era, by far.

D

Though the Vikings picked him in the 4th round (97th overall) of the 1979 NFL Draft, Dils didn't make his first start until his second year, filling in for the injured Tommy Kramer. In his start, he won a crucial game with playoff implications over the Washington Redskins. Dils would only get two starts over the next two seasons, but that changed in 1983 when he enjoyed the most playing time he would ever see in his NFL career. In twelve starts, Dils passed for 2,840 yards and 11 touchdowns, leading the Vikings to a 5–7 record with Dils at the helm. During the 1984 season, Dils was traded to the Rams, with whom he threw 1 TD and 1 interception in just 7 pass attempts. He would start nine games over the next three years with the Rams, passing for 9 TDs and 8 interceptions.

Dils moved to Atlanta for one last season in 1988, starting three games for the Falcons. In eleven years with the NFL, Steve Dils passed for 5,816 yards, 27 touchdowns, and 32 interceptions. He had one comeback win and five game-winning drives.

Steve Dils had one of the most productive and memorable seasons in Pac-8 history, won ten games as a starter in the NFL—including one that led the Vikings to the Playoffs—and had a career in professional football lasting over a decade. That is a successful football career in any book.

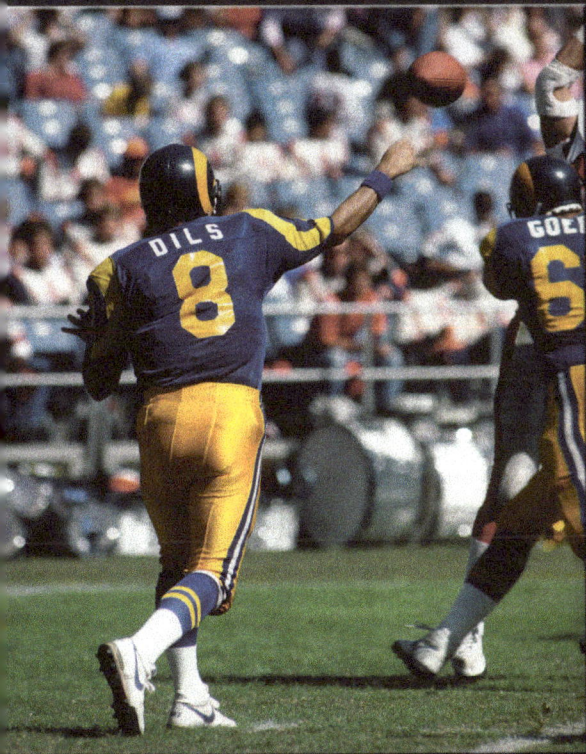

DIXON, DENNIS

As a senior in 2002 at California's San Leandro High School, Dixon threw for 2,426 yards and 30 touchdowns, leading his team to a 12–1 record and a 4-A state championship game. Upon graduation, Dixon had passed for 5,951 yards and 79 TDs earning his teams a combined 36–3 record with his only losses coming from three straight championship games. He was a four-star recruit in football and a highly recruited baseball player as well, initially drafted in the 20th round of the 2003 Major League Baseball Draft by the Cincinnati Reds.

Dixon passed on the baseball offer to instead pursue a scholarship to the University of Oregon. After he gray-shirted in 2003, Dixon backed up Kellen Clemens as a freshman in 2004, seeing minor playing time. He was slated to back up Clemens again in 2005, but when Clemens suffered a broken ankle, Dixon split time with fellow sophomore Brady Leaf and helped the Ducks to the Holiday Bowl versus Oklahoma.

As a junior in 2006, Dixon led the Ducks to a 4–0 start but was benched in favor of Leaf after losing to Cal. Oregon lost three of their last four games without

D

Dixon at the helm. Despite his shortened season, Dixon still finished with 219.3 total yards per game, good for fourth best in the Pac-10. He was a second-team Academic All-Conference athlete and graduated with a 3.27 GPA and a degree in sociology before his senior football season even started. Dixon was drafted yet again by Major League Baseball, this time in the 5th round by the Atlanta Braves. He hit .176 in 74 at bats for two of their rookie-league teams and would return to Oregon for his senior season in 2007.

In his senior year, everything came together for Dixon. He was named USA Today's National Player of the Week after his performance against powerhouse Michigan when he achieved 368 yards and 4 touchdowns. The next week he had 3 total TDs against Fresno State and then 367 yards passing and 4 TDs the following week against Stanford. At that point Dixon was in contention for the Heisman Trophy, but a torn ACL late in the season sidelined him for the remainder of the year. He still managed to pass for 2,136 yards with 20 touchdowns and only 4 interceptions and rushed for 583 yards and another 9 touchdowns. Dixon's 67.7 pass completion percentage topped the conference, and he was awarded the 2007 Pac-10 Offensive Player of the Year. Before his injury, the Ducks moved up to no. 2 in the BCS poll but lost their last two games with Dixon removed. Unfortunately, he had to watch from the sidelines as the Ducks defeated South Florida in the Sun Bowl.

Dixon was selected in the 5th round (156th overall) of the 2008 NFL Draft by the Pittsburgh Steelers. His first NFL pass was to Hines Ward, completed for the receiver's 800th career reception. While that would be his only pass or field action during his rookie season, Dixon earned a ring when the Steelers won Super Bowl XLIII.

D

After starter Ben Roethlisberger and backup Charlie Batch were both injured, Dixon found himself moving from third-string to starter on November 29, 2009, in a game against the Baltimore Ravens. He passed for a touchdown and ran for another but then threw an interception in overtime and lost the game.

Dixon started 2010 at number two on the quarterback depth chart since Roethlisberger was suspended for the first four games of the season. When fill-in starter Byron Leftwich went down with a knee injury in preseason, Dixon found himself as the opening day starter. He defeated Atlanta in that first game and was on his way to another victory the following week versus Tennessee when he tore his meniscus, landing him on the injured reserve list and ending his season. That would be the last time Dixon played in the NFL.

In 2012 Dixon was a member of the Baltimore Ravens practice squad. Although he never suited up on their roster, he earned another ring as part of the team after they won Super Bowl XLVII. Dixon reunited with his former Oregon Ducks coach Chip Kelly after signing a two-year deal with the Philadelphia Eagles in 2013, but he was released before the season began. Later that year, Dixon was signed to the Buffalo Bills practice squad and in 2014 signed to the Arizona Cardinals practice squad.

Although Dixon only passed for 402 yards with 1 passing and 1 rushing TD in four NFL games, he left the sport with two Super Bowl rings, seventeen first-place Heisman Trophy votes—fifth overall in final voting—a finalist position for the Davey O'Brien Trophy, a Draddy Trophy, a Johnny Unitas Golden Arm Award, a Maxwell Award, and a Walter Camp Award.

DOMRES, MARTY

Domres played at Columbia University, where he set fifteen new passing records. The anthropology major led the Ivy League in total offense in both 1967 and 1968. He concluded his collegiate career as one of the best players the school had ever seen with 4,495 yards passing, good for third most in Ivy League history (at the time). Domres also set twelve Ivy League records, three Eastern, and one national for most total offensive plays in a career (1,133), and he was inducted into the Columbia Lions Hall of Fame in 2008.

Domres was a 1st round pick (9th overall) by the San Diego Chargers in 1969. Unfortunately for

Domres, the Chargers starter John Hadl was in the midst of back-to-back Pro Bowl seasons in 1968–69 and would continue to tear up the Chargers' record books over the next half decade. After starting only six games in three years, Domres requested a trade, and the Baltimore Colts acquired Domres to backup Johnny Unitas.

Domres replaced the aging legend Johnny Unitas as the starter in week six of the 1972 season, after the Colts GM Joe Thomas ordered coaches to bench the veterans in favor of getting his younger players more experience. Domres would see most of his NFL action over the next four seasons with Baltimore, starting in twenty-four games and throwing for over 3,400 yards and 21 touchdowns.

In 1976 Domres would move to San Francisco where he would see limited action behind starter Jim Plunkett and backup Scott Bull. Domres landed another new home in 1977, this time in New York. Domres started two games for the Jets behind the highly touted youngster Richard Todd.

In his nine professional seasons, Domres completed 399 of 809 passes for 4,904 yards with 27 touchdowns and 50 interceptions. He rushed for another 679 yards, scoring 10 times.

MARTY DOMRES

QUARTERBACK
COLTS

DOUGLAS, BOBBY

Bobby Douglass grew up in Kansas with a football coach father, so it was only fitting that he attended the University of Kansas for football. He was named as an All-Big-8 Conference selection in both 1967 and 1968 and as an All-American in 1968. The lefty passed for 1,316 yards and 12 touchdowns his senior season, leading his Jayhawks to a 9–2 record and the 1969 Orange Bowl. Douglass finished seventh in the Heisman Trophy voting that season.

Douglass was a 2nd round pick (41st overall) of the Chicago Bears in 1969. He would start seven games, rushing for 408 yards in his rookie campaign, but wouldn't really become the main fixture at quarterback until 1971. In 1972 the fleet-footed Douglass set the record for most rushing yards in a season by a quarterback with 968 yards on 141 carries, and that was in only a fourteen-game season. He scored 8 TDs on the ground and led the entire league with a 6.9 yards-per-carry average.

D

His incredible record stood for thirty-four years and was broken in a sixteen-game season. The next season, Douglass would rush for another 525 yards and set another record, scoring 4 rushing TDs in a single game against the Packers. All of this in an era when quarterbacks weren't supposed to run and typically didn't.

Douglass was traded to the San Diego Chargers during the 1975 season and would see another new team in 1976, eventually landing with the New Orleans Saints. He had a bit of a revival as a passer in the Super Dome, throwing for 1,288 yards, the most of his career. Douglass spent one more season in New Orleans before moving to Green Bay for his final season in 1978.

Although he wasn't known for his arm, Bobby Douglass used his feet to run his way into the record books and NFL highlight films. In his decade-long career, Douglass rushed for 2,654 yards on 410 carries, good for an amazing 6.5-yard average every time he carried the ball. He had 22 career rushing TDs to go with his 36 career passing scores.

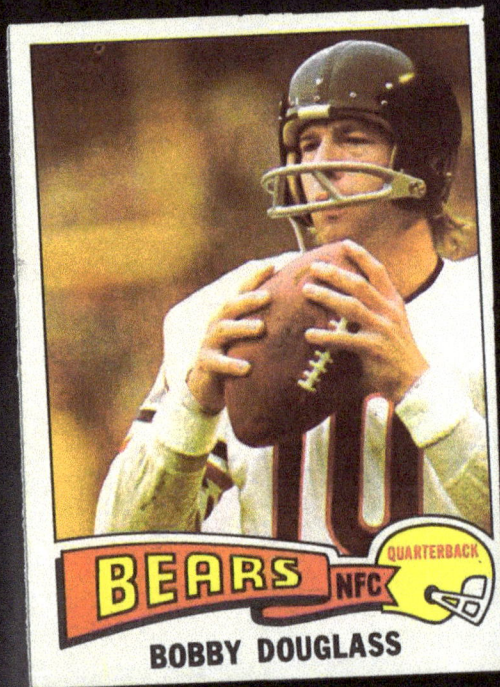

BEARS NFC QUARTERBACK

BOBBY DOUGLASS

DOWLING, BRIAN

In 1963, as a junior at St. Ignatius High School in Cleveland, OH, Brian Dowling left the City Championship game at halftime with a bruised kidney and a broken collarbone, and his team lost the game. That would stand as the only game he ever lost in high school football. As a senior the following season, he got revenge and beat the same team in the next City Championship game by a 48–6 routing. Dowling threw 4 touchdown passes and ran for a 71-yard score, ending his high school career with a 36–1 record.

In high school basketball, Dowling led his team to the City title by sinking four 3-pointers in the championship game's final thirty-four seconds to overcome a thirteen-point deficit. As a sophomore playing tennis, he made the state finals in doubles, and he made the Regional finals in singles as a senior.

D

Dowling had multiple offers from NCAA Division I schools but decided on Yale University with his father's help. As a freshman he led the junior varsity football team to a perfect 6–0 record, averaged 24.5 points on their basketball team, and managed to also compete in tennis.

Dowling missed all but the first football game of his sophomore year because of a season-ending knee injury, then he broke his wrist in preseason practice as a junior and missed the first three games of that year. He came back strong in week four, led the team to the Ivy League Championship, and beat Harvard in a come-from-behind victory.

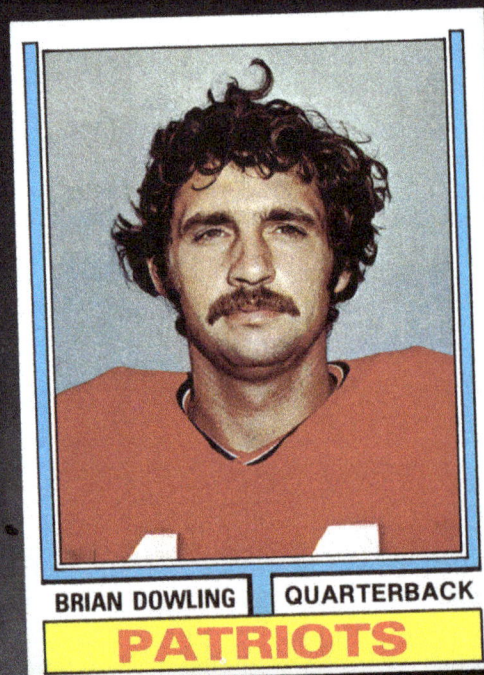

BRIAN DOWLING | QUARTERBACK
PATRIOTS

In his senior season, Dowling rewrote the Yale record books, totaling 1,554 yards passing with 19 TDs and 313 yards rushing that added another 6 TDs on the ground. Again, he led Yale to a perfect record and his second Ivy League title. Overall, Dowling was 16–1–1 in his college career, his only loss coming in a game he couldn't finish as a sophomore due to injury.

Dowling was drafted in the 11th round by the Minnesota Vikings in 1969, but he wouldn't make it past the practice squad. He then laced up for the Bridgeport Jets of the Atlantic Coast Football League, a minor league team of the New York Jets.

D

The next season, Dowling would sign with the New England Patriots but again remained on the practice squad until 1972, when he finally saw the field. In his NFL rookie campaign, Dowling would complete 29 out of 54 passes for 383 yards, 3 touchdowns, and 1 interception.

In 1974 Dowling signed with the Charlotte Hornets of the new World Football League, where he would throw for 523 yards, 2 touchdowns, and 11 interceptions as a backup from 1974 to 1975. In 1976 he moved north to Canada to try out for the Toronto Argonauts but didn't make the team.

Dowling would return to the NFL four years later in 1977 and catch on with the Green Bay Packers as a third-string quarterback. He got into a game and attempted one pass to finish his professional career.

Even though his whole professional career looks more like the statistics of one good game and doesn't stand out in the annals of NFL history, nobody can deny his tenacity and dedication to the sport of football. He left marks and memories in high school and college that are still talked about, and he's a member of the Cleveland Sports Hall of Fame as one of the greatest all-around athletes to ever come out of Cleveland.

DRUCKENMILLER, JIM

Druckenmiller could already bench press 250 pounds and squat over 300 by the time he was a senior at Northampton High School in Pennsylvania (per a BiggerFasterStronger.com article with Dr. Greg Shepard). Although he passed for over 1,000 yards with 11 TDs his senior season, Druckenmiller didn't get much attention from colleges, so he decided to attend Fort Union Military Academy after high school in 1990. There, he could work on the nuances of his football game without losing a year of college eligibility. His hard work paid off, and he played well enough and studied hard enough to impress coaches at Virginia Tech.

Even though Druckenmiller was voted Offensive MVP of the Hokies 1992 spring game, he decided to redshirt his freshman year. The next two

D

seasons he saw limited playing time behind Maurice DeShazo, attempting just 38 passes for 209 yards. Druckenmiller kept hard at work honing his quarterback skills, and at the gym, his bench press topped 320 pounds, and he was squatting 450. According to Dr. Shepard's aforementioned article, Druckenmiller was getting frustrated sitting on the bench and took his aggression out in the weight room.

It all paid off his junior season when Druckenmiller won the starting job and led the Hokies to a 10–2 record and Big East title. He passed for 2,103 yards with 14 TDs in the season and defeated the Texas Longhorns in the Sugar Bowl. Druckenmiller proved himself even more his senior year when he passed for 2,071 yards with 17 TDs and only 5 interceptions and added 205 yards rushing. He led the Hokies to another 10–2 record and consecutive Big East titles. Druckenmiller earned All-Big East honors and won the 1996 Big East Offensive Player of the Year.

When Peyton Manning returned to Tennessee for his senior season, it cemented Druckenmiller as the top quarterback in the 1997 draft. The San Francisco 49ers selected Druckenmiller as the 26th overall pick in the 1st round, the first time they

D

had selected a quarterback in the 1st round since Steve Spurrier thirty years prior.

The 49ers intended on grooming Druckenmiller as future Hall of Famer Steve Young's successor, and when Young was forced to miss a game with a concussion, Druckenmiller was called on for his first start, beating out Jeff Brohm. He completed just 10 of 28 passes with 1 TD and 3 INTs. He saw playing time in three more games, throwing another interception and no more touchdowns. Druckenmiller finished his rookie year completing 21 of 52 passes for 239 yards with 1 TD and 4 picks.

In his second season (1998), Druckenmiller faced drastically diminished playing time, seeing action in only two games, and never attempted a pass. He was relegated to third string behind Steve Young and Ty Detmer. San Francisco GM Steve Walsh didn't think highly of Druckenmiller and traded him to Miami in 1999 for a conditional draft pick. While playing behind Dan Marino and Damon Huard, Druckenmiller never saw the field. The Dolphins released him after preseason in 2000.

In 2001 Druckenmiller signed with the Los Angeles Avengers of the Arena Football League as a backup to former Oregon State star Erik Wilhelm and Oregon Duck standout Tony Graziani. He later signed with the Memphis Maniax of the XFL and became one of the only starters in the league to play the entire season without injury or replacement. Druckenmiller finished the season completing 109 of 199 passes for 1,499 yards with 13 TDs and 7 INTs and was one of the most promoted and popular players in the league.

D

After not playing in 2002, Druckenmiller was invited in 2003 to try out for the Colts' third-string position behind starter Peyton Manning and backup **Brock Huard**. The Colts chose to go with Jim Kubiak instead, and Druckenmiller's professional football career was finished.

Druckenmiller remained in Memphis after playing for the Maniax. He has had two knee surgeries and bulging disks in his back, and he can no longer run due to injuries suffered in his football career.

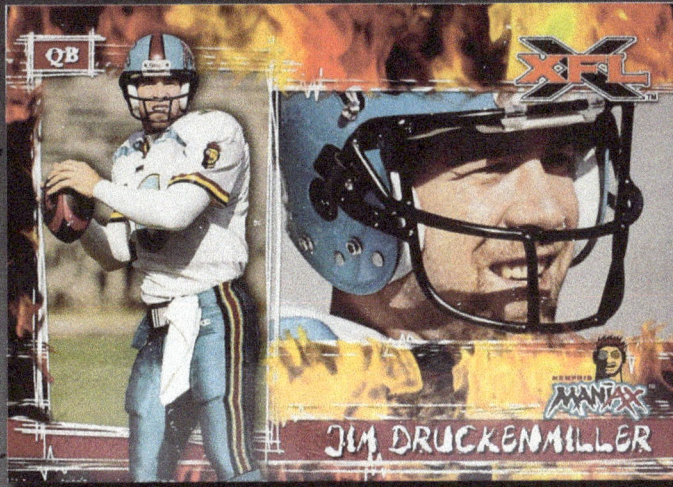

DUFEK, JOE

Joe Dufek defines persistence and dedication. In 1980 he was a third-string quarterback at Yale University and attempted just 19 passes for 79 yards. In 1981 Dufek moved up to second-string yet still only threw the ball 35 times for 191 yards, with 3 TDs and no picks.

The name Dufek may sound very familiar to college football enthusiasts. Joe's father, Don Dufek Sr., was a star fullback with the University of Michigan Wolverines from 1948 to 1950. Joe Dufek's brother, Don Jr., was an All-American defensive back at Michigan from 1973 to 1975, and his other brother, Bill, played offensive line for

D

the Wolverines from 1974 to 1978, also an All-American. All the Dufeks made it to the NFL.

Joe Dufek got a chance to join his brother on the Seattle Seahawks as an un-drafted player in 1983. His older brother, Don Dufek, spent eight seasons as a special teams captain and safety for the Seahawks. Joe didn't make the squad but was signed by the Buffalo Bills for quarterback depth insurance when their megastar new draft pick Jim Kelly jumped ship to the new USFL league.

Dufek made the Bills roster in 1983 but didn't get to use his arm on the field. By 1984 Bills starter Joe Ferguson was aging and Dufek got the call to start five times. In 150 pass attempts, he completed 74 for 829 yards with 4 touch-downs and 8 interceptions. Dufek also added a rushing touchdown. Dufek re-turned to the Bills for 1985 but was cut partway through the season. He caught on with the Chargers to finish out the season but never saw action on the field. Dufek tried out for the Raiders in 1986 but was released in camp and called it a career.

FASANI, RANDY

Did Randy Fasani turn down the Jets and other NFL teams to pursue a passion for law enforcement, replacing one dream with another?

Fasani graduated from Del Oro High School in Loomis, California, as an All-American. With 5,299 yards passing and 53 TDs and 654 yards rushing for another 16 TDs in his high school career, Fasani was considered a top recruit in the nation.

After many Division I-A offers, Fasani chose to stay near home in California and attend Stanford University. After redshirting his freshman year (1997), Fasani was put into games in goal line situations to utilize his legs, and he scored 3 touchdowns. With his 6'3", 230-pound build, Fasani also played some tight end in 1998. Placed behind senior starter Todd Husak in 1999, Fasani only made 6 pass attempts at quarterback and played the inside linebacker position. He also made honorable mention Academic All-Pac-10 that year. In his junior year, Fasani started eight games at quarterback. Using both

F

his arm and legs, the dual-threat Fasani passed for 1,400 yards with 11 TDs and rushed for another 123 yards with 2 TDs. In 2001 Fasani duplicated the eight starts from his junior year but improved his offensive output. He passed for 1,479 yards with 13 TDs and only 4 INTs and rushed for another 174 yards with a score, earning honorable mention on the All-Pac-10 team.

Fasani was selected in the 5th round of the 2002 NFL Draft by the Carolina Panthers. He competed with Chris Weinke for the spot to back up veteran Rodney Peete. Fasani made the roster but only saw action in four games, starting one. He finished his rookie season completing 15 of 44 passes for 171 yards with 0 TDs and 4 INTs and 95 yards rushing. He was released the next season, and his one start against the Buccaneers would be the only one of his career.

In 2003 Fasani had the opportunity to play with the New York Jets via a trade with the Panthers, but he decided to return home instead. He had lost the passion to play football and wanted to go back to his family and pursue his other dream of becoming a police officer. Fasani had been on more than a few police ride-a-longs while in the NFL and fell in love with it.

Fasani follows his passions to the fullest. He wanted to play in the NFL, and through determination and hard work, he made it happen. He wanted to become a police officer, like his father-in-law and two cousins, and quit football to chase that dream, becoming a member of the Visalia, California, police force. He later rediscovered his passion for football after becoming the head coach at Ripon Christian High School and eventually found his way home to coach at his old high school.

FLICK, TOM

Imagine if your client list included Boeing, Hallmark, Starbucks, Microsoft, NASA, and the Pentagon. Tom Flick learned leadership and motivational skills from being a quarterback and parlayed them into a very successful career as a motivational speaker after his time in pro football.

A three-sport star at Interlake High School in Bellevue, Washington, Tom Flick led his Saints to a perfect 10–0 record his junior year. He finished the season in the KingCo Championship, and his team reached a no. 2 ranking in the state. Flick repeated the feat his senior year and led the Saints back to the state championship. Although he was recruited by several colleges, Flick chose to stay near home and attend the University of Washington.

After Being stuck behind Warren Moon his freshman year, Flick decided to redshirt his sophomore season in 1978—Moon's senior year. In his first season as a starter, Flick led the Huskies to a 9–3 record and an appearance at the 1979 Sun Bowl.

In his senior season, Flick led his Huskies to another nine-win season (9–2), the Pac-10 Championship, and a 1980 Rose Bowl appearance. During the season he completed the longest TD pass in school history, 84 yards, to Willie Rosborough versus Air Force. Flick also set a school and NCAA record for highest completion percentage in a game (94.1 percent) when he completed 16 of 17

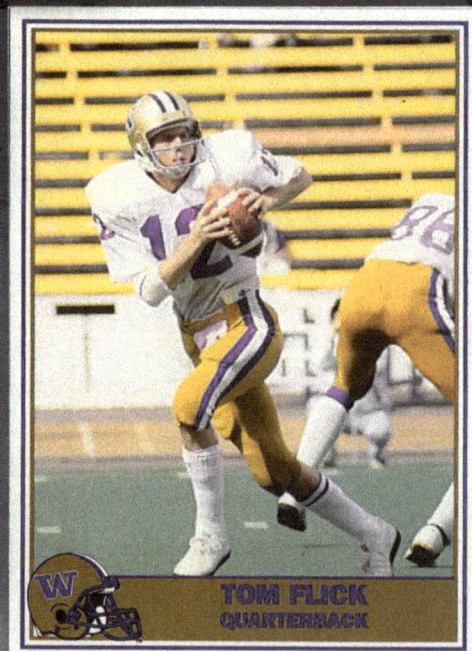

TOM FLICK
QUARTERBACK

F

passes against Arizona, all while he was suffering from a concussion. Flick's career 60.3 percent completion ratio topped the school record books, and his 2,460 yards passing in 1980 also established a new UW high. Flick won the Flaherty Award, KIRO Player of the Year, Pac-10 Sports Report Player of the Year, and was selected to play in two all-star games: the East-West Shrine game and the Japan Bowl. Flick finished the year voted the team's most inspirational player, a seed which would sprout into a career in his post-playing days.

Flick was selected in the 4th round (90th overall) by the Washington Redskins in the 1981 NFL Draft. First-year coach Joe Gibbs personally wanted Flick drafted. As a backup to Joe Theisman, Flick didn't see much playing time his rookie year, but he completed 13 of 27 passes for 143 yards and 2 TDs. In 1982 Flick was traded to the Patriots and landed at third string behind starter Steve Grogan and backup Matt Cavanaugh. In 1984 Flick moved on again, this time to Cleveland. He earned the backup position behind starter Paul McDonald. With McDonald playing virtually every down from scrimmage, Flick only attempted 1 pass and completed it for 2 yards. With the drafting of highly touted Hurricane Bernie Kosar, Flick was relegated to the third string position in 1985 and didn't appear in any games that year.

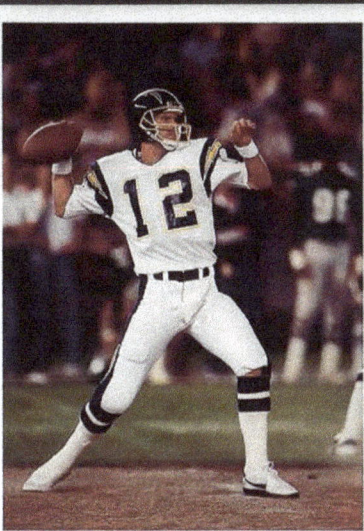

In 1986 Flick signed with the San Diego Chargers as Dan Fouts's backup. Fouts missed three games due to injury, which led to the first NFL starts of Flick's career. He won one of the three games and passed for

12   TOM FLICK   QB

Height: 6-3   Birthdate: August 30, 1958
Weight: 191   Birthplace: Patuxent River Naval
College: Washington   Air Station, Maryland
                     Acquired: FA-1986

F

361 yards with 2 TDs and 8 INTs in his brief time as a starter. In his lone victory on November 9th, Flick was named the game's MVP for his performance, with 16 completions in 22 pass attempts. He beat the Super Bowl-bound Denver Broncos and out-dueled his counterpart John Elway.

In the strike-riddled 1987 season Flick signed with the New York Jets but didn't see any playing time on the field. Flick retired with 47 completions in 106 attempts for 506 yards. He passed for 2 touchdowns and ran for another while throwing 10 interceptions over his career.

Flick was always known and respected as a leader on the football field and continued utilizing that attribute after life on the turf. He founded Flick Communications in 1989 and began speaking at educational and public events. He has since traveled around the world, inspiring leadership and change. Flick has been hired by some of the top organizations and companies in the world as a motivational speaker.

FURRER, WILL

Furrer was a baseball player at Pullman High School in Washington and didn't even play organized football until his sophomore year. With his strong arm, he may have been the starting quarterback his junior year if it were not for the varsity starter being none other than Timm Rosenbach, another future NFL quarterback. But when Timm went off to Washington State, Furrer became the starter his senior season and picked up right where Timm left off, earning himself a scholarship to Virginia Tech.

As a redshirt freshman, Furrer had an up-and-down season with the Hokies in 1988. He passed for 1,384 yards with 6 touchdowns and 16 interceptions. By his junior year in 1990, Furrer was on his way to setting school records. The lefty passed for 2,122 yards and a school-record 19 touchdowns, completing over 58 percent of his passes, and was named the team MVP.

F

Furrer wasn't just sharp on the field; he dominated in the classroom as well. He was a recipient of the 1991 National Football Foundation and College Hall of Fame Scholar Athlete Award his senior year, made the Dean's List six times, and won the John Schneider Award for the team's top scholar-athlete.

Furrer finished his college career as Virginia Tech's all-time leader, with 494 completions and 53 touchdown passes. He was inducted into the school's sports Hall of Fame in 2015.

Furrer was selected in the 4th round of the 1992 NFL Draft by the Chicago Bears, the fifth quarterback taken in the draft. Furrer saw just one start during his rookie campaign and playing time in one other game, completing only 38 percent of his passes with 0 TDs and 3 interceptions. The Bears released him the next season, and Furrer signed with the Phoenix Cardinals but, positioned behind veterans Steve Beuerlein and Chris Chandler, didn't see any playing time. The Broncos signed him next

F

in 1994, but behind perennial All-Pro John Elway and reserve Hugh Millen, Furrer remained sidelined in Denver too.

In 1995 Furrer crossed the pond and played for the Amsterdam Admirals in the World League. He completed 51 of 85 passes for 542 yards and 4 TDs in a platooning role with Jamie Martin, and it was enough to be signed by the Houston Oilers later in the year. In Houston Furrer got one more shot to play at the top level of professional football. In seven games, he completed 48 of 99 passes for 483 yards and 2 touchdowns with 7 interceptions.

Furrer went abroad again to become the Admirals' starter in 1996, his best season as a professional quarterback. He completed 206 of 369 passes for 2,869 yards and 20 touchdowns, earning him All-World League honors. His stellar playing earned him another look from the NFL, and he signed with the Rams in 1997. With rookie Tony Banks starting all sixteen games and earning All-Rookie team honors, Furrer got no playing time. He gave it one more shot in 1998, signing with Jacksonville and joining his former Admirals teammate Jamie Martin, but starter Mark Brunell was having another great season, and Furrer didn't see any field action.

Although he only passed for 572 yards and 2 touchdowns in the NFL, Furrer left his impression on the game, setting records at Virginia Tech and in the WLAF for Amsterdam and being recognized as a top scholar-athlete of his time.

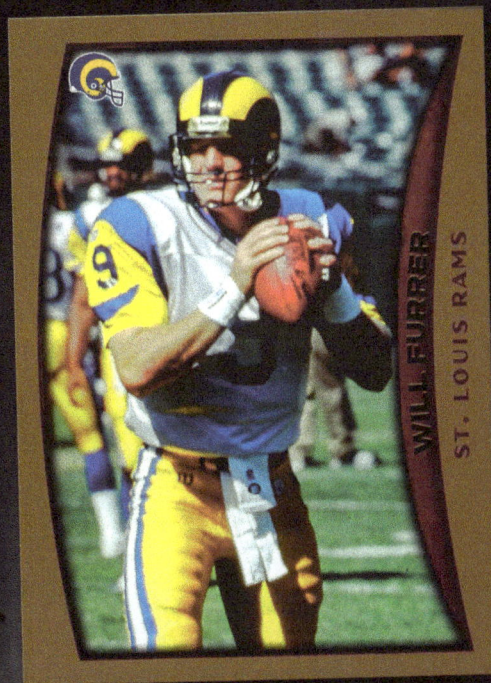

WILL FURRER

ST. LOUIS RAMS

FUSINA, CHUCK

On November 13, 1978, Chuck Fusina appeared on the cover of Sports Illustrated alongside the words "Penn State Rolls On," an appropriate headline considering he led his Nittany Lions to two consecutive 11–1 seasons.

Born and raised in Pittsburgh, it was only fitting that Fusina, the Sto-Rox High School star, stayed in-state to attend the powerhouse that was Penn State. Fusina earned the starting role by his sophomore year (1976) and helped lead the Nittany Lions to a 7–5 record and a Gator Bowl appearance. Fusina chased perfection in his junior year, finishing the season 11–1 with a fifth-place standing in the nation. With 2,221 yards passing and 15 TDs, Fusina recorded a 146.4 passer rating and had a year for the Penn State record books in 1977.

Not only did Fusina have another incredible season his senior year, it may have been even better than his junior campaign. He led Penn State to an 11–0 record in the regular season but narrowly

missed perfection with a 14–7 loss to Alabama in the Sugar Bowl. His efforts earned him both the 1978 Consensus All-America and Maxwell Awards. Fusina finished college with a career record of 29–3 as a starter and was runner-up in the Heisman Trophy voting.

Fusina was selected in the 5th round of the 1979 NFL Draft by the Tampa Bay Buccaneers. As Doug Williams's backup, Fusina only got on the field in one game his rookie season. Because of Williams's continued success, Fusina only played in six more games over the next two seasons, attempting just 5 passes.

In 1983 Fusina left the NFL for the newly formed USFL where he had a better opportunity to shine than he had stalled behind Williams in Tampa. It was the right choice for Fusina, as he blossomed under Philadelphia/Baltimore Stars coach Jim Mora. Fusina began an immediate aerial assault on the United States Football League. In 1983 he passed for 2,718 yards with 15 touchdowns. The following season he led the Stars to the USFL title with 3,837 yards good for 31 touchdowns and only 9 interceptions. Fusina was named the USFL Most Outstanding Quarterback, the Sporting News USFL Player of the Year, and the USFL Championship Game MVP. Topping the 3,000 passing yard mark again in 1985, Fusina led the Stars to their second consecutive championship and helped establish them as the top team in the history of the USFL.

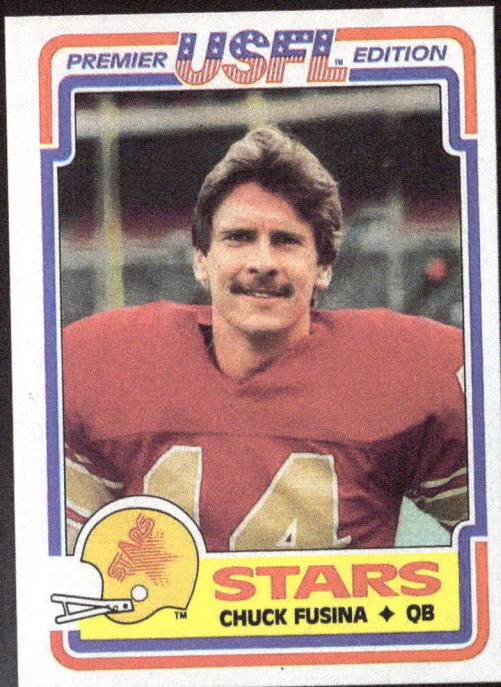

The USFL folded the next year, and Fusina would return to the NFL, signed by the Green Bay Packers in 1986. As a backup to Randy Wright, Fusina saw playing time in seven games, completing 19 of his 32 pass attempts for 178 yards. He retired the following season.

Although he never started an NFL game and only collected a single touchdown in the league, Fusina made history in professional football. While in the USFL, Fusina threw for 66 touchdowns, more than any other quarterback in the league, and passed for over 10,000 yards in just three seasons with the Stars.

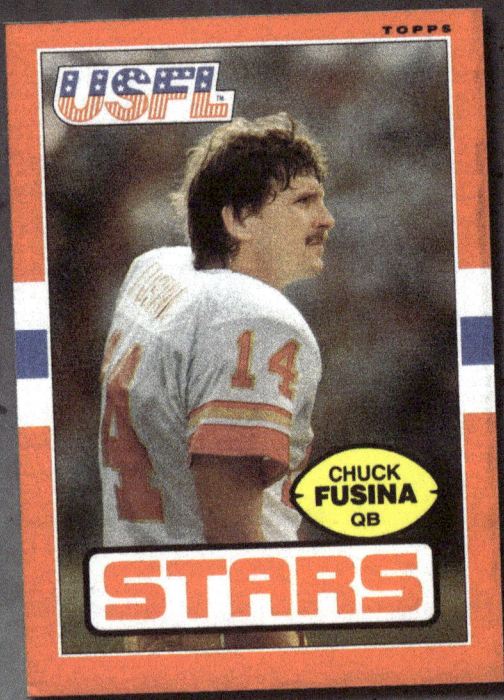

Fusina was inducted into the Pennsylvania Sports Hall of Fame in 2015.

GILBERT, GALE

Imagine being on five Super Bowl teams. Now Imagine the pain of not winning with a single one.

The Red Bluff, California, native was already a phenomenal athlete by age twelve, but it wasn't football that thrust him into the spotlight; it was baseball.

G

Gilbert was the catcher for his baseball team when they advanced to the 1974 Little League World Series, but they lost the championship to Taiwan on national television.

Gilbert stayed in-state and attended the University of California, playing under legendary Golden Bear alumnus Joe Kapp. Gilbert saw minimal playing time his first two years and had an injury redshirt. In his 1982 sophomore season Gilbert became the starter and passed for 1,796 yards with 12 touchdowns. He was part of arguably the most popular game in college football history commonly referred to as "The Play." Leading his Golden Bears against John Elway's Stanford Cardinal, Gilbert's team was down by one point with four seconds remaining when they began a series of five laterals on a kick return to score a touchdown between the Stanford band as they marched on the field prematurely.

As a junior, Gilbert led the Pac-10 in pass completions (216), pass attempts (365), and passing yards (2,769) in 1983. Gilbert passed for 4,462 yards and 19 touchdowns over his final two seasons at California. He accumulated 6,566 yards with 32 touchdowns and 48 interceptions over his college career.

Gilbert was not drafted but did sign as a free agent with the Seattle Seahawks in 1985 and made the team as the third-string quarterback behind Dave Krieg and Jim Zorn. He didn't get to see the field during his rookie season, but the following year Jim Zorn was released, and Gilbert got his first taste of NFL action. As Dave Krieg's backup, Gilbert saw limited playing time in nine games, primarily as the placekick holder on field goals and PATs, but he did complete 19 of 40 pass attempts for 218 yards throughout the season. On September 23rd, Gilbert threw his first touchdown in dramatic fashion, completing a 37-yard screamer

G

to Daryl Tuner in the final seconds of the game against the Rams.

Gilbert started two games in his second season (1986) and threw for 485 passes with 3 TDs and 3 picks, losing both contests. In the strike-laden 1987 season, Gilbert didn't see any playing time behind Dave Krieg, Jeff Kemp, and Bruce Mathison, and he was put on injured reserve. Then he hit rock bottom.

Gilbert got caught up in the celebrity life of football. In Seattle in the 1980s, Seahawks and Sonics players were celebrities. It was all the city had before the rise of grunge and famous rock stars around every coffee shop corner. Gilbert was young and made poor choices. He lost his job as a backup quarterback. He lost himself because of infidelities. He was arrested.

Before he knew it, Gilbert was sitting at home in 1988 watching NFL games from his couch instead of from the sidelines. He witnessed quarterbacks getting hurt left and right and knew he still had the skills to fill in for one of them, so he put together a highlight tape with his attorney and sent it to every NFL team except Seattle and San Francisco. The Bills bit.

Buffalo had been interested in Gilbert since scouting him during his days at the University of California. They invited him in for an audition in 1989, and he passed. Unfortunately, the good luck turned bad. Gilbert broke a rib in preseason and was put on injured reserve, missing the whole year. Finally, in November of 1990, Gilbert saw his first regular season action in nearly four years. He completed 8 of 15 passes for 106 yards with 2 TDs and 2 interceptions.

Although he didn't see any playing time in 1991–92 and just a single game in

G

1993, Gilbert was a part of the four consecutive Buffalo Bills Super Bowl teams.

The next season, Gilbert signed on with the San Diego Chargers, getting his first start in almost eight years. He filled in admirably in several other games and completed over 61 percent of his passes for 410 yards with 3 TDs and 1 INT. San Diego lost the Super Bowl to San Francisco in 1994, the fifth consecutive Super Bowl loss that Gilbert was a part of, making him the only player in NFL history with that regrettable honor.

After one more season in San Diego in which he started his last NFL game, Gilbert called it a career. In a decade of professional football, Gale Gilbert went to five Super Bowls, passed for 1,544 yards and 9 touchdowns, lived like a celebrity in Seattle, shared quarterbacking duties with Hall of Famer Jim Kelly, and got paid to do what he loved for longer than most quarterbacks could ever dream of.

Gale's son Garrett plays in the NFL and has had time with the Patriots, Rams, Lions, Raiders, Browns, Panthers, and Cowboys, among others. Gale's other son Griffin was a tight end at TCU.

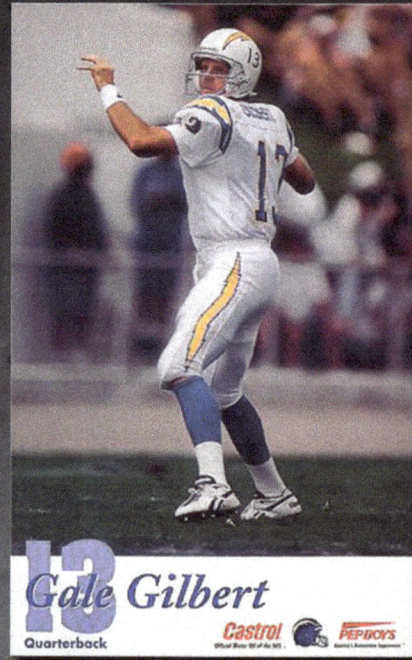

Gale Gilbert
Quarterback
Castrol   PEP BOYS

GRAZIANI, TONY

In 2007 Tony Graziani became the highest paid player in the history of the Arena Football League. But before that, his road led from California to Oregon to the NFL and almost everywhere in between.

Graziani started at quarterback for Thomas Downey High School in Modesto, California. He led his team to the Central California Conference Title (shared) in 1991 and finished his high school career with 3,956 yards passing and 35 touchdowns.

Graziani enrolled at the University of Oregon and sat behind Ducks starter Danny O'Neil until he got his chance. As a freshman, Graziani made the most of his brief opportunity when he filled in for the injured O'Neil. With 287 yards passing, he led the Ducks to

G

their first victory over USC at the Coliseum in over twenty years. In 1995 he had his first full season and helped lead Oregon to the Rose Bowl with 2,604 yards passing and 13 TDs and another 236 yards on the ground with 4 TDs. After O'Neil departed in 1996, Graziani was poised to have his breakout year with high hopes from scouts, but his injuries added up, and he only played half the season. In six games Graziani was headed for a banner year with 1,353 yards passing, 8 TDs to only 4 INTs, and a 131 passer rating.

Graziani showed enough promise when healthy to earn himself a shot at the big time. He was drafted in the 7th round (204th overall) of the 1997 NFL Draft by the Atlanta Falcons. He got one start his rookie year, filling in for an injured Chris Chandler. Graziani found himself at third on the quarterback depth chart in 1998 behind Chandler and veteran Steve DeBerg, but he still managed to find playing time in four games, starting one. He won his start and passed for 199 yards with no TDs and 2 INTs in the year. As Chris Chandler's primary backup in 1999, Graziani saw action in eleven games, starting three for the injured Chandler. Graziani compiled a 1–2 record with 759 yards passing, 2 touchdowns, and 4 interceptions. Late in the season, he had a come-from-behind, game-winning drive during the fourth quarter against New Orleans in which he passed for 162 yards and a last-minute touchdown.

G

The Falcons released Graziani in 2000, and he signed with the Cleveland Browns. The Browns allocated Graziani to the Barcelona Dragons of NFL Europe to get more developmental practice. For the Dragons, Graziani completed nearly 60 percent of his passes while throwing for 1,377 yards and 8 touchdowns. Despite his improved play in Barcelona, the Browns cut Graziani before the 2001 season.

Although the NFL cut had hurt at the time, it opened a new door for Graziani that few quarterbacks in his position had ever gone through, and of those that had, none of them dominated in their new league like he did. In 2001 Graziani signed with the Los Angeles Avengers of the Arena Football League (AFL), competing with former NFL quarterbacks Todd Marinovich and Jim Druckenmiller to be Erik Wilhelm's backup. After completing 62.2 percent of his passes and throwing 7 TDs to only 1 INT as a backup, Graziani earned the starting spot for the next season. In 2002 Graziani started every game and had 3,568 yards with 67 touchdowns and only 9 interceptions passing with another 6 rushing touchdowns in fourteen games. He was even better in 2003, completing 60.4 percent of his passes for 4,290 yards with 96 touchdowns—yes, 96! He led the Avengers to an 11–5 record and playoff berth. 2004 was almost unbelievable for any quarterback, but not Graziani. He improved again, putting up absurd, almost unbelievable numbers. He completed 65.3 percent of his 510 pass attempts for 4,265 yards and led the league with 99 touchdowns and only 5 interceptions. Let's look at those stats again: 99 TDs to 5 INTs. Graziani led his team to a 9–7 record and the playoffs again, earning himself All-Arena honors for his efforts.

G

In 2005 Graziani became the AFL's highest paid player ever after signing with the Philadelphia Soul. For the third consecutive year, he topped 4,000 yards passing and threw for 90 touchdowns. Although he had an injury-plagued 2006 season, Graziani managed almost 3,000 yards passing and 41 touchdowns and led the Soul to their first playoff game in franchise history. 2007 started off hot for Graziani as he had the Soul undefeated at 5–0 and had thrown 24 touchdowns with only 3 interceptions, including an 8-touchdown performance against the Colorado Crush. Unfortunately, he hurt his shoulder and missed the next five games. He still finished the year with 2,832 yards passing, 64 touchdowns, and 8 interceptions, landing the Soul in the playoffs again, where they won their first playoff game. In 2008 Graziani started off strong once again and set a Soul record with 9 touchdown passes in a single game. He suffered an ankle injury in week three and missed the next four games. When he returned, he was injured again. Then he would return in another game only to suffer a concussion. Although he missed a big portion of the season, Graziani still completed 66.7 percent of his passes for 1,128 yards with 30 touchdowns and only 4 interceptions. He helped the Soul to a 13–3 record, kicking in the door they'd been knocking at for the last couple years, and winning ArenaBowl XXII.

With the injuries piling up and age not helping them heal any faster, Graziani retired from professional football. He left the game on top as a champion. He ended his career with 999 yards passing and 2 TDs in the NFL, 1,377 yards and 8 TDs in NFL Europe, and 23,606 yards and 494 TDs in the AFL. Twelve years of professional football and over 500 touchdowns, not bad for a 7th round draft pick with only one full season of college play under his pads.

GREISEN, CHRIS

Chris Greisen has been everything from a Mid-America Intercollegiate Athletics Association (MIAA) Player of the Year to a two-time AFL Player of the Year, from NCAA Division II National Champion to UFL Champion. Oh yeah, and Greisen played in a little league called the NFL.

At Sturgeon Bay High School in Wisconsin, Greisen led his team to the 1993 WIAA State Championship. They lost the game 25–20, and after a knee injury, Greisen lost a lot of upper division college scholarship offers.

Greisen attended the Division II Northwestern Missouri State University on a scholarship. He didn't see much playing time his freshman and sophomore years, attempting just 59 passes over his first

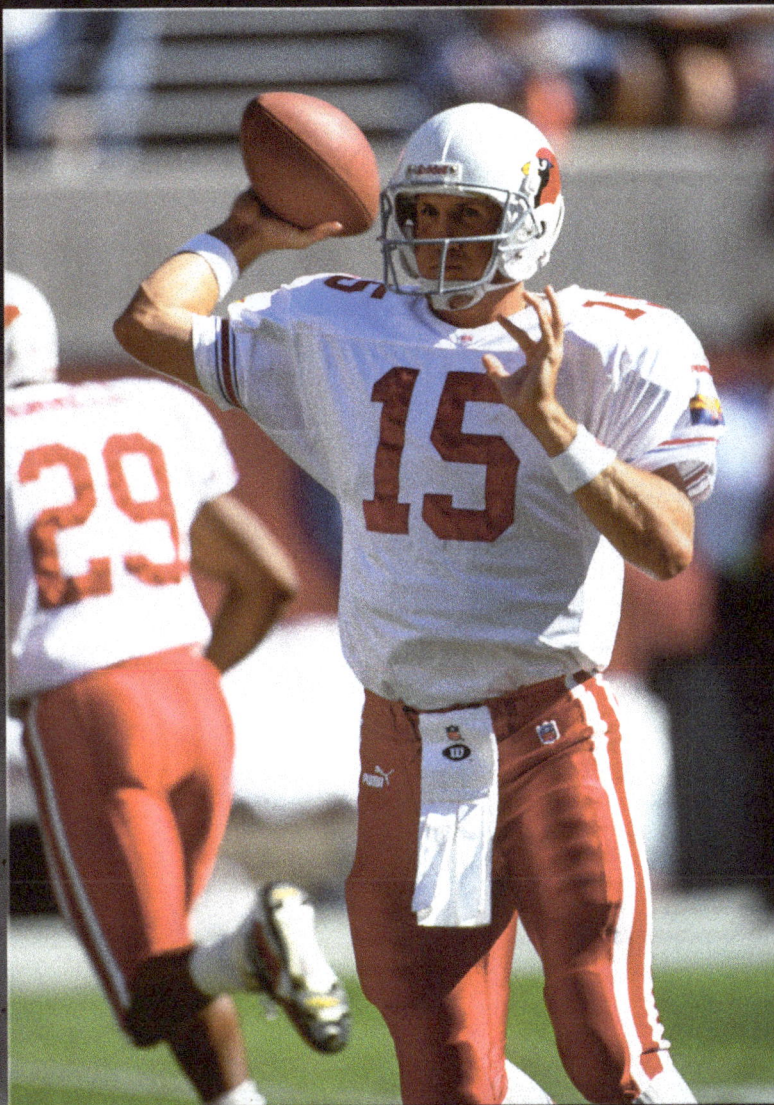

G

two seasons, but Greisen did earn Academic All-MIAA honors as a sophomore. He became the starter his junior season and started re-writing the school's record books. He finished 1997 with 2,456 passing yards for 23 TDs and 7 INTs. In his senior year (1998), Greisen's 2,937 yards passing with 25 touchdowns and another 5 rushing touchdowns led his Bearcats to a 15–0 record and their first ever NCAA Division II National Championship. His efforts earned him the 1998 MIAA Player of the Year honors, and Greisen finished his college career with a 27–1 win-loss mark and nine school passing records.

Greisen was selected in the 7th round (239th overall) by the Arizona Cardinals in the 1999 NFL Draft. As a third-stringer behind Jake Plummer and Dave Brown, Greisen appeared in just two games his rookie season, completing 1 of 6 passes. He remained in that role the next season and then was inactive the entire 2001 season. In 2002 he made the third-string position again, this time behind Josh McCown and Preston Parsons, but was released after preseason. He finished the year on the Washington Redskins practice squad.

Greisen signed with the Rhein Fire of NFL Europe in 2003. Splitting time with Nick Rolovich, Greisen passed for 843 yards and 10 TDs to help the Fire reach the World Bowl XI game.

In 2004 Greisen signed with the Green Bay Blizzard of the AF2, the Arena Football League's developmental league. He quickly proved that he belonged back in the primary AFL league after throwing for 2,718 yards and 61 touchdowns. In 2005 Greisen returned to the AFL and signed a two-year contact with the Dallas Desperados. But he spent most of those two seasons backing up Clint Stoerner and Clint Dolezel, passing for just 142 yards and 3 TDs.

G

In 2007 Greisen proved that he was a quarterbacking force to be reckoned with. He led the Georgia Force to a 14–2 record and won the Southern Division Championship. Greisen completed 393 of 531 passes for 4,871 yards, an incredible 74 percent completion rate. With his 117 passing touchdowns, he earned first-team All-Arena and the AFL Offensive Player of the Year, not to mention establishing a new league record for passing touchdowns in a season. 2008 was almost a repeat of the previous season. Greisen led his Force to a 10–6 record and won the Southern Division Championship. He completed 68.2 percent of his passes, going 399 for 585 while racking up 4,965 yards with 97 touchdowns. The team folded in 2009, so Greisen looked elsewhere for quarterback duties.

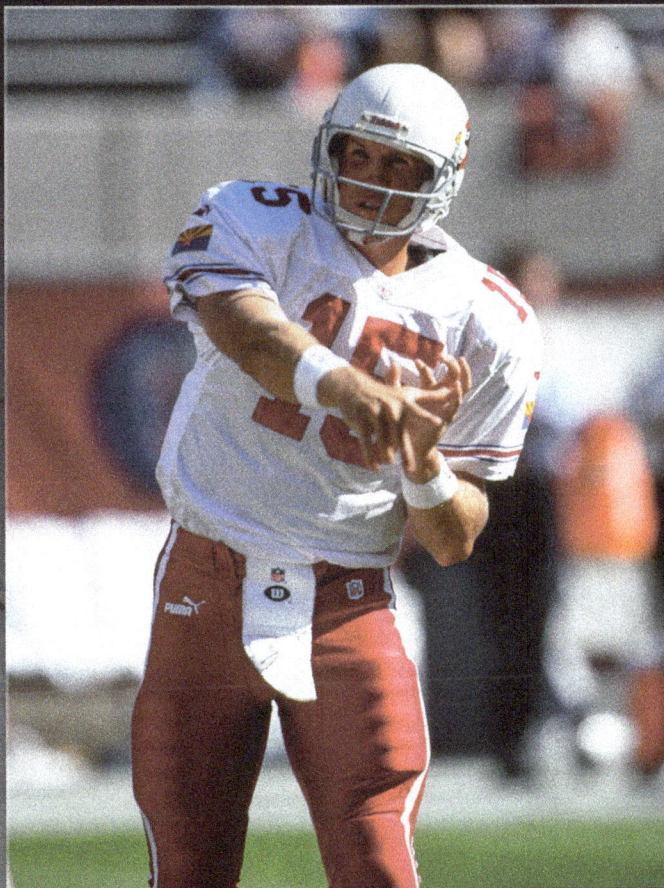

Greisen found the new United Football League (UFL) and signed with the Florida Tuskers for their inaugural season in 2009. As a backup to fellow NFL alumnus Brooks Bollinger, Greisen didn't see much playing time and was limited to only 20 pass attempts.

Greisen returned to the AFL in 2010, where he had so much prior success,

G

and signed with his hometown team, the Milwaukee Iron. He captained the Iron to an 11–5 record and the Midwest Division championship, then on to the AFL conference championship where they lost to the Spokane Shock. Greisen's 5,139 passing yards in the season set a new AFL record, earning him both the first-team All-Arena and the AFL Offensive Player of the Year for the second time in his career. He passed for 107 touchdowns and only 11 interceptions.

Immediately following the conclusion of the 2010 AFL season, Greisen re-signed with the Florida Tuskers for his second stint in the UFL. Again, he would back up Bollinger, but when Bollinger got injured, Greisen filled in for the last three games of the season, leading the team to victory in all three and helping take Florida to the UFL Championship game. Although Greisen passed for 346 yards and had 2 rushing TDs, the Tuskers lost to the Las Vegas Locomotives.

Also in 2010, after leading the AFL's Milwaukie Iron to within one game of the championship title and leading the UFL's Florida Tuskers to within one quarter, Greisen signed with the Dallas Cowboys practice squad. Because of the Cowboys starter John Kitna's nagging injury, they needed more depth at the quarterback position, and Greisen was added to the roster on New Year's Eve. He didn't see any action, but he did complete the trifecta of being on the active roster for three different professional teams in three different leagues in the same year.

Greisen returned to the UFL for the 2011 season and signed with the Virginia Destroyers, who assumed rights to the Florida Tuskers' players after the team folded. He helped the Destroyers to the UFL Championship game, his third con-

G

secutive appearance. Greisen completed 21 of 31 passes, and Virginia won the title, making it his first championship win since his senior season in college thirteen years earlier.

Once again, the workhorse Greisen played in a second professional football season for the second year in a row. The Dallas Cowboys came calling in December when their starter Jon Kitna was placed on injured reserve. Even though Greisen first played in the NFL in 1999, he still had the practice squad eligibility of a nine-game limit since he had only been active for eight total games. New Year's Eve came rolling around and Greisen was activated to the roster, just like the previous season exactly one year earlier. He did not get any field action in the game.

In 2012 Greisen returned to the UFL for one more season in the pro ranks. He was having a solid year and completed over 60 percent of his passes for 845 yards with 5 TDs when the league ceased game operations for financial reasons.

Though he only threw the ball 16 times for 69 yards with 1 TD and no INTs in the NFL, Chris Greisen's football legacy will remain complete, from high school to Division II college to four professional football leagues.

After retiring, Greisen became a high school head coach and also runs the Chris Greisen Quarterback Academy in both Dallas, Texas, and Green Bay, Wisconsin.

Chris's younger brother Nick Greisen was a linebacker in the NFL for the Giants, Jaguars, Ravens, and Broncos.

HACKENBERG, CHRISTIAN

If you look for Christian Hackenberg in the NFL statistical records, you won't find him. Although he was a 2nd round draft pick, he never played a down in the NFL.

Hackenberg was a five-star recruit at Fork Union Military Academy in Virginia. He was ranked by ESPN as the best pro-style quarterback coming out of high school and was ranked no. 2 pro-style quarterback in the nation. Hackenberg turned down offers from Alabama, Florida, Rutgers, South Carolina, Virginia, Tennessee, and others to play for Penn State.

Hackenberg was named the Nittany Lions starting quarterback as a true freshman in 2013. His 311-yards-passing game against Eastern Michigan broke Penn State's single-game freshman record and propelled him toward winning one of his five Big 10 Freshman of the Week honors. He was named 2013 Big 10 Freshman of the Year and set ten school freshman records.

H

As a sophomore in 2014, Hackenberg led the Big 10 with 484 pass attempts and 270 completions. He led his Nittany Lions to an overtime win against Boston College in the Pinstripe Bowl. As a junior in 2015, Hackenberg passed for 252 yards and only 6 interceptions, leading his team to another bowl game. He finished his college career with 8,318 yards and 48 touchdowns.

Hackenberg was selected in the 2nd round (51st overall) of the 2016 NFL Draft by the New York Jets. He signed a four-year, $4.66 million contract with a large signing bonus. He played in a couple preseason games but fell to fourth-string on the Jets depth chart behind Ryan Fitzpatrick, Bryce Petty, and Geno Smith. Hackenberg was inactive for the first fifteen games of the season but was activated to the roster for the final game when Geno Smith and Bryce Petty suffered injuries. He did not get into the game.

2017 looked brighter for Hackenberg as he started training camp, competing for a roster spot with Josh McCown and Bryce Petty with no clear front-runner for the starting position. Hackenberg played in all four preseason games and even started on two of them. He threw for over 300 combined yards but also committed two pick-sixes. He wound up third on the quarterback depth chart but was on the sidelines, suited up for the first game due to Bryce Petty's being injured. He was deactivated upon Petty's return the next week but returned to active status in week fourteen when McCown was placed on injured reserve with a broken hand. Hackenberg backed up Petty the final three games of the season but did not see any playing time. Although he was a member of the New York Jets, Hackenberg did not get to throw a pass during a regular season NFL game.

Hackenberg was traded to the Oakland Raiders in 2018 but released less than a month later. He then signed with the Philadelphia Eagles and started a preseason game before being waived at final cuts. Two days later Hackenberg signed with the Cincinnati Bengals practice squad and remained there for nearly the rest of the season.

Hackenberg showcased his skills at the new Alliance of American Football quarterback camp in November 2018 and was subsequently drafted by the Memphis Express in the second round of the 2019 AAF Quarterback Draft. He started the first three games and saw his most significant playing time since college. After passing for only 277 yards and three interceptions with notouchdowns, he was replaced with Zach Mettenberger by head coach Mike Singletary.

In 2020 Hackenberg decided to pursue a baseball career as a pitcher and has since become a high school football coach.

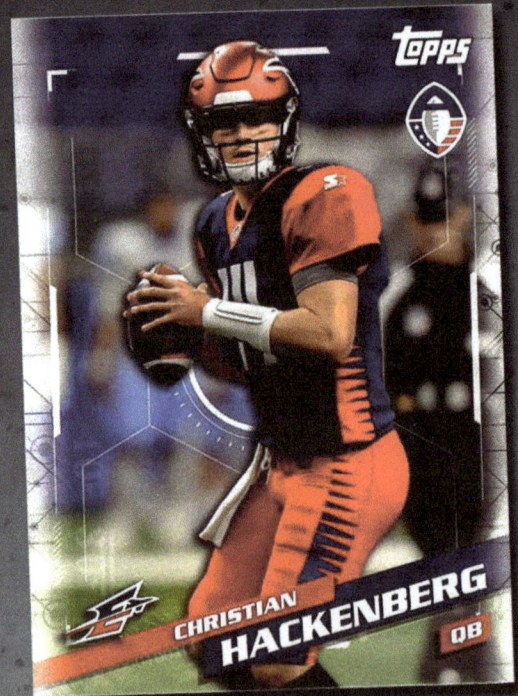

HARRELL, GRAHAM

Graham Harrell played football under his father at Ennis High School in Texas. He started for three years and led his school to the Class 4-A state title by the time he was a sophomore. By the end of his senior season, Harrell had rewritten the Texas high school state record books. He graduated as the leader in single-season passing yards (4,825 yards) in only thirteen games, career passing yards (12,532), single-season touchdown passes (67), career touchdown passes (167), and single-season pass completions (334).

Harrell attended Texas Tech and redshirted his freshman season with the Red Raiders in 2004. In 2005 he backed up Cody Hodges, who led college football in passing yards. Harrell won the starting job his sophomore year and started paving the road for his historic college career. Harrell brought Texas Tech to a 7–5 record and an appearance at the 2006 Insight Bowl. Then he led his Red Raiders to overcome a 31-point deficit to defeat Minnesota in the largest comeback victory in NCAA FBS Bowl history. Harrell's 445 yards passing and 3 total touchdowns earned him the game's Offensive MVP. His 4,555 passing yards and 38 TDs were the most ever by a sophomore in the Big 12 conference. Besides the yards and touchdowns, Harrell also led the NCAA with 412 pass completions and 617 pass attempts.

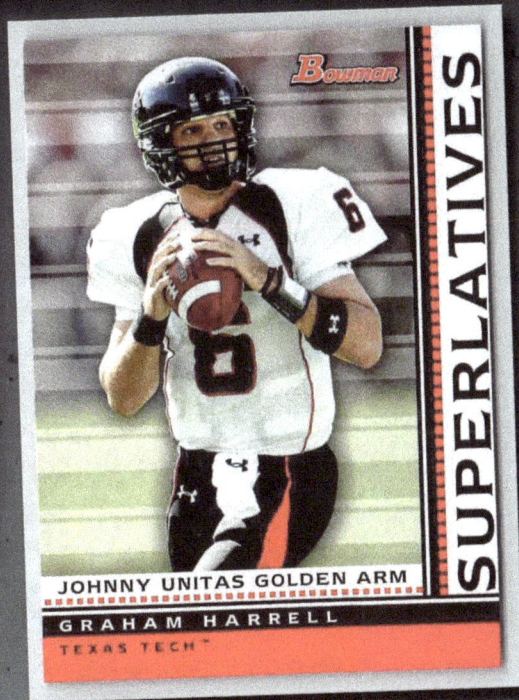

SUPERLATIVES

JOHNNY UNITAS GOLDEN ARM

GRAHAM HARRELL

TEXAS TECH

Harrell's junior year in 2007 was even more jaw-dropping as he continued his assault on the Big 12's and NCAA's record books. With Michael Crabtree and Danny Amendola as his receivers, Harrell and company finished the season with an 8–4 record and made an appearance at the Gator Bowl. Once again, Harrell led the nation in passing with 512 completions, 713 attempts, 5,705 yards, 48 touchdowns, and an obscene 71.8 pass completion percentage. Harrell concluded his amazing season by winning the Sammy Baugh Trophy for college football's best passer.

Not only did NCAA records start to fall to Harrell in 2008, but so did Big 12 opponents. After beating Eastern Washington Harrell was awarded the AT&T ESPN All-American Player award. While defeating Kansas State, Harrell broke Texas Tech's all-time passing yardage record and won two player-of-the-week awards after the game. In October he moved past Phillip Rivers into third place for all-time career passing yards and surpassed Ty Detmer a few games later for second place on the list. In his final regular season game against Baylor, Harrell shattered two fingers in the first half of the game and was advised to sit out the remainder. Harrell considered the trainer's advice but made him tape up his hand so he could finish the game. Harrell won the game by throwing 309 yards passing and 2 TDs, which clinched a share of the Big 12 title . The following day, Harrell went in for hand surgery, and seventeen pins and two plates were placed into his hand to help heal nine breaks. Harrell was cleared to play in the 2009 AT&T Cotton Bowl, which would be his last collegiate game, and a very historic one at that. He overtook Colt Brennan to become the NCAA all-time career passing touchdown leader with 134. Harrell reached 5,111 yards on the year to become the first NCAA player with multiple 5,000-yard passing seasons. He also set new NCAA marks with most 400+ yard games

(20), most 400+ yard games in a season (11), most passes completed in a season (512), most pass completions on average per game in career (31.2), and several others. With his 2008 efforts, Harrell was awarded the Johnny Unitas Golden Arm Award and an invitation to Washington, DC, to meet President George W. Bush. Harrell finished fourth in the Heisman Trophy race, and his teammate Michael Crabtree finished fifth.

Harrell concluded his college career with 1,403 completions for 15,793 yards and 134 touchdowns. His career quarterback rating was an astonishing 154.3.

Amazingly, Harrell was not drafted in the 2009 NFL Draft. Some say it was because he was the by-product of a pass-happy spread offense that was about the system, not the player. Regardless, it surprised many fans and supporters. Harrell had a workout for the Cleveland Browns but was not signed despite praise from coach Mangini. He later signed a contract with the Saskatchewan Roughriders of the Canadian Football League but would ask for his release before the next season to further pursue his NFL options.

Harrell signed with the Green Bay Packers and joined their practice squad in 2010. Near the end of the season, Harrell was signed to the active roster after Aaron Rogers was injured. Harrell did not get to play, but he got a ring with the Packers' Super Bowl XLV victory over the Pittsburgh Steelers.

Harrell was signed to the Packers practice squad again in 2011 and activated again late in the season. This time around, he was named Aaron Rogers's primary backup after Matt Flynn's departure. The next season (2012), Harrell made the Packers team and got his first taste of NFL action. Unfortunately, the taste wasn't too sweet as he tripped on his center and fumbled the handoff in the redzone. He played in four games total, completing 2 of his 4 passes for 20 yards. Harrell struggled in preseason the next summer and was released. Harrell signed with the New York Jets soon after and got into a preseason game in relief of Matt Simms. He was released with the last cuts and the Jets' signing of Brady Quinn.

Although he only threw 4 passes in the NFL, it wasn't the end of Harrell's football career. Harrell wasted no time and became a member of Washington State's coaching staff in 2014. In 2016 Harrell was named offensive coordinator and quarterback coach at the University of North Texas, whose poorly-ranked offense he improved in two seasons to become one of the nation's top ranked in 2017–18. Harrell has since been named the offensive coordinator for Purdue, and his coaching stock continues to rise.

HENSON, DREW

All Drew Henson did was play quarterback for the Dallas Cowboys in the NFL and third base for the New York Yankees in Major League Baseball. Just a couple small feats and franchises to write home about.

Drew Henson was an All-State football, baseball, and basketball player at Brighton High School in Michigan. Not only was he an All-American quarterback, but he also had 47 tackles and 5 interceptions as a defensive back his sophomore season and received All-American honors as a punter, averaging over 45 yards per punt. Henson's 5,662 passing yards finished second of all time in Michigan state records. His record-setting 52 touchdown passes included a state-record 26 in a single season (1997).

Henson was a four-time All-State selection in baseball and finished

high school setting national records for career home runs (70), runs batted in (RBIs) (290), and runs scored (259). A dual threat on the diamond, Henson also pitched. He collected 163 strikeouts his junior year and 174 more his senior season to accompany a 0.86 earned run average (ERA) and a 14–1 record. Henson received the USA Today High School Player of the Year honors, Gatorade High School Player of the Year, and Baseball America 1998 High School Player of the Year.

1998 was a busy year for Henson. He was drafted in the 3rd round (97th over-all) by the Yankees and started his summer with the rookie-level Gulf Coast Yankees. Henson also accepted a scholarship to play for the University of Mich-igan. As a true freshman, he battled a then-unknown kid named Tom Brady for the starting quarterback job. He became Tom's backup and saw limited action over seven games.

In 1999 Henson was still dedicated to both major sports. On the turf, he tan-gled with Brady for the starting job again, and both quarterbacks platooned for the first seven games of the year before Brady finished the season. Henson completed 47 of 90 passes for 546 yards and 3 TDs. On the diamond, Henson was promoted to the High-A Tampa Yankees where he batted .280 with 13 homeruns and 37 RBIs in sixty-nine games.

With Tom Brady leaving for the NFL in 2000, the starting quarterback job was finally Henson's alone. He did not disappoint in his junior season. Although he missed the first three games while healing from a foot surgery, he led his Wol-verines to a 9–3 season and a win against Auburn in the Citrus Bowl. In his eight games, Henson completed over 60 percent of his passes (131 of 217) for

1,852 yards. He connected for 16 touchdowns and only 4 interceptions.

Henson began his 2000 baseball season in Tampa again but was quickly pro-moted after recording a .333 batting average. After hitting 7 homeruns for AA-Norwich, Henson was traded to the Cincinnati Reds in a big four-player deal that sent pitcher Danny Neagle to the Yankees.

In 2001 the Yankees wanted Henson back. They traded with the Reds for him and offered him a six-year deal to forgo the NFL. Henson accepted and didn't return to Michigan for his senior season either. It was time to focus on one sport. Henson's batting average dipped to .228 at AAA-Columbus in 2001. In seventy-one games, he batted .222 with 11 homeruns. Henson's batting aver-age slightly improved in his first full minor league season in 2002, hitting .240 in 521 at bats, again at the AAA level. He did show signs of good power, though, hitting 30 doubles and 18 homeruns with 65 RBIs in 128 games. The Yankees brought Henson to New York for September callups, and he got his first taste of the Major Leagues; playing in three games, he got 1 at bat and struck out. Henson's batting average didn't improve in 2003. Playing again at AAA-Columbus, he batted only .234 but still showed he had a powerful swing, hitting 40 doubles and 14 homeruns with 78 RBIs in 133 games. The Yankees called Henson up at season's end, and he got his first Major League hit. Unfor-tunately, he only got 1 hit in 8 at bats, scoring 2 runs in five games. That would be it for his baseball career. Henson didn't see any more progress in baseball with the Yankees and decided to resume his football career while he still had a prospect in the NFL.

The Houston Texans took a chance on Henson and selected him in the 6th round (192nd overall) in the 2003 NFL Draft, hoping that he would return to the NFL soon. After announcing his retirement from baseball in 2004, the Dallas Cowboys traded their 3rd round (2005) pick to the Texans for Henson.

Making way for Henson, the Cowboys released another former baseball player, Chad Hutchinson. However, Henson had some tough competition behind starter Tony Romo and veteran Vinny Testaverde. With Romo hurt, Henson would see his first playing time when backup Testaverde left the Ravens game with an injury. He completed a perfect 6 of 6 passes for 47 yards and a TD. With Testaverde still infirm, Henson got his first NFL start on Thanksgiving Day 2004. After only completing 4 of 12 passes and throwing a pick-six in the first half, coach Parcells replaced Henson with Testaverde in the second half. Henson wouldn't see the field again his rookie season.

With a poor training camp in 2005, Henson fell to third on the quarterback depth chart behind Romo and veteran Drew Bledsoe and would not be activated all season. Coach Parcells allocated Henson to NFL Europe the following season to further his skills.

Playing for the Rhein Fire in 2006, Henson finished as the second rated passer in the league. He completed 109 of 203 passes for 1,321 yards and 10 touchdowns with only 3 interceptions. He returned to the Cowboys for training camp, but Parcells decided to stick with just his two veterans, and Henson was waived. Henson was signed to the Vikings practice squad.

He re-signed with the Vikings in 2007 but was cut in training camp and once

H

again relegated to their practice squad.

In 2008 Henson signed with the Lions. He was cut in training camp and sent to the practice squad another time until the Lions starter Jon Kitna was injured. Henson found himself in a Lions uniform back on an active NFL roster for the first time since 2004. He was cut a month later when the Lions signed veteran Duante Culpepper. Henson was then re-signed to the practice squad. Days later the carousel continued, and Henson made the active roster. This time around, Henson finally got back on the field. Four years after his first game on Thanksgiving Day with the Dallas Cowboys, Henson got to relieve Culpepper in the fourth quarter on Thanksgiving Day with the Detroit Lions. Henson completed 1 of 2 passes. Then he got into one more game for a play and got sacked. The Lions drafted Matthew Stafford as the first overall pick in 2009, and Henson was released.

Henson's journey is one of dedication and amazing athletic talent. He followed his passion, twice, and played at the ultimate level of professional sports, twice!

HIPPLE, ERIC

Eric Hipple saw playing time as a freshman at Utah State and was setting school career records before his collegiate career even concluded. As a junior in 1978, he led the entire Pacific Coast Athletic Association (PCAA) conference with 18 touchdowns: 9 passing and 9 rushing. As a senior the following year, Hipple led his conference and was seventh in the nation with a 60.3 completion percentage. His 140.8 passer rating also topped the PCAA conference and placed him sixth in the nation. Hipple finished his college career with 6,073 yards passing, a 117.3 passer rating, and 34 passing and 11 rushing touchdowns.

Hipple was drafted in the 4th round (85th overall) in 1980 by the Detroit Lions, the team he would remain with for his entire decade-long NFL career. He wouldn't get any real action his

rookie season backing up Gary Danielson who started all sixteen games. However, Hipple would win the starting job the following season, starting ten games and leading the Lions to a 6–4 record under his command. Although he threw 15 interceptions, Hipple also threw 14 TDs and ran for 7 more, combining for 21 total TDs and accounting for at least one score in each of his starts. Hipple would split time with Danielson in 1982, getting just four starts and throwing for 411 yards.

In an alternating cycle of up-and-down seasons, Hipple would bounce back in 1983 to start all sixteen games, leading his Lions to a 9–7 winning season. In 1984 he only started one game and finished with 246 yards on the year. In 1985 Hipple again rebounded to start fifteen games, producing his best season. He would finish with 2,952 yards and 17 passing touchdowns. Hipple's best game of the year came on Thanksgiving Day (November 28, 1985) in a victory versus the Jets in which he threw 4 touchdowns. 1986 would be the last season that Hipple saw much field action. He passed for 1,919 yards with 9 TDs to his 11 picks. He led the league with a 63 percent pass completion ratio but finished his

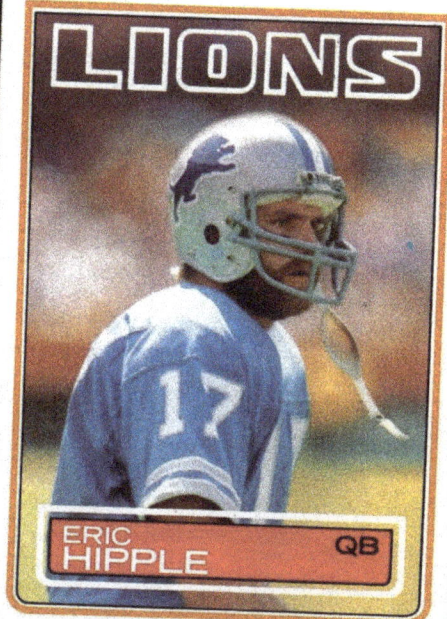

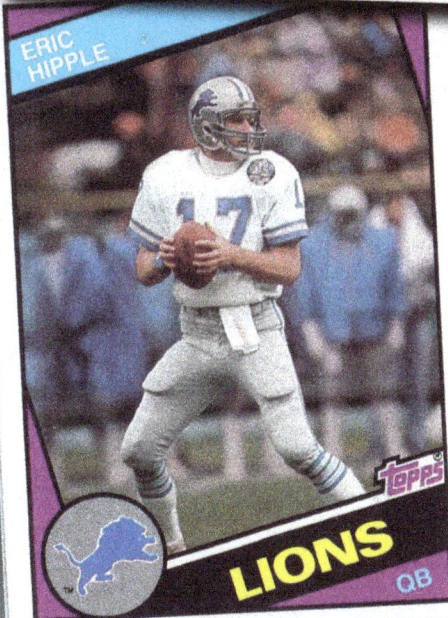

H

ten starts with a 3–7 record.

After the Lions drafted Chuck Long with their 1st round pick in 1986, Hipple's fate was sealed. He missed the entire 1987 season with a sprained thumb injury and would see very limited action in 1988, attempting only 27 passes. Hipple returned for a final season in 1989 in a third-string role behind new draft pick Rodney Pete and veteran Bob Gagliano. He would get one last start but went just 7 for 18 with 90 yards and 3 interceptions. Hipple would finish his career with 10,711 yards and 55 touchdowns in fifty-seven starts.

In 2000 Hipple's fifteen-year-old son committed suicide. As a result, Hipple is now a motivational speaker, author, and suicide prevention activist.

HOLCOMB, KELLY

Holcomb was a three-sport star at Fayetteville, Tennessee, lettering in football, baseball, and basketball. On the basketball court, he led his school to the 1990 Tennessee state championship.

Staying close to home. Holcomb attended Middle Tennessee State University. He started all four years, and in his first start as a true freshman, he was immediately thrust into the national spotlight against no. 1 ranked Florida State. Holcomb completed 20 of 28 passes for 188 yards against a secondary that featured two All-American and future NFL defensive backs. He completed 130 of 209 passes for 1,763 yards his freshman season. Holcomb would earn All-OVC (Ohio Valley Conference) for his sophomore and senior seasons. He won the MVP

in the Blue-Grey game as a senior and passed for 2,154 yards with 15 touch-downs, cementing himself as MTSU's all-time passing leader with 7,064 yards. Holcomb would be elected to the MTSU Hall of Fame in 2008.

Holcomb was not drafted by the NFL. He spent the 1995 season on the Tampa Bay Buccaneers practice squad, never suiting up for a game. Yet he knew that he had the athletic chops to make it to that top level, so he took his skills abroad in 1996 to showcase for the Barcelona Dragons of the World League of American Football. Holcomb proved in Spain what he could do at a professional level. He completed 191 of 319 passes, good for nearly a 60 percent comple-tion ratio, and had 2,382 yards and 14 touchdowns in only ten games. Holcomb had the season he needed to get back on the NFL's radar.

The Indianapolis Colts signed Holcomb following the Drag-ons' 1996 season. He landed at third on the quarterback depth chart, behind starter Jim Harbaugh and reserve Paul Justin, and didn't see any playing time his rookie year. In 1997 Holcomb saw some mop-up work and got one start in which he lost. With the arrival of heralded rookie Peyton Manning in

1998, Holcomb wouldn't see any more playing time as a Colt during the regular seasons.

In 2001 Holcomb signed with the Cleveland Browns. He saw action in one game, completing 7 out of 12 passes for 114 yards and a TD. The next season, Holcomb went 1–1 in two starts, throwing 8 TDs behind no. 1 draft pick Tim Couch. In 2003 Holcomb would replace the struggling Couch, starting eight games and having the most productive season of his NFL career. Holcomb had a career game in the AFC Wild Card matchup against rival Pittsburgh. He passed for 429 yards on January 5, 2003, good for third most in playoff history. In the season, Holcomb completed almost 64 percent of his passes for 1,797 yards and 10 touchdowns, proving to be a very reliable backup.

With Couch gone, the Browns signed veteran Jeff Garcia and drafted Luke McCown in 2004, leaving Holcomb fighting for playing time. He made his way into four games, starting two and throwing 7 TDs in his brief field action.

Holcomb signed with the Buffalo Bills in 2005 and started half the season. He split the starting role with the Bills' 1st round pick from the previous year, J. P. Losman, and won half of his starts. Holcomb completed over 67 percent of his passes for 1,509 yards and 10 touchdowns. Once again, he proved to be one of the most reliable backups in the game. In 2006 Losman took over as the regular starter, and Holcomb never saw the field.

Holcomb was traded to the Eagles in 2007 but didn't get any playing time. The Eagles then traded him early in the year to the Vikings for a 6th round pick.

With Minnesota, Holcomb started three games, losing them all.

Holcomb retired in 2008 after an eleven-year NFL career. He completed 63.3 percent of the passes he threw for 5,916 yards with 39 touchdowns and 38 interceptions. Soon after retirement, Holcomb went back to his college roots and became the color commentator for MTSU radio.

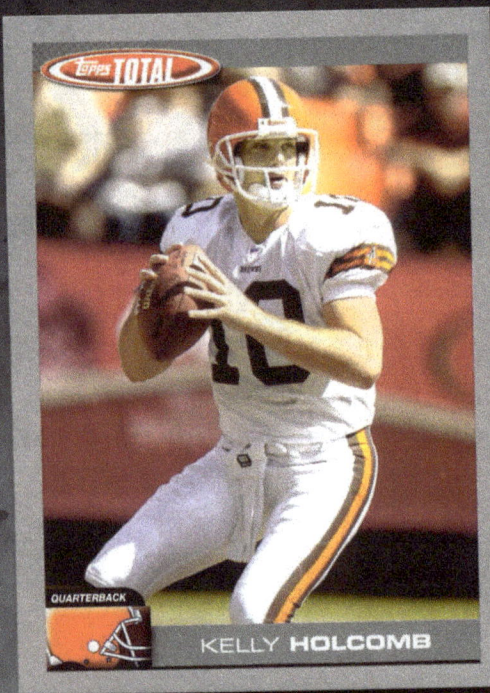

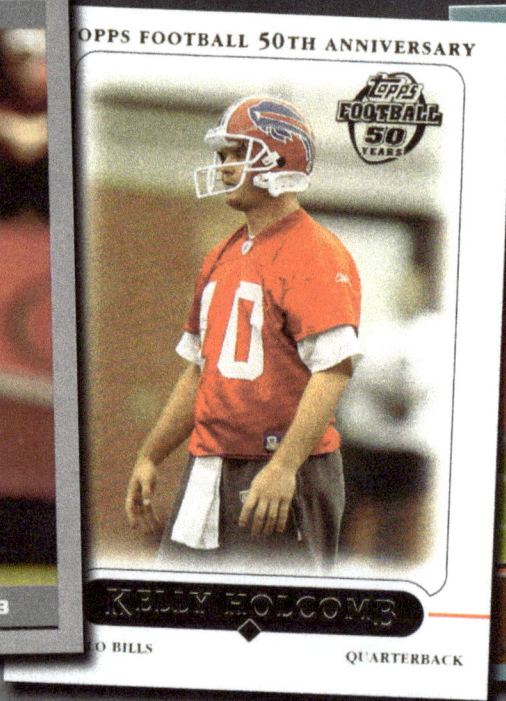

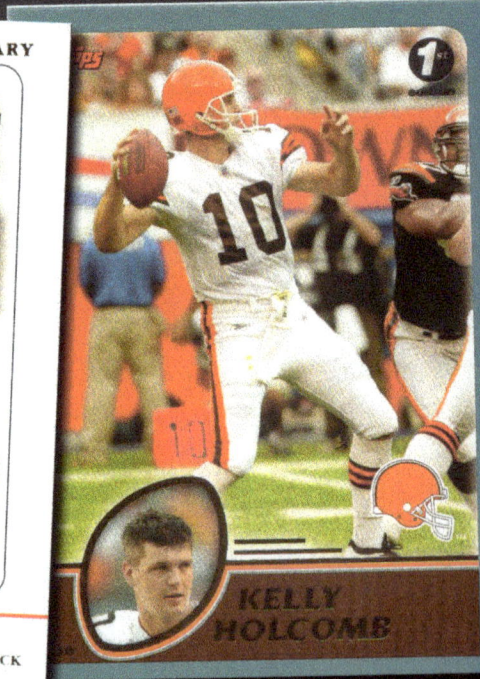

HUARD -BROTHERS

Brothers Damon and Brock Huard took Washington by storm in the 1990s. Both played for their father, the head coach at Puyallup High School, and both won high school Player of the Year awards; both played at the University of Washington, and both made it to the NFL.

The elder of the two brothers, Damon, lettered in football and basketball. He played tight end as a sophomore because the starting varsity quarterback was future NFL mainstay Billy Joe Hobert, who would also attend the University of Washington. After his stellar 1990 senior season, Damon was an All-American and was named the Powerade Washington State Player of the Year.

Like his older brother before him, Brock lettered in both

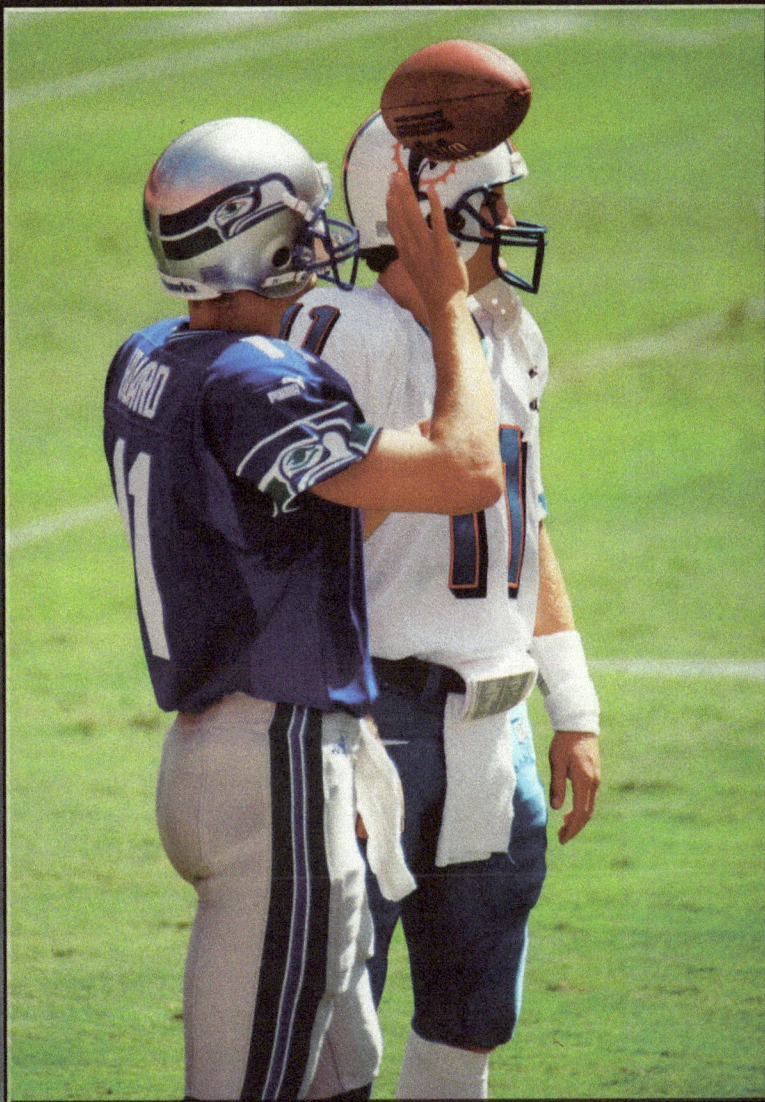

basketball and football at Puyallup High School. In his high school career, Brock completed 237 of 408 passes with 45 touchdowns and only 10 interceptions. As a senior in 1995, Brock was All-State and was named the Gatorade National Player of the Year, Class AAA State Player of the Year, and a High School All-American by ESPN, Schutt, *Parade* magazine, *Super Prep*, and others. He graduated with a 4.0 GPA.

Damon redshirted his freshman year at the University of Washington in 1991, when his former high school teammate Billy Joe Hobert led the Huskies to a National Championship season. Hobert left for the NFL draft after the 1992 season, and Damon took over as the starter in 1993. From that point on, Huard remained the starter for the duration of his college career. As a junior in 1994, he led his Huskies to snapping the University of Miami's fifty-eight-game home winning steak in an 18-point win at the Orange Bowl. In his senior season, Huard passed for 2,415 yards with only 6 interceptions and a 143.3 quarterback rating. He led Washington to a first place (tie) finish in the Pac-10 and an appearance at the Sun Bowl. Damon finished his collegiate career as the University of Washington's all-time

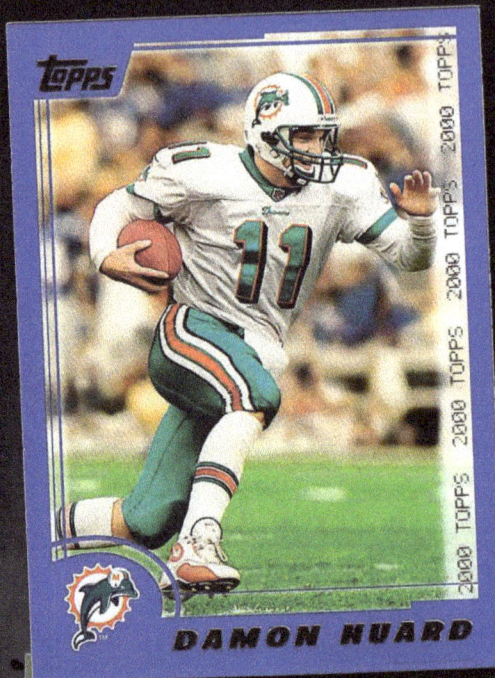

DAMON HUARD

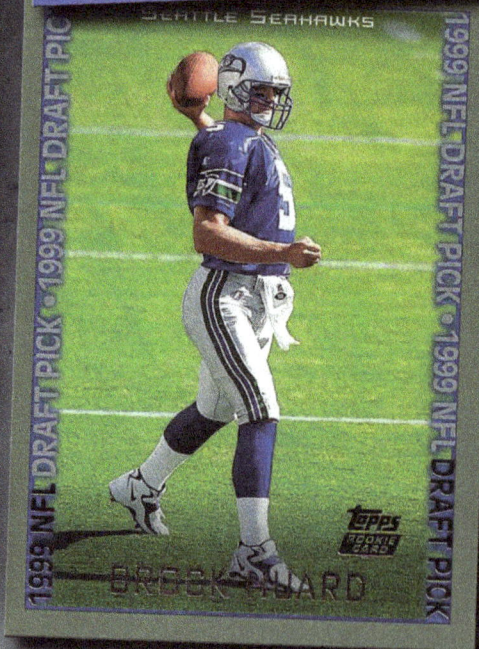

BROCK HUARD

leader in career passing yards with 5,692.

Brock Huard was one of the most highly recruited quarterbacks in the nation, turning down offers from UCLA and other top Division I schools to follow in his older brother's footsteps and play at the University of Washington. Brock red-shirted his freshman year since his brother Damon was the starter. Brock took over in 1996 and, along with team MVP Corey Dillon, helped the Huskies to a 9–3 record and an appearance at the Holiday Bowl. Much in line with his brother's senior year, Brock threw only 5 interceptions as an (athletic) freshman.

WASHINGTON HUSKIES

vs
ARMY
SAT., SEPT. 23, 1995
BAND DAY/OKTOBERFEST

28   26   E   20

TUNNEL   SEC.   ROW   SEAT

Despite missing some time with an ankle injury, Brock passed for 2,140 yards and a school-record 23 touchdowns his sophomore year of 1997, leading Washington to an 8–4 record and a 51–23 whooping of Michigan in the Aloha Bowl. Brock's junior season in 1998 didn't fare as well, and his numbers went down a little while Washington suffered its first non-winning season (6–6) since 1975. Brock was named an Academic All-American in his final two seasons, and he finished his college career setting school records with 51 lifetime touchdowns, four 300-yard games, and 151 consecutive attempts without an interception. Brock even beat out his brother Damon by only 50 yards for a record 5,742 career passing yards.

H

Damon Huard went undrafted in 1996. He was later signed by the Cincinnati Bengals but waived in training camp. Damon spent the year out of football then signed with the Miami Dolphins in 1997. He began the season on their practice squad but soon was elevated to the active roster and spent the rest of the season as third quarterback on the Dolphins' depth chart. Damon began 1998 with the Frankfurt Galaxy in the NFL Europe league, where he passed for 1,857 yards with 12 TDs and 7 interceptions. His solid play abroad earned him the third-quarterback spot with the Dolphins again, and he saw his first NFL action on the field, completing 6 of 9 passes. In 1999 he began the season as a backup again and was the field goal holder on special teams. Because of an injury to Hall of Famer Dan Marino, Damon started his first NFL game on October 24, 1999. He went on to win his first three starts and finished with a 4–1 overall record in five starts, passing for 1,288 yards and 8 touchdowns. With the signing of Jay Fiedler, Damon saw only one start in 2000, beating the Colts. History was made that day as Damon and his brother Brock were the first brothers to ever start on the same weekend in the NFL.

Brock was selected in the 3rd round of the 1999 NFL Draft by the Seattle Seahawks, the team just miles away from where he grew up and went to college. In his first preseason game, Brock threw a touchdown on his very first pass attempt. He made the squad but, like his brother, spent the season as third on the quarterback depth chart and didn't see any field time. Moving up to the number two spot behind start Jon Kitna the next season, Brock saw his first NFL action against his brother Damon's team, the Miami Dolphins. On November 26, 2000, Brock started against the Broncos while his brother started against the Colts, creating NFL history. Unfortunately, Brock suffered a season-ending knee injury during the game. The brothers reunited on January 9th when the Dolphins played the Seahawks in a Wild Card playoff matchup. Although Brock was inactive from his injury, the two brothers met on the field, and the game was historic for other reasons as well. It would be the final game played in Seattle's Kingdome before it was demolished, and it was future Hall of Famer Dan Marino's final win in the NFL. The next year, Brock backed up new arrival Matt Hasselbeck and appeared in just one game.

In 2001 Damon Huard would leave the Dolphins and sign with the New England Patriots as a free agent. He spent his time in training camp competing against second-year, 199th overall pick Tom Brady for the backup job behind All-Pro Drew Bledsoe. When Bledsoe was injured, Brady became the starter and Huard moved to Brady's backup role. He won his first Super Bowl ring after the Patriots beat the Rams in Super Bowl XXXVI. Damon saw his first field action as a Patriot the next season (2002), getting in for drives in two games.

In 2002 the Seattle Seahawks traded Brock Huard to the Indianapolis Colts

H

where he didn't see any field action backing up iron man Peyton Manning. In 2003 Brock played in two games, completing 2 of 3 passes for 22 yards.

In 2003 Damon Huard saw action in two more games with the Patriots and spent a little time on their practice squad. Damon, leading the Patriots, faced none other than his brother's Indianapolis Colts in the AFC Championship. New England advanced to win Super Bowl XXXVIII and Damon received his second Super Bowl ring.

In 2004 Brock Huard returned to the Seattle Seahawks but spent the entire year on injured reserve and never saw the field again. He finished his pro career completing 60 of 197 passes for 689 yards with 4 touchdowns and 2 interceptions.

2004 took Damon Huard to the Kansas City Chiefs. He would settle in as the team's third-string quarterback for his first two years in red and yellow, not seeing any field time. In 2006 Damon replaced injured starter Trent Green and won five of the next eight games. He passed for 1,878 yards with 11 touchdowns and only 1 interception, leading the league at a 0.4 interception percentage. Huard started in 2009, playing in nine games before injuries to his back and hand limited his playing time later in the season. He still had the most productive season of his career, completing 62 percent of his passes for 2,257 yards and 11 touchdowns. Huard traded starts and injury occurrences with Brodie Croyle in the beginning of 2008, limiting Huard to just 477 yards and 2 TDs in three starts. Damon injured his thumb halfway through the season and was placed on injured reserve, ending his season. He would never see the field again. After a brief tryout of the 49ers in 2009, Huard was cut, and subsequently he retired. In his eleven-year NFL career, Damon Huard completed over 60 percent of his passes for 6,303 yards and 33 touchdowns.

After retiring form playing, Brock Huard has stayed close to the game. He has done TV and radio broadcasting for Fox Sports Network XFL games, ESPN College Football, Fox College Football, Seattle's KIRO sports talk radio, and NFL games on Fox.

Damon Huard has remained close to the game as well. He returned home to the University of Washington to become the Chief Administrative Officer of the Huskies football program. Like his younger brother, Damon has also done radio, serving as a color analyst on Huskies game broadcasts. His son Sam is also a quarterback and has followed in his dad's footsteps, playing at the University of Washington.

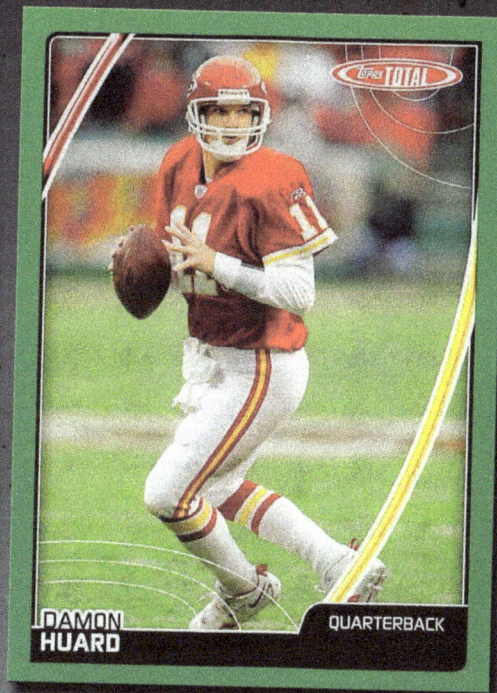

HUFF, GARY

Gary Huff is Florida football. He graduated from Leto Senior High School in Tampa, Florida, played college football at Florida State in Tallahassee, then later returned to Tampa to play professional football with the Buccaneers.

At Florida State, Huff played both football and baseball. As a junior in 1971, he batted .372 in seventeen games as a shortstop and third-baseman with the the Seminoles. He finished his collegiate baseball career with a .297 batting average in 101 at bats with 2 triples and 2 home runs. As memorable as his career on the diamond was, it didn't come close to his skill between the sidelines.

The first Florida State football player to earn Academic All-American honors, Huff's award resume didn't stop there. After several All-American honorable mention nods as a junior, he solidified himself as one of the nation's best as a senior.

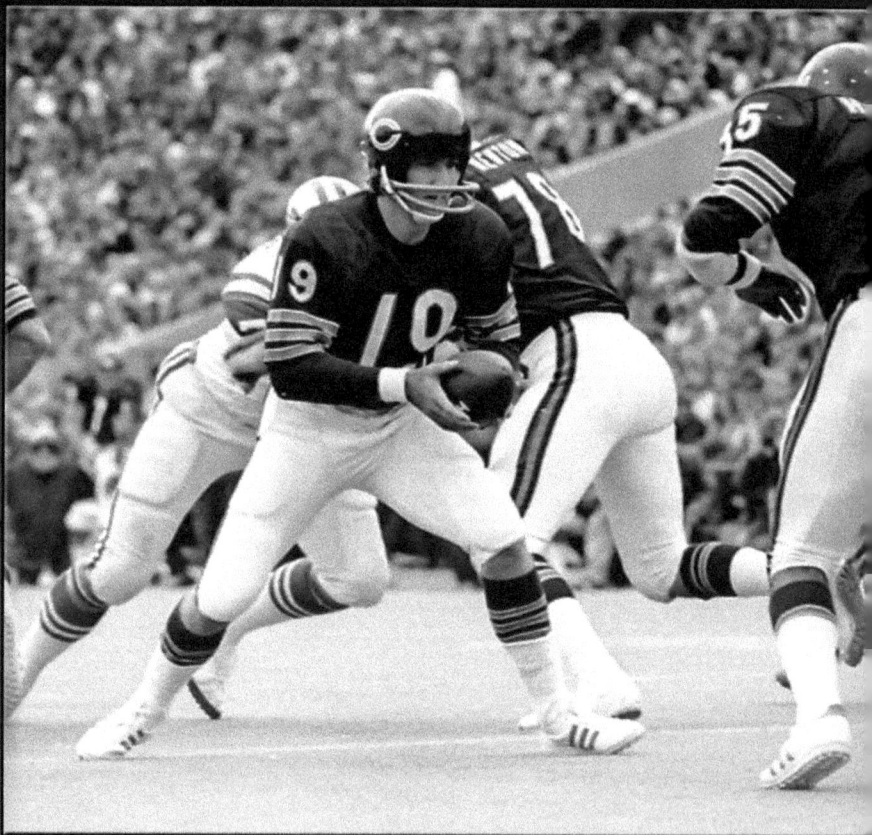

H

Huff earned first-team All-American honors from the American Coaches Association, *College & Pro Football Weekly*, *Churchman's*, Football Writers Association, *Gridiron*, and *Time* magazine and second-team honors from *Football News* and *United Press International*. Huff passed for over 2,700 yards and 23 TDs his junior year and topped that with 2,893 yards and 25 TDs his senior season. He led the nation in touchdowns both his junior and senior seasons. Huff played in the first Fiesta Bowl in 1971, where he threw three TDs and established a first in college history with three receivers each topping the 100-yard receiving mark. Huff set more than thirty FSU passing records, many of which still stand. He had 6,378 career passing yards and 52 touchdowns and was elected into the Florida State Hall of Fame in 1983.

Huff was drafted in the 2nd round (33rd overall) by the Chicago Bears in 1973. He started two games his rookie season, throwing 8 interceptions to 3 touchdowns. His sophomore campaign had the most playing time he would see in his career, starting eleven games and throwing for 1,663 yards, however his ratio of 6 touchdowns to 17 interceptions didn't bode well for a long future with the organization. After starting nine games in 1975, Huff wouldn't see any real playing time in 1976, and his career with Chicago would come to an end.

Huff returned to Florida in 1977, where he had played so well in high school

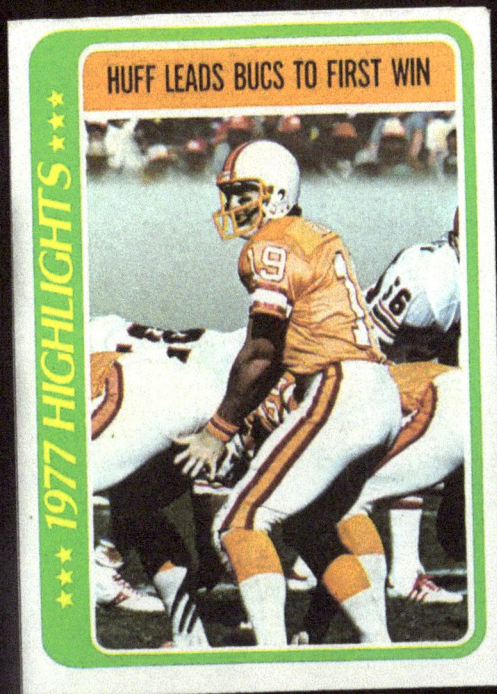

1977 HIGHLIGHTS

HUFF LEADS BUCS TO FIRST WIN

and college. He had the distinction of leading the new Buccaneers franchise to their first ever win, a 33–14 routing over the Saints. In his six starts, he only won one more game that season and finished with 3 touchdowns to 13 interceptions. With the Buccaneers selecting Doug Williams as their 1st round pick in 1978 and signing veteran backups Mike Boryla and Mike Rae, Huff saw very little field action. He threw just 36 passes, completing 15 for 169 yards with 1 TD and 3 interceptions. Huff caught on with the San Francisco 49ers in 1980–81 as a backup, but he didn't see any playing time.

Huff immediately began coaching and became the offensive coordinator for Indiana University in 1983, but he would leave the college ranks the next season for pro ball, this time as a coach with the Memphis Showboats of the new USFL. In 1985 Huff would actually be listed on the official Showboats roster as a player and a coach. He didn't see the field as a player, and it officially ended his thirteen-year playing career. However, his post-playing career was just getting started.

When the USFL folded, Huff became the quarterback coach for the Houston Oilers in 1986. He moved back to the college ranks in 1987 to take an offensive coordinator position with the University of Kansas, but that would prove short-lived when he landed a position as CFO with the Los Angeles Raiders. From 1987 to 1993, Huff was one of only three people (at that time) to have played, coached, and administered professional football.

In the twilight of his career, Huff returned to Florida State to become the senior athletic director.

HUSAK, TODD

The California native Husak played in just one NFL game, throwing 2 passes and completing both for −2 yards, and rushed one time for −1 yard. He didn't have a pro career, but he can still say he was among the 6 percent of high school athletes to play college ball and among the 1.6 percent of those who get a shot at the ultimate level of football.

Husak played college ball at Stanford where he did nothing short of set records and amaze his teammates. Known as a "smart" quarterback, Husak quickly picked up on offensive systems. He lettered as a true freshman and was the starter by his junior year in 1998. Husak led the Pac-10 with 233 pass completions and 18 touchdowns. He passed for 3,092 yards and led the Cardinal to their first Rose Bowl appearance since 1972, earning him first-team

All-Pac-10 honors. As a senior in 2000, he led Stanford to the Hula Bowl and was named co-MVP of the game. Husak finished his football career at Stanford ranked fifth of all-time with 6,564 yards passing and 41 touchdowns.

The Washington Redskins noticed Husak's intelligence both on and off the field and selected him in the 6th round of the 2000 NFL Draft. He made it into one game that year and was released by the next season. Husak made the Denver Broncos' roster in 2001 but saw no action on the field.

In 2002 Husak joined the Berlin Thunder of the NFL Europe league, where he quickly became the starter. He completed 208 of his 356 pass attempts for 2,386 yards and 14 touchdowns, leading his team to the World Bowl Championship. His performance grabbed the attention of several NFL teams, and Husak spent the next few years on the New York Jets' and the Cleveland Browns' practice squads as a reserve.

Husak retired from professional football in 2004 and worked as an assistant coach with Stanford. In 2008 he became the color commentator for Stanford football radio broadcasts.

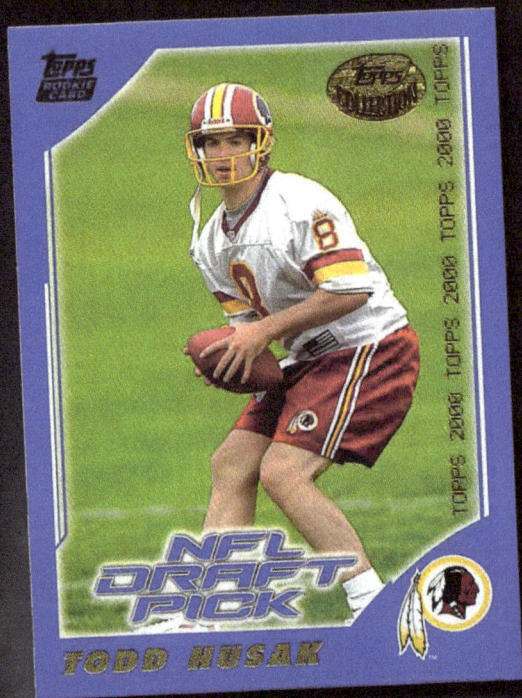

HUTCHINSON, CHAD

Hutchinson was actually more of a baseball star at Torrey Pines High School than a football star. He didn't even start playing football until his freshman year in high school, beginning at linebacker and only moving to the quarter-back position his senior year. In baseball Hutchinson had a 94 mph fastball and a perfect 11–0 record as a senior with a 1.20 ERA and 116 strikeouts, earning him the Gatorade National Baseball Player of the Year award.

Hutchinson chose a football scholarship from Stanford University over a professional baseball contract when the Atlanta Braves drafted him. As a redshirt freshman in 1996, he was named starting quarterback and earned MVP honors when he helped lead the Cardinal to a 38–0 win over Michigan State in the Sun Bowl. His 60.9 completion percentage topped the Pac-10 conference.

Hutchinson also starred as a

starting pitcher on the Stanford baseball team as a true freshman in 1996, and his 7–2 record helped lead the Cardinal to a 41–19 mark and an appearance in the NCAA West Regional. He received first-team All-American freshman honors.

As a sophomore in 1997, Hutchinson passed for 2,101 yards and 10 TDs, and his 189 pass completions placed third in the conference. He had a 340-yard performance against the Oregon Ducks and tied a school record with 4 touchdowns. In baseball that same year, Hutchinson notched an 8–3 record with 110 strikeouts and helped Stanford reach the College World Series.

Chad
HUTCHINSON

After another stellar baseball season in his junior year, Hutchinson was selected again in the Major League Baseball draft. He left Stanford in 1998, leaving behind two years of football eligibility, to sign with the St. Louis Cardinals for a four-year, $3.5 million contract. Hutchinson began the season in low Class-A New Jersey and was promoted to advanced Class-A after just three starts.

In 1999 Hutchinson split time between the AA and AAA levels and did well enough to be called up to St. Louis after only his first full season in the minors. He did not appear in any games, but he would earn another shot. In 2000 Hutchinson spent more time in the minors before being shelved with elbow problems for two months. He began the 2001 season in the majors with the

Cardinals and pitched in three games before being sent to AAA for the remainder of the season.

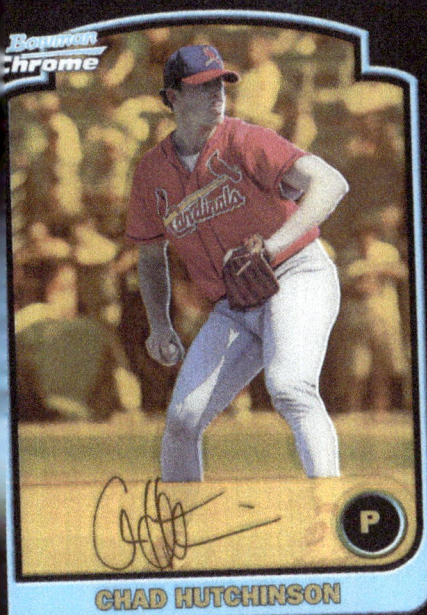

After reaching the majors and struggling in his last season, Hutchinson turned back to football. He held an open workout in 2002 that the Cowboys, Chiefs, and Bears attended. A bidding war ensued, and Hutchinson signed with the Cowboys as an undrafted free agent in a contract that included a "no baseball" clause.

As a twenty-five-year-old rookie, Hutchinson got thrown into the starting position after struggling starter Quincy Carter was benched. Hutchinson lost his first game to the Seattle Seahawks, a contest in which his teammate, Emmitt Smith, broke the NFL's all-time rushing record. Later that season, Hutchinson passed for 301 yards and 2 touchdowns against Jacksonville. He finished his rookie campaign completing 127 of 250 attempts for 1,555 yards and 7 TDs. He set an NFL rookie record in the process by throwing 95 straight passes without an interception.

With the arrival of new coach Bill Parcels in 2003, all positions were open to competition, and Hutchinson lost his starting spot to former starter Quincy Carter and saw limited action, throwing only 2 passes and completing one. In

2004 a new group of quarterbacks were brought in, including another former-baseball player, Drew Henson, and veteran Vinny Testaverde. Both Quincy Carter and Hutchinson were subsequently released.

In 2004 Hutchinson played with the Rhein Fire of NFL Europe to work on his accuracy and mechanics. He completed 126 of 207 passes for 1,356 yards and 5 TDs before missing the final two games of the season with a sprained right shoulder. After rehabbing his shoulder, Hutchinson signed with the Chicago Bears as a free agent for the 2004 NFL season when their starter, Rex Grossman, suffered a season-ending knee injury. Hutchinson started five games and threw for 903 yards with 4 TDs and 3 Interceptions. After a subpar preseason performance and rookie Kyle Orton's signing, Hutchinson was released before the 2005 season began, ending his professional football career.

Professional athletics runs in the Hutchinson family. Chad's father Lloyd was an outfielder in the Philadelphia Phillies' farm system, his brother Trevor was a pitcher in the Florida Marlins organization, and his wife is the sister of former MLB player Todd Walker. Chad Hutchinson is part of an elite class of athletes who have played in both the NFL and MLB.

JOHNSON, RANDY

Born and raised in San Antonio, Randy Johnson stayed close to home to play quarterback at Texas A&I (later known as Texas A&M). Johnson was a four-year starter for the Javelinas and a two-time All-American in 1964 and 1965. Blocking for him on that team was future NFL Hall of Famer Gene Upshaw. Johnson led the team in both passing and rushing in 1964 and led the entire Lone Star Conference in passing, earning him the conference MVP. In his senior season, Johnson was the MVP in both the Blue-Grey Classic game and the Senior Bowl.

Johnson had several distinctions and firsts in his post-college and NFL careers. He was the first Texas A&I player ever taken in the 1st round of the NFL draft—selected by the Atlanta Falcons as the 16th pick in 1966—however, Johnson was also selected by the Denver Broncos in the 4th round of the AFL draft. After choosing to sign with Atlanta, Johnson became

J

the very first quarterback to ever start for the newly formed Atlanta Falcons.

Starting eleven games in his rookie year, Johnson passed for 1,795 yards with 12 TDs and 21 interceptions. The next season he saw the most playing time in his career, starting twelve of fourteen games, passing for 1,620 yards with 10 touchdowns and another 21 interceptions. Johnson would spend three more years in Atlanta splitting playing time with Bob Berry.

Johnson signed with the Giants in 1971 and would spend the season as Fran Tarkenton's backup, getting just one start. He remained in New York for two more seasons, backing up Norm Snead, before having the statistically best season of his career in 1973. Filling in for the injured Snead, Johnson completed 99 passes for 1,279 yards with 7 TDs and 8 interceptions.

In 1974 Johnson would take his resume to the new startup World Football League. Sharing quarterback duties with Norris Weese, Johnson completed 113 of 197 passes for 1,368 yards and 11 touchdowns. His performance would earn him another shot in the NFL, and Johnson left the WFL to sign with the Washington Redskins in 1975. Backing up mainstay starter Billy Kilmer, Johnson only started two games, losing both. In 1976 Johnson signed with the Packers for one last year on the turf. He started one game and got the victory.

In his decade-long NFL career, Johnson completed 647 of 1,286 passes for 8,329 yards with 51 touchdowns and 90 interceptions. He also rushed for another 573 yards and 10 touchdowns.

Johnson spent the later years of his life in seclusion and passed away in 2019.

KIEL, BLAIR

To say quarterbacking ran in the Kiel family is an understatement. Blair's brother was a quarterback at Butler University. His nephew Gunner Kiel began with Notre Dame then transferred to Cincinnati University, nephew Drew Kiel was a quarterback at Illinois State, and yet another nephew, Dusty Kiel, quarterbacked at Indiana University. Blair Kiel himself was a quarterback up until the day he died.

Blair Kiel was the third-ranked quarterback in the nation coming out of Columbus East High School in Indiana. Notre Dame coach Dan Devine liked what he saw in Kiel and offered him a full scholarship. Kiel earned the starting quarterback and starting punter positions during his freshman year in 1980 and helped lead the Irish to a 9–0–1 record and no. 2 ranking in the nation before losing the season finale and the Sugar Bowl.

During his senior year in 1983, Kiel helped the Irish to a victory

K

over Boston College in the Liberty Bowl. He was featured on the August 29, 1983, cover of *The Sporting News* headlined "Blair Kiel, Irish Quarterback Aims for National Title." Kiel played in every single game during his four years at Notre Dame, and the Irish faithful will always remember him for executing a 96-yard touchdown, which still remains the longest play in school history.

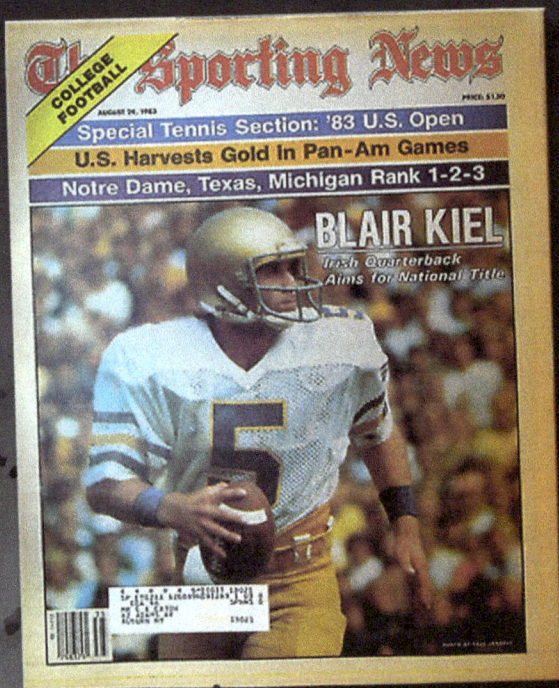

Kiel was selected in the 11th round of the 1984 NFL Draft by the Tampa Bay Buccaneers. He saw action in ten games during his rookie season but only as the placeholder for kicks. With the addition of future Hall of Famer Steve Young in 1985, Kiel was relegated to third string and didn't see any field time.

Kiel signed with the Colts in 1986 and made the team as the third-string quarterback behind Jack Trudeau and Gary Hogeboom. Kiel finally got a chance to throw the ball in Indianapolis and completed 11 of 25 passes for 236 yards and 2 TDs. The Colts re-signed Kiel the following season, again as the third-string quarterback. With injuries to Trudeau and Hogeboom, Kiel got his first NFL start in 1987.

The Packers picked up Kiel in 1988 as insurance behind Don Majkowski and Randy Wright. Kiel only saw playing time in a single game and didn't attempt

K

a pass, but he continued with the Packers and earned his second NFL start in 1990 after Majkowski suffered an injury. Between his one start and three other games of relief work, Kiel would attempt the most passes of his career that season. He completed 51 of 85 passes for 504 yards with 2 TDs and 2 INTs. In 1991 the Packers signed veteran Mike Tomczak, and Kiel would be stuck at third on the depth chart behind Tomczak and Majkowski. Kiel found his way into four games and started one. With the addition of Brett Favre in 1992, Kiel would see the last of his playing days in Green Bay.

Kiel tried out for the Atlanta Falcons in 1992 but was released, so he decided to try his hand up north in the CFL. He didn't fare well, throwing 3 interceptions in just 28 pass attempts. In 1993 Kiel gave professional football one more go, this time around with the Arena Football League. Kiel signed with the Cincinnati Rockers and saw the most playing time of his professional career. He completed 92 of 181 passes for 899 yards with 9 touchdowns. He retired the next season.

Even though he only started three games in his NFL career, Kiel was grateful just to play quarterback at the top level. His Notre Dame teammate Allen Pinkett once said, "Gerry Faust came in (in 1981) and benched him (Kiel) a couple times. Blair never complained, he never made a scene, and he was always a leader. If there's one thing I'll always remember about Blair, it was his ability to keep his head up and deal with circumstances that were beyond his control."

Kiel worked as a private quarterback coach after his playing days until he passed away from a heart attack in 2012. He was only fifty years old. He never gave up on the quarterback position and never truly stopped playing.

KLINGLER, DAVID

Before David Klingler earned a master's degree in Evangelical Theology and a PhD in Old Testament studies, he was earning records, awards, and trophies for some of the best college quarterback play in the history of humankind.

Born and raised in Houston, Texas, Klingler stayed at home to attend the University of Houston in 1988. He only attempted 7 passes his freshman year sitting behind Andre Ware, but he completed 6 of them. It was a sign of things to come. His sophomore year was more of the same, stuck behind the soon-to-be Heisman Trophy winner Andre Ware. Klingler did see action in eight games, though, completing 68 of 114 passes for 865 yards with 8 TDs and only 1 INT.

1990 came around and Ware was gone as a no. 1 pick in the NFL draft, so the starting quarterback spot was Klingler's. Klingler immediately proceeded to set the NCAA and Houston

school record books on fire. While leading his Cougars to an 11–1 record, Klingler rewrote college quarterback history along the way. On November 17, 1990, he passed for 11 touchdowns in one game to set a record across all colleges at all levels and divisions. Two weeks later, Klingler set the NCAA single-game passing yards record with 716. On the season he set the NCAA single-season touchdown record with 54—a record that stood for sixteen years.

During his remarkable junior season, he led the NCAA not only with TDs, at 55 in total, but also with 374 pass completions, 643 pass attempts, and 5,221 total yards. Klingler also led the Southwest Conference (SWC) in virtually every passing category possible. His unforgettable season earned Klingler the Sammy Baugh Trophy and third place in the Heisman Trophy voting behind Ty Detmer and Raghib Ismail.

Klingler continued his assault on college football his senior season in 1991. His 278 pass completions and 497 pass attempts both led the NCAA, and his 55.9 pass completion percentage, 3,388 passing yards, and 29 TDs all led the SWC. During his college career, Klingler completed 726 of

K

1,262 passes for 9,430 yards and 91 touchdowns, all of which set new school records. Houston retired Klingler's number 7 jersey.

Klingler was selected as the 6th pick in the 1st round of the 1992 NFL Draft by the Cincinnati Bengals. As a backup to Boomer Esiason, Klingler didn't see much playing time his rookie season. He started four games, winning only one, but then with Esiason gone in free agency, the starting job was Klingler's to lose. The Bengals signed veteran Jay Schroeder and drafted Erik Wilhelm out of Oregon State for insurance. Klingler would start thirteen games, losing ten of them. He passed for 1,935 yards with 6 TDs and 9 INTs and rushed for another 282 yards. In 1994 Klingler got one more shot as starter, but after several subpar performances he lost his job to the newly acquired Jeff Blake. In seven starts, Klingler completed 131 of 231 passes for 1,317 yards and duplicated his previous season's numbers of 6 TDs and 9 INTs. Klingler played the season with an injured elbow and shoulder, which required surgery after the season's end.

Klingler was informed that his career was all but over after undergoing elbow surgery. Prior to his injury Klingler could throw the ball 85 yards in the air, but after his procedure he struggled to toss it 35 yards. However, after

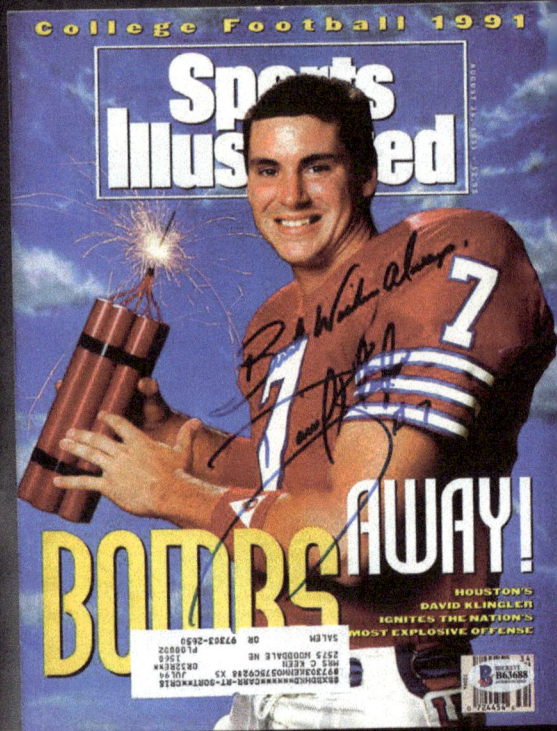

K

rehabbing the physical injury and enduring mental distress, Klingler kept pushing forward, defying the doctor's conclusions and the odds that were stacked against him. Behind Jeff Blake's Pro Bowl season in 1995, Klingler's arm wasn't tested much, as he only saw time in three games, completing 7 of 15 passes. The Bengals released Klingler after the season.

Klingler signed with the Oakland Raiders in 1996 and made the team as the third-string quarterback behind starter Jeff Hostetler and backup Billy Joe Hobert. Klingler played relief in one game, completing 10 of 24 passes for 87 yards. He made the Raiders team again in 1997, this time as the primary backup for newly signed veteran Jeff George. George proved very durable and had a great season, allowing Klingler to play in only one game.

Klingler gave the game one last shot in 1998, signing with the Green Bay Packers. Vying for a spot as Brett Favre's backup, Klingler competed against Ty Detmer, T. J. Rubley, and veteran Jim McMahon. Klingler was cut before the season opener and ended his six-year NFL career with 3,994 yards passing, 16 TDs, and 22 INTs.

After football life, Klingler devoted his time and passion to the afterlife. He graduated from the Dallas Theological Seminary with his impressive, aforementioned degrees, and by 2010 would become the director of the school's Houston extension. Klingler put the same energy, dedication, and passion into his religious beliefs as he did his football career. In 2012 Klingler was elected as assistant professor of biblical studies at Southwestern Baptist Theological Seminary's Harvard School in Houston. He is currently an associate professor of bible exposition at the Dallas Theological Seminary.

KRUCZEK, MIKE

To say Kruczek had pinpoint accuracy isn't too much of a stretch. His 68.9 completion percentage in 1974 broke the NCAA record previously held by Hall of Famer Roger Staubach (though it was broken again in 1978 by Guy Benjamin).

Kruczek didn't play much at Boston College until his junior year because his teammate, Gary Marangi, was busy tearing up the school record books. As a junior, Kruczek won the starting job upon Marangi's departure for the NFL and then rewrote the school's new record books. In 1974 Kruczek completed 104 of 151 passes for an incredible 68.9 percent and a 143.6 passer rating. He almost duplicated the feat in 1975, completing 107 of 164 attempts for 65.2 percent and a 126.8 passer rating, leading him to an All-American selection. Kruczek finished college with a career 66.8 completion percentage and 134.8 passer rating,

K

establishing many new Boston College passing records. Kruczek was inducted into the Boston College Athletics Varsity Club Hall of Fame in 1981.

Kruczek was drafted in the 2nd round (47th overall) of the 1976 NFL Draft by the Pittsburgh Steelers. He was thrust into the starting lineup to fill in for an injured Terry Bradshaw and quickly distinguished himself by winning six consecutive starts and setting a new rookie record, which would stand for a decade. Unfortunately, his memorable six starts would be his only in four seasons with the Steelers, attempting just 38 more passes while backing up Bradshaw, the future Hall of Famer.

Kruczek signed with Washington in 1980 and got one last chance to start an NFL game with the Redskins. Although he completed 22 of 31 passes for an amazing 71 percent that season, he would not see an NFL field again as a player.

However, Kruczek's NFL career did not end as a player. He began his coaching career as the Florida State Seminoles' quarterbacks coach from 1982 to 1983. Kruczek would move back to the pro ranks in 1984, maintaining the same coaching position with the Jacksonville Bulls of the new USFL. For the next nineteen years, he would begin as the quarterbacks coach, move to offensive coordinator, and become head coach for the University of Central Florida.

Kruczek would return to the NFL in 2004 as a quarterbacks coach with the Arizona Cardinals for a few years before moving on to coaching for the California Redwoods (which later became the Sacramento Mountain Lions) of the United Football League. Kruczek is still coaching at the college and high school ranks in his fourth decade in the sport.

LEWIS, JEFF

"Jeff Lewis was a great teammate and brought great energy to me and [the] team. He will be missed. My condolences to Jeff's family."
—John Elway

Jeff Lewis left behind a quarterback legacy that began early in high school. At Horizon High School in Phoenix, Lewis was a three-sport star who earned All-Conference and All-City selections in football, baseball, and basketball. In football, Lewis gained over 1,000 yards rushing in both his junior and senior seasons and, in baseball, hit .492 his senior year.

Lewis received a scholarship from Northern Arizona University and, after a redshirt freshman year, became a four-year starter. For his junior year (1994), Lewis earned second-team All-Big Sky and third-team Division I-AA All-American. In his incredible forty-one

L straight starts, the durable Lewis completed 785 of 1,315 passes for 9,655 yards with 67 touchdowns, all good for second place on the Lumberjacks' all-time records list. Lewis also set an NCAA record for his career interception ratio of 1.82 percent. He would be inducted into the school's Hall of Fame in 2003.

Lewis was selected in the 4th round (100th overall) by the Denver Broncos in the 1996 NFL Draft. He made the team as third in the quarterback depth chart behind starter John Elway and backup Bill Musgrave. Lewis saw limited time on the field, connecting 9 of 17 passes for 58 yards. Although Lewis moved up a slot to the number two quarterback position in 1997, he only attempted 2 passes behind the incumbent All-Pro John Elway. One of Lewis's 2 passes was completed to his teammate and the other to the opposing team for an interception. He missed the entire 1998 season with a torn ACL suffered while playing a pickup basketball game.

Denver traded Lewis to Carolina in 1999 for two draft picks. Carolina coach George Seifert saw potential in Lewis and wanted him to eventually replace starter Steve Beuerlein. Beuerlein, however, didn't budge and started every game over the next two seasons, leaving Lewis with only 35 attempts on the field. In 2000 Beuerlein was released, and Lewis was named the starter. Unfortunately, he had a bad preseason, and after a game in which he threw 3 interceptions in 4 pass attempts, he was released.

In 2002 Lewis was given a shot with the New Orleans Saints but was released during the preseason. He never got a chance to start a game in his five-year NFL career, but Lewis did earn two rings as part of the Super Bowl XXXII and XXXIII winning teams.

In 2003 the Arena Football League expanded to add the Colorado Crush, owned by Lewis's old teammate John Elway. Elway signed Lewis who would compete for a starting quarterback job with John Dutton but eventually lost out and served as his backup. Lewis completed 26 of 47 passes for 344 yards with 7 TDs and 3 INTs.

Lewis would eventually return to Northern Arizona University, where he had enjoyed his Hall of Fame collegiate career, to become an assistant coach. On January 5, 2013, Lewis died at his home in Phoenix, Arizona. Autopsy reports revealed that Lewis died of an accidental drug overdose after mixing the sleep aid Ambien and morphine. He had also been recently diagnosed with a heart condition. At the time of his passing, Lewis was the wide receivers coach at his alma mater, and his sudden death was a tragic shock felt around the university and by his past teammates and coaches.

" 'This loss is felt throughout NAU Athletics, where Jeff's impact as a player, a coach, and an outstanding person will always be remembered,' Northern Arizona University Vice President for Intercollegiate Athletics said. 'We were deeply grateful for his return to the football program and wish our time together could have been longer. Our thoughts go out to his family at this difficult time.' "   —*As reported by John Bena, Mile High Report, January 5, 2013*

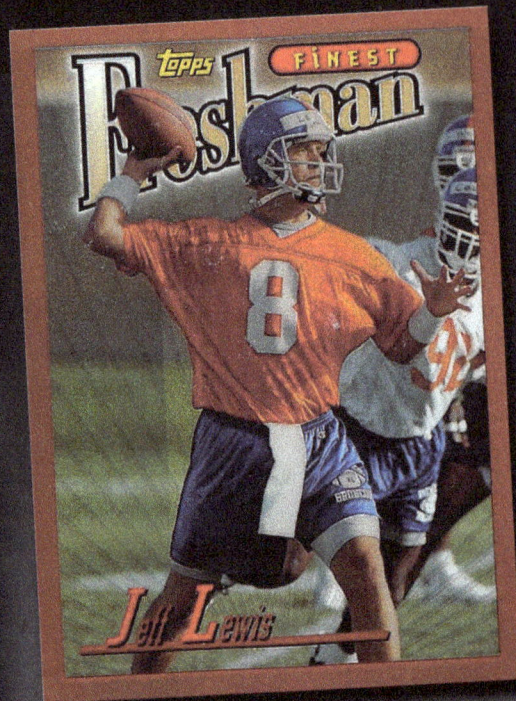

LUCK, OLIVER

When it comes to Oliver Luck, the question of his career in football should be what hasn't he done, rather than what has he done. Aside from his own college and pro football playing career, Luck was the XFL's first commissioner, president of the World League of American Football (WLAF), the first president and GM of the Houston Dynamo of Major League Soccer, and father of 2012's no. 1 overall NFL draft pick Andrew Luck. And that hasn't even scratched the surface.

After a stellar high school career in Cleveland, Oliver Luck attended West Virginia University. Playing behind senior Dutch Hoffman his freshman year, Luck saw limited action on the field but was starting by his sophomore season in 1979. With Luck at the helm, the Mountaineers more than doubled their win total, improving from 2–9 the prior year to 5–6. In his junior season, Luck elevated WVU again, helping the team to a 6–6 record and earning Academic All-American honors. His 19

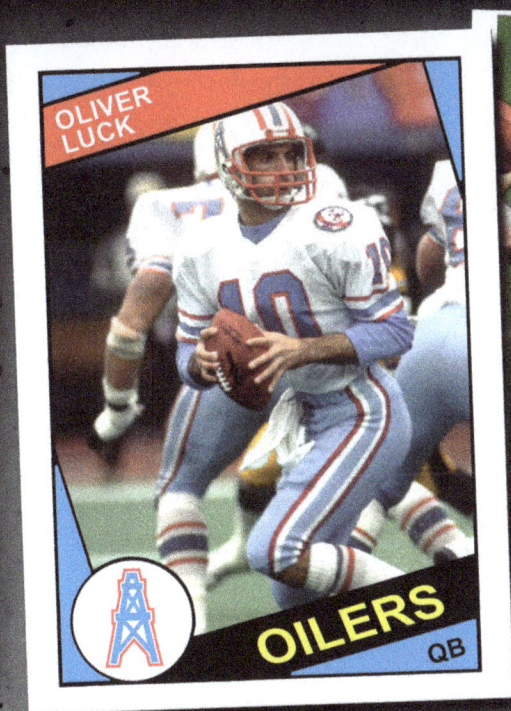

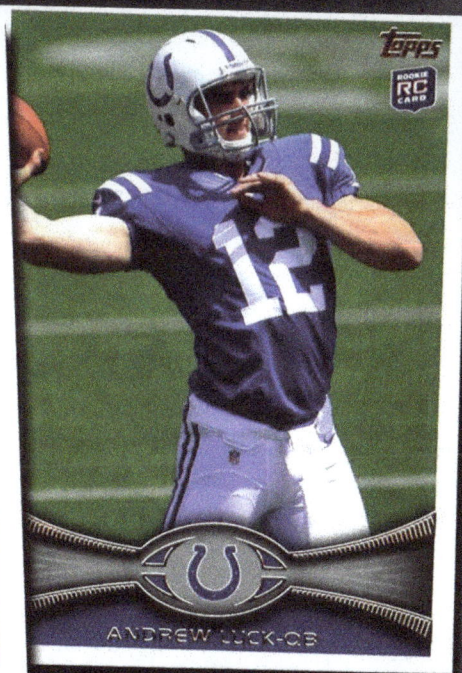

touchdown passes set a new school record in the process, and he was named the team's MVP.

In his senior year (1981), Luck led the Mountaineers to a 9–3 record and a seventeenth place finish in the NCAA, the schools best finish since 1969. Luck took his team to the Peach Bowl where they defeated the Florida Gators with a score of 26–6. Luck was named Academic All-American and team MVP for the second consecutive year and set more school records.

Luck finished his West Virginia career with several new school records attached to his name. He established new career marks with 43 touchdown passes, 466 completions, 911 pass attempts, and 5,765 passing yards. He graduated magna cum laude in 1982 and would be inducted into the Academic All-American Hall of Fame in 2000.

Luck was selected in the 2nd round (44th overall) of the 1982 NFL Draft by the Houston Oilers. Luck didn't see any playing time during his rookie year behind Archie Manning and Gifford Nielsen; not to mention the season was shortened by the players' strike.

In 1983 Luck was elevated to starter after Manning and Nielson shared a combined 0–10 record as starters. Luck started six games, winning Houston's only two victories on the year. He passed for 1,375 yards with 8 TDs and 13 INTs. It was the most playing time that he would see in his career.

1984 brought the arrival of Warren Moon, and the quarterback landscape in Houston would be forever changed. Moon was lights out, and unless he suf-

Lfered an injury, no backup stood a chance of playing. From 1984 to 1986, Luck would serve as Moon's primary backup, and in that three-year stretch, Luck would see action in only thirteen games, starting just three.

Luck retired from playing in 1987 with 2,544 passing yards, 13 TDs, and 21 INTs to his credit. He was a gifted backup for five years, but his true contributions to the game had not yet begun.

Luck immediately resumed his education and earned a law degree from the University of Texas School of Law just a year later and graduated with honors. After studying the legal system while abroad in Germany, Luck found his way back to football and became the general manager of the Frankfurt Galaxy of the WLAF in 1991. In 1995 he became the GM of the Rhein Fire and was named the league's president and Chief Executive Officer the next year. Luck oversaw the league's rebranding to NFL Europe in 2000.

In 2001 Luck was named CEO of the Houston Sports Authority. He oversaw the operations, construction, and management of Minute Maid Park (home of the Houston Astros, MLB), Reliant Stadium (home of the Houston Texans, NFL), and the Compaq Center (home of the Houston Rockets, NBA).

Luck became the athletic director for his alma mater, West Virginia University, in 2010. In his tenure, Luck made significant changes to the school's sports programs, including a move from the Big East Conference to the Big 12 Conference, taking the school off major probation, instituting beer sales at football games, facilitating media rights for a twelve-year, $86 million deal, adding the men's golf program, which had been absent for thirty-two years, and organizing funds to build the school's new baseball stadium.

In 2014 Luck took a newly-created position with the NCAA as the executive vice president of regulatory affairs, in which he governed all regulatory functions, including academics, memberships, eligibility, and enforcements.

#10 Oliver Luck QB

Luck returned to the pro football ranks in 2018, becoming the new XFL's first commissioner and CEO. After an incredible launch—widely regarded as one of the best new league launches in decades—the league folded due to the Covid pandemic.

In 2023 Luck was named executive director of the new ASUN-WAC Football Conference, which is set to start play in 2023.

And one other small detail about Oliver Luck. He is the father of no. 1 pick and legendary Colts quarterback Andrew Luck. And if he didn't have enough on his plate, Oliver Luck also continuously coaches youth sports.

LUTHER, ED

Was it difficult for Ed Luther to be the backup quarterback for Dan Fouts, who was widely considered one of pro football's finest passers? "It's been very, very frustrating," Ed Luther said. "You just take it day by day, year by year."
—As quoted in the New York Times, October 3, 1983

As a three-year starter at San Jose State University, Luther had not yet felt the full frustration of being a backup quarterback. By his sophomore year (1977), Luther started slinging the ball all over the field and finished the season completing 126 of 268 passes for 1,527 yards passing and 11 TDs, all of which topped the Pacific Coast Athletic Association (PCAA). Luther then flipped the team's win ratio from a 4–7 campaign in 1977 to a 7–5 record his junior year of 1978, and led the league again with 205 pass completions in 386

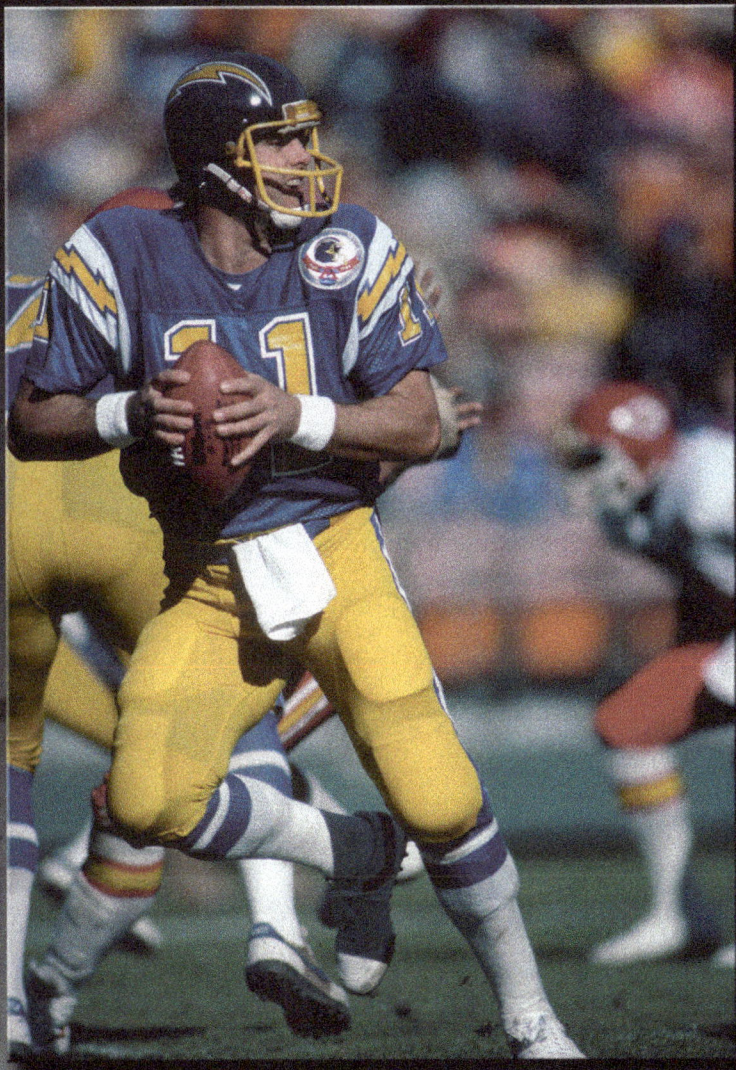

attempts for 2,275 yards. Lutherimproved even more his senior season in 1979 and led his team to another winning record. His 241 pass completions in 415 attempts for 3,049 yards and 20 TDs all led the PCAA, for the third consecutive year in several of those categories.

Luther finished his college career with 600 completions for 7,190 yards and 47 touchdowns, rare numbers from a quarterback in the run-heavy era of the 1970s. He was selected in the 4th round (101st overall) of the 1980 NFL Draft by the San Diego Chargers.

From 1980 to 1983, Ed Luther did not get a single start. In fact, he only threw the ball twenty-two times while stuck behind the iron man Dan Fouts, who never missed a game. But Luther's time finally came in 1983. After suffering a hit by George Martin and Lawrence Taylor, Fouts removed himself from a game against the Giants because of a hurt shoulder. Luther came in cold and proceeded to complete 9 of 13 passes for 94 yards, leading his Chargers to two scores and a victory. The Giants underestimated Luther; "Maybe I'd heard of him," said Bill Currier, the Giants' strong safety. "When he came in, I never thought he'd be able to read our defenses. We had mixed our pass coverages so well, disguised them so that even Fouts was having a hard time. But Luther did the job." Lawrence Taylor, the Giants' linebacker, wished that Fouts had stuck around. "He was sore," said Taylor. "He couldn't throw the ball downfield. Then this guy (Luther) comes in with the fresh, strong arm. He was tough."   —As quoted in the New York Times, October 3, 1983

Luther started six games in 1983 but only won one more after his initial comeback against the Giants. He passed for 1,875 yards with 7 TDs and 17 INTs in-place of the injured Fouts. The next season, he saw three more starts filling in for Fouts and passed for 1,163 yards with 5 touchdowns and a much lower interception total of only 3. The Chargers released Luther the following season.

Luther signed with the Jacksonville Bulls of the USFL in 1985. After starter Brian Sipe was injured in the opening game, Luther played the remainder of the season, completing 60 percent of his 400 passes for 2,792 yards with 15 TDs and 21 interceptions. The team finished 9–9. The USFL folded and ceased all operations shortly after.

Luther returned to the NFL for one more shot in 1986 and signed with the Indianapolis Colts. Behind Jack Trudeau and Gary Hogeboom, he never got on the field. Luther called it a career the next season. He totaled 245 pass completions for 3,187 yards with 12 TDs and 23 INTs in his NFL career.

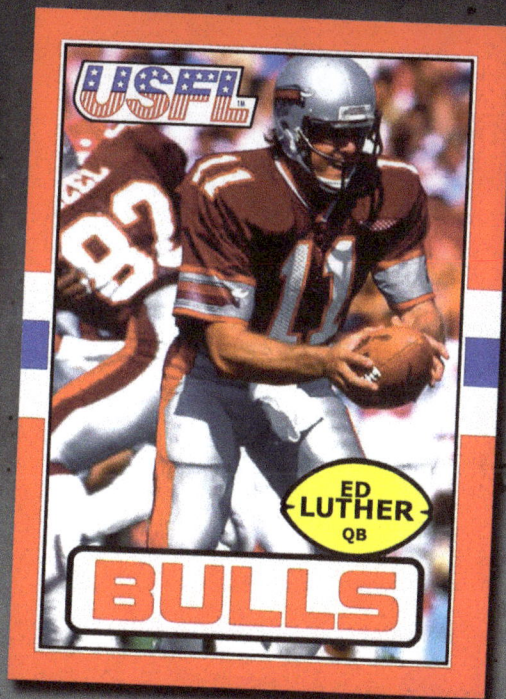

MARANGI, GARY

Gary Marangi grew up in Elmont, New York, where he was a football and lacrosse star. In his senior year, Elmont won the Long Island lacrosse championship after going a perfect 21–0. His year in football was also perfect, going 8–0 on the season.

Marangi had a stellar collegiate career at Boston College. He completed 235 of 447 passes for 2,739 yards and 19 touchdowns and also rushed for 512 yards and 5 touchdowns. As a senior in 1973, Marangi was second in the nation with a 60.4 completion percentage, which put him on many pro scouts' radars.

Marangi was the second player ever drafted by the

newly formed World Football League, but he decided to pursue the NFL instead. He was drafted in the 3rd round (70th overall) of the 1974 NFL Draft by the Buffalo Bills. During his rookie season, he backed up Joe Ferguson, only seeing action in three games. However, the first pass that Marangi ever threw in the NFL was a touchdown to receiver J. D. Hill in a game against the Miami Dolphins.

Marangi got a little more field time in 1975, appearing in five games for the Bills. In 1976 starter Joe Ferguson, who was one of the leading quarterbacks in football at the time, suffered a back injury in week seven and was sidelined for the season. Marangi got the call to finish out the season and would see the most playing time in his career. The Bills were 0–7 with Marangi at the helm, and he threw 7 TDs with 16 interceptions. It would be the last time Marangi saw action on an NFL field. Chronic shoulder problems and multiple surgeries took a severe toll on Marangi's performance. He was traded to Green Bay but didn't pass the physical to make the team. In 1977 he suited up for four games with the Cleveland Browns but never got on the field.

Marangi stayed away from football for nearly twenty-five years, but teaching led him back to the game. Marangi was a teacher and the offensive coordinator at Sachem East High School and a quarterbacks coach at Connetquot High School before becoming the dean and head football coach at Patchogue-Medford High School in Medford, New York.

MARTIN, TEE

Martin, an Alabama native, learned behind starter Peyton Manning at Tennessee during his freshman and sophomore years. Then he earned the opportunity to shine as the starter his junior year when Manning departed for the NFL. In 1998 Martin led the Volunteers to a perfect 13–0 record and a win at the Fiesta Bowl over Florida State, claiming Tennessee's first NCAA National Championship since 1951. He broke several records that season, including Chuck Long's mark for 22 straight completions in a game in 1984. Martin's 24 straight completions (over three games) broke the NCAA record previously shared by USC's Rob Johnson and Maryland's Scott Milanovich.

Martin steered the Volunteers to their second consecutive BCS Bowl game in 1999 as a senior.

Tennessee lost the title game to third-ranked Nebraska, but Martin caught the attention of the NFL, and his career of 4,592 passing yards, 32 passing touchdowns, and 16 rushing touchdowns caught the hearts of the fans.

Martin was drafted in the 5th round (163rd overall) of the 2000 NFL Draft by the Pittsburgh Steelers and saw action in one game his rookie year. Although he didn't attempt any passes he did rush once for 8 yards. After his release the following season, Martin joined the Rhein Fire of NFL Europe, passing for over 1,000 yards to help them to a 7–3 record and an appearance in the World Bowl. He lost to fellow 2000 draft pick Todd Husak and the Berlin Thunder, but it earned Martin a slot on the Philadelphia Eagles practice squad.

Martin got one more shot in the NFL in 2003 with the Oakland Raiders, backing up the previous season's league MVP Rich Gannon. Martin saw action in two games, completing 6 of 16 passes for 69 yards and rushing for 28 more. Martin would be released by the Raiders, but it wouldn't be the end of his professional career. Martin signed with the Winnipeg Blue Bombers of the Canadian Football League and passed for 458 yards over two seasons from 2004 to 2005.

After high school coaching stints and stops at New Mexico University, Kentucky, and USC to coach quarterbacks and wide receivers, Martin would eventually return to the NFL fifteen years later as a receivers coach with the Tennessee Titans in 2019–20 before moving to Baltimore for similar duties in 2021.

MCDONALD, PAUL

There's a McDonald family known for producing great hamburgers, and then there's one that produced great quarterbacks. Paul McDonald's youngest son, Matt, started for Bowling Green from 2020 to 2022, passing for nearly 6,000 yards and 36 touchdowns. Middle son, Andrew, played for New Mexico State from 2012 to 2013 and had a senior season with 2,497 yards and 15 TDs. The eldest son, Mike, was a backup at USC from 2006 to 2007, behind John David Booty and Mark Sanchez, and part of two national championships.

Paul McDonald was an All-State quarterback from Bishop Amat Memorial High School and received a scholarship from the University of Southern California, where he backed up future NFL draftees Vince Evans and Rob Hertel. By his junior season in 1978, McDonald claimed the starting job and held on to it tightly. With a running back core that included Charles White and Lynn Cain, McDonald led the Trojans to a (shared) National Championship title. His 1,690 yards passing led the Pac-10, and

19 TDs tied a USC single-season record. McDonald's 150.6 quarterback rating was second in the NCAA, and his senior season was even better. Along with a backfield that included two Heisman Trophy winners, Charles White and Marcus Allen, McDonald led the Trojans to another (shared) national title. With 2,223 passing yards, 18 TDs, and a conference-leading 150.8 quarterback rating, McDonald finished sixth in the Heisman Trophy voting.

McDonald finished his collegiate career with a 22–1–1 record, back-to-back national championships, and the NCAA record for lowest interception percentage in a career at 2.3 percent. He only threw 13 interceptions in 561 attempts, which included a Pac-10 record of 143 straight passes without an interception.

McDonald was selected in the 4th round (109th overall) of the 1980 NFL Draft by the Cleveland Browns. Although he got into several games and even ran a few times, McDonald didn't get to pass the ball his rookie season. He saw more playing time in 1981, completing an impressive 35 of 57 passes with 4 TDs, but had yet to start a game. Finally, in 1982 McDonald saw his first three starts, filling in for the inured Brian Sipe. His 993 yards and 5 TDs helped the Browns win two of the three contests McDonald started and propelled them to the playoffs. He started the first round of the playoffs with a great performance, passing for 281 yards with a TD and no INTs, but it wasn't enough to hold the Raiders back from eliminating his team.

Brian Sipe regained his health in 1983, and McDonald resumed his backup role, starting in just two games. In 1984 Sipe departed to play with the New Jersey Generals of the new USFL, so the starting job was vacated for McDonald, who turned down USFL offers himself to stay in Cleveland. He started

every game in 1984, passing for 3,472 yards with 14 touchdowns and an un-characteristic 23 interceptions. After a poor start, the Browns made a coaching change midseason and finished 5–11. McDonald was sacked 53 times. The Browns drafted Bernie Kosar in the 1st round of 1985 and traded for veteran Gary Danielson, which left McDonald in the third-string position at quarterback. After not letting him see the field at all that season, the Browns released McDonald.

The Seattle Seahawks signed McDonald in 1986 as an emergency quarterback behind starter Dave Krieg and backup Gale Gilbert, but he was released after training camp when the team decided to keep just two quarterbacks. Later in the season, the Cowboys picked up McDonald as a backup after they lost Danny White to injury for the season. He got into one game but didn't attempt a pass. McDonald was re-signed in 1987, but with the players' strike, he lost out on any playing time to Fresno State record-setting rookie Kevin Sweeney, who was successful in his new starting role until the striking players returned. McDonald would retire the following season after accumulating 5,269 yards with 24 TDs and 37 INTs in a career that lasted for over eight years and eighty-five games.

McDonald became the color commentator for USC radio broadcasting and won awards for that role in 2002 and 2004. He has since written a book called *Thru the Tunnel: True Stories of Sports and Life That Empower Your Spirit* and contributed to a documentary film titled *A City Divided* about the UCLA-USC rivalry.

MCGWIRE, DAN

What *didn't* Dan McGwire accomplish in high school sports? That should be the question. The California native was an All-American at Claremont High School. After completing 203 of 328 passes for a 61.9 percent average, 3,172 yards, and 33 touchdowns as a senior, he led his team to California's East Sectional Title (out of 550 teams) and even punted for a 40-yard average. McGwire was awarded California's 1985 Offensive Player of the Year and 1985 California State MVP. In his three-year varsity high school career, McGwire passed for 6,559 yards and 65 touchdowns. He also averaged double digits in scoring and rebounding in his last two seasons of basketball.

Standing at 6'8", Dan McGwire was the tallest quarterback to ever compete at the college level. He began his college playing career at the University of Iowa where he completed 47 of 84 passes for 680 yards and 6 TDs over his freshman and sophomore seasons. He transferred back home to California to attend San Diego State and went on a record-smashing spree. As a junior in 1989, McGwire passed for 3,651 yards with 16 TDs and a 131.7 passer rating, ranking fifth in the NCAA in pass completions and pass attempts and third in the nation in passing yards. As a senior in 1990, McGwire got even better. He threw for 3,833 yards, completing over 60 percent of his passes. His passing yards, attempts, and completions were all good for third best in the NCAA, and his 27 touchdowns and rating of 148.6 both ranked fourth in all of Division 1A football.

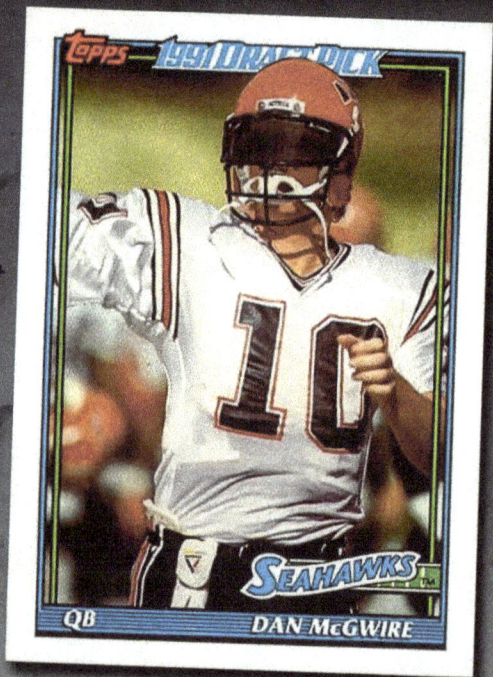

McGwire was the no. 1 pick of the Seattle Seahawks in 1991. He was the first quarterback selected (16th overall), even taken before Hall of Famer Brett Favre. McGwire beat out Kelly Stouffer to back up Dave Krieg his rookie season and was expected to soon replace the aging veteran. He got his chance to start in his second season, only for the opportunity fall short due to a season-ending hip injury. In 1993, McGwire's third season, the Seahawks drafted Rick Mirer out of Notre Dame with their 1st round pick, showing little patience for Dan McGwire to mature. When Mirer went down with an injury in 1994, McGwire saw the most playing time of his pro career. In three starts and seven total appearances, he completed 51 of 105 passes for 578 yards, 1 touchdown, and 2 interceptions. Four years with the Seahawks would be it for McGwire. He signed with Miami in 1995 but only got to attempt one pass on the field behind future Hall of Famer Dan Marino.

In five NFL seasons, McGwire would complete 74 of 148 passes for 745 yards, 2 touchdowns, and 6 interceptions, starting just five games. Although his professional career wasn't highlighted with records or accolades, what McGwire did in high school and college to get to the pro level will never be forgotten.

Athletic prowess isn't limited to Dan McGwire; it seems to run in the family. He has three daughters, two of whom have played Division I college basketball, and Dan is also the younger brother of former Major League record-setting home run slugger Mark McGwire.

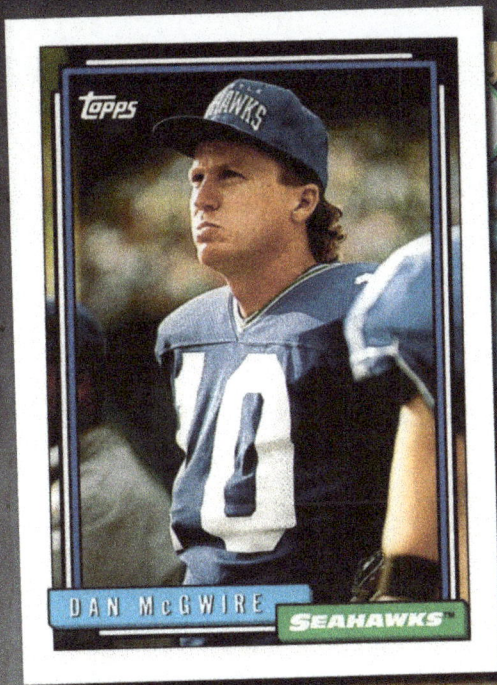

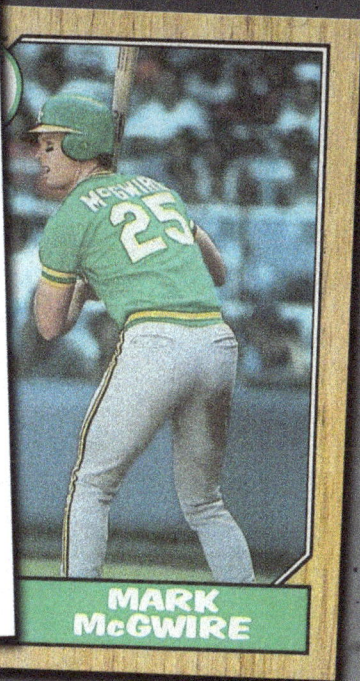

METTENBERGER, ZACH

As a senior at Oconee County High School in Watkinsville, Georgia, Zach Mettenberger passed for 2,106 yards and 19 touchdowns. He was ranked as the eleventh best pro-style quarterback recruit by Rivals.com.

Mettenberger stayed local and attended the University of Georgia in 2009, but he was kicked off the team for disciplinary reasons. He transferred to Butler Community College in 2010 where he passed for 2,678 yards with 32 TDs and only 4 interceptions and led the team to an 11–1 record and to the JUCO National Championship game.

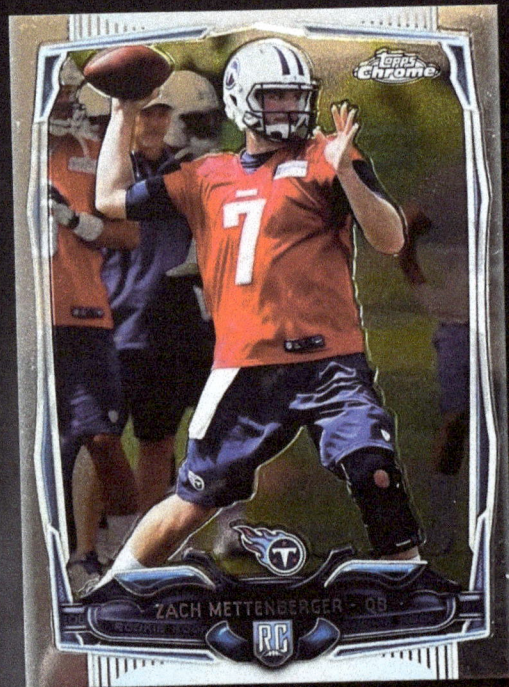

In 2011 Mettenberger transferred to LSU. In his first season as a Tiger, he saw limited action but would become the starter his junior year. In 2012 he passed for 2,609 yards and led his team to a 10–3 record and an appearance at the Chick-fil-A Bowl against Clemson.

Mettenberger's senior season was one for the record books. He completed 192 of 296 passes for a 64.9 completion percentage and connected for a 10.4 yard-per-attempt average, good for first in the SEC. He threw for 3,082 yards and 22 touchdowns with only 8 interceptions, becoming the first ever LSU quarterback to throw for over 2,500 yards in consecutive seasons. Again, he led his team to a bowl game, and although Mettenberger was sidelined with a torn ACL he suffered in the last regular season game, LSU still defeated Iowa in the Outback Bowl. Mettenberger ended his LSU career with 5,783 yards and 35 touchdowns.

Mettenberger was selected by the Tennessee Titans in the 6th round (178th overall) of the 2014 NFL Draft. He got his first start against the Texans. In a losing effort, he was 27 of 41 for 299 yards, 2 touchdowns, and an interception. In his next start on Monday Night Football, he threw 2 TDs, hitting Nate Washington for an 80-yard score, but, again, it was a losing effort. Unfortunately, Mettenberger injured his shoulder in the game and missed the rest of the season. Although his numbers were decent by any rookie standard, with 1,412 yards, 8 touchdowns, and 7 interceptions in six starts, the Titans were 0–6 under Mettenberger's helm.

Mettenberger started four games in 2015 and played parts in three more while starter Marcus Mariota was out with an injury. He passed for 935 yards with 4 touchdowns and ran for another, but he also had 8 interceptions. He was released before the next season.

The San Diego Chargers claimed Mettenberger off waivers from the Titans in 2016 but released him after training camp. He was then claimed off waivers by the Pittsburgh Steelers but was only activated for four games and didn't see any

ZACH METTENBERGER
QB

playing time. He was released before the next season began.

In 2019 Mettenberger was a 4th round draft pick by the Memphis Express of the newly formed Alliance of American Football league. He began the season as a third-string quarterback behind Christian Hackenberg and Brandon Silvers. After Silvers suffered an injury and Hackenberg played poorly, Mettenberger became the starter. He was having a good season, completing 36 of 54 passes for a 66.7 completion percentage with 475 yards and 5 total TDs and only 1 interception, until injury hit. The Express signed Johnny Manziel and placed Mettenberger on injured reserve. The league folded before the 2019 season and Mettenberger found quarterback work in the Spring League—a developmental league that played an abbreviated season consisting of showcase events for scouts.

Mettenberger has since coached in high school and is a coaching analyst for the University of Alabama.

MILLEN, HUGH

After passing for 1,217 yards and 8 touchdowns at Santa Rosa Junior College in California, Hugh Millen transferred to the University of Washington after his sophomore year. Taking a chance as a walk-on under legendary coach Don James, Millen beat out freshman and future NFL mainstay Chris Chandler for the starting job.

Although he finished his junior year with only 1,051 yards passing, 5 touchdowns, and 9 interceptions, Millen led the Huskies to an Orange Bowl victory over Oklahoma in 1984. The win became known as the infamous "Schooner Game," in which the underdog Huskies rallied to beat the Oklahoma Sooners 28–17, and propelled Washington to an 11–1 record and a no. 2 national ranking. Not too bad for a walk-on. In

his senior season, Millen passed for 1,565 yards with 6 TDs and 14 interceptions and won the National Football Foundation Scholar-Athlete award.

Millen was selected in the 3rd round (71st overall) of the 1986 NFL Draft by the Los Angeles Rams but was sidelined his entire rookie year after fracturing his ankle. His second season didn't fare much better, as he got into one game, attempting 1 pass and completing it for no yards, then he missed most of the season with a back injury. Because of all the time Millen lost to injuries, Jim Everett became entrenched as the Rams' starter, which made Millen expendable.

Millen signed with the Falcons in 1988 and would spend the next three seasons primarily backing up their no. 1 pick, Chris Miller out of Oregon. In his three-year stretch, Millen would see action in eleven games, starting three and attempting 144 passes for 1,074 yards and 2 touchdowns.

In 1991 Millen signed with the Patriots as a free agent and, in week four, would replace the injured starter, Tommy Hodson, for the remainder of the season, producing Millen's best year in the NFL. He completed 246 of 409 passes, good for 60.1 percent, topped 3,000 yards, and threw 9 TDs to 18 interceptions. The following year, Millen would share quarterback time with Tommy Hodson, Scott Zolak, and Jeff Carlson, but he still led the club with 1,203 passing yards and 8 TDs, doing so with a third-degree sprained shoulder all season. After the Patriots suffered another poor season, they wanted a complete overhaul and traded Millen to the Dallas Cowboys.

Millen was signed for quarterback depth since Dallas star Troy Aikman was healing from surgery for a herniated disc. Millen was third on the depth chart behind future coach Jason Garrett, but he would never see playing time and was later cut to make room for veteran Bernie Kosar, who was signed after being cut by the Cleveland Browns. Millen was quickly signed by the Miami Dolphins, who lost Dan Marino for the year with an Achilles tendon injury, but did not appear in any games.

Millen would play his final two seasons backing up John Elway with Denver in 1994–95. In eight games, he threw for 1,090 yards with 3 TDs and rushed for 2 more. He completed 63 percent of his passes as a Broncos reserve. In 1996 Millen would sign with the Saints for one more shot but be released before the season's start, and it would finalize his decade-long professional career.

Quarterback blood runs deep in the Millen family. Hugh has two quarterback sons. His oldest, Cale, was recruited by several Division I colleges and played for Oregon in 2019 then transferred to the University of Connecticut in 2021. Millen's younger son, Clay, passed for 1,910 yards and 10 TDs with a 149.8 passer rating as a freshman with Colorado State in 2022.

MOROSKI, MIKE

Mike Moroski's father, Hank, was a college basketball star. He was the first player in Cal Poly history to become a four-year starter and All-Conference in all four years. Hank twice led the California Athletic Association in scoring, and he is one of only two players with a retired number at the university. His son took a different path to athletic stardom.

Mike Moroski and his father were equally gifted, but Mike's expertise was on the football field rather than the basketball court. Like his father, Mike was also a star college player. At the University of California Davis (UC Davis), Mike Moroski was also a four-year starter, and from 1975 to 1978, he established himself as one of the top quarterbacks in Division II-A football. In his junior season, Moroski carried his team to the Division II semifinals in 1977. He was a two-time Far West Conference Player of the Year. As if that weren't enough, Moroski was also a pitcher on the Aggies baseball team.

Despite playing at a smaller, lower-division college, Moroski's talent caught the attention of several NFL teams. He was selected in the 6th round (154th overall) of the 1979 NFL Draft by the Atlanta Falcons, but his first four seasons with the Falcons didn't offer Moroski much playing time behind starter Steve Bartkowski.

Moroski finally got his first NFL starts in 1983, winning one and losing one. He saw playing time in all sixteen games, whether in relief work or kick-holding scenarios, and he completed over 64 percent of his passes for 575 yards. The next season, he played in all sixteen games again, this time starting five of them. Moroski had his most productive NFL season and completed 102 of 191 passes for 1,207 yards with 2 TDs and 9 INTs.

In 1985 Moroski signed with the Houston Oilers and competed with Oliver Luck for the backup slot behind starter Warren Moon. He saw a decline in playing time, only appearing in five games, then 1986 brought Moroski another new team. He signed with the 49ers to become Joe Montana's backup, and he started two games while Montana was sidelined with an injury. He split the decisions and completed 42 of 73 passes for 493 yards. Moroski described his time in San Francisco in an interview with the *Marin Independent Journal*: "What I learned from Bill Walsh is that the key to building a program is having

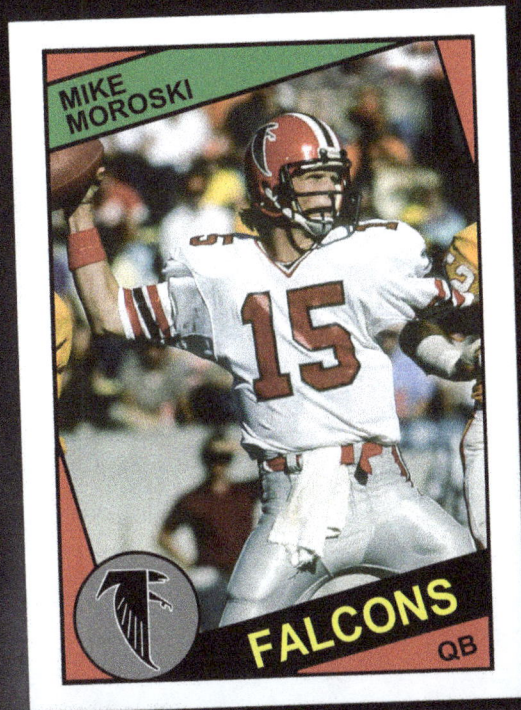

great people. I believe that from my own experience in college and the pros, and especially accentuated with my one year with the San Francisco 49ers, who were people-oriented."

Moroski retired the next season. During his eight years in the league, he played in sixty-nine games and passed for 2,864 yards with 8 touchdowns. However, his football career was far from over.

Moroski returned to his alma mater and coached for the Aggies from 1987 to 2012. During his tenure, Moroski's offensive knowledge helped UC Davis to eight NCAA Division II postseason appearances and four national semifinal appearances. In 2001 Moroski won National Assistant Coach of the Year.

Moroski left his old school in 2012 to pursue the head coaching position that he'd been longing for, and he got that opportunity at the College of Idaho. The Yotes' football program had been on hiatus for thirty-seven years, and Moroski was the man to bring it back. Starting fresh and with no recruits, Moroski went to work and by his fourth season had a winning record. By season six they had a perfect 10–0 record and made it all the way to the National Association of Intercollegiate Athletics (NAIA) Quarterfinals. Moroski's teams have finished first place in the Frontier Conference every year since.

MUSGRAVE, BILL

m

Bill MUSGRAVE

When a high school sophomore wins All-Conference honors as a safety, you wouldn't expect for him to duplicate the honor at a different position the next season, but that's exactly what Bill Musgrave did. At Grand Junction High School, Musgrave moved to starting quarterback his junior year. He then proceeded to win All-Conference honors for the next two seasons. After recording a state-record 30 touchdown passes, Musgrave was named the Colorado High School Athlete of the Year in 1985 and awarded the *Denver Post's* Gold Helmet Award for the state's top scholar-player in football.

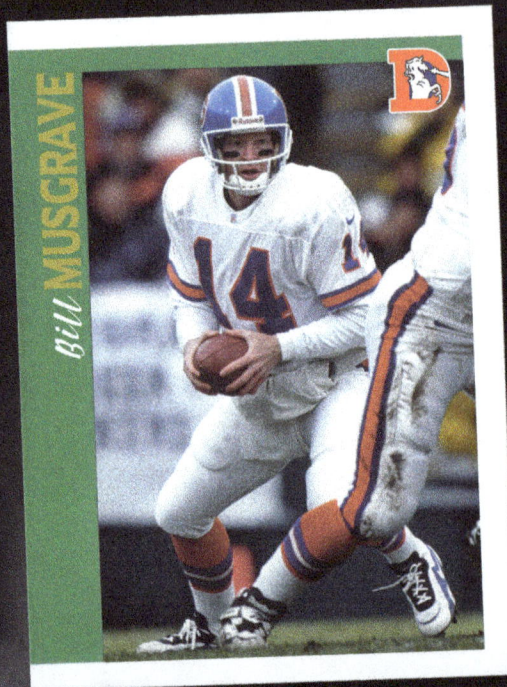

When Musgrave accepted a scholarship from the University of Oregon, they had only four winning seasons in their last twenty-two and hadn't seen a bowl game since the early 1960s. He immediately became the starter as a freshman in 1987 and led the Ducks to a no. 16 ranking. As a sophomore, Musgrave was off to a stellar start and had settled his Ducks into a top 20 ranking with a 6–1 record when he broke his collarbone. The team proceeded to lose their remaining four games and missed bowl game contention yet again.

Musgrave had his best season as a junior in 1989. He amassed 3,081 yards passing and 22 touchdowns, both of which topped the Pac-10. Both his 401 pass attempts and 231 completions also led the conference. Musgrave threw for a school-record 489 yards against the BYU Cougars' Ty Detmer who passed for 470 yards. The duo set an NCAA record for most passing yards in a game by two players. Musgrave led the Ducks to a 7–4 record and their first bowl game in over two decades. Behind the arm of Musgrave, Oregon won the Independence Bowl 27–24 over Tulsa.

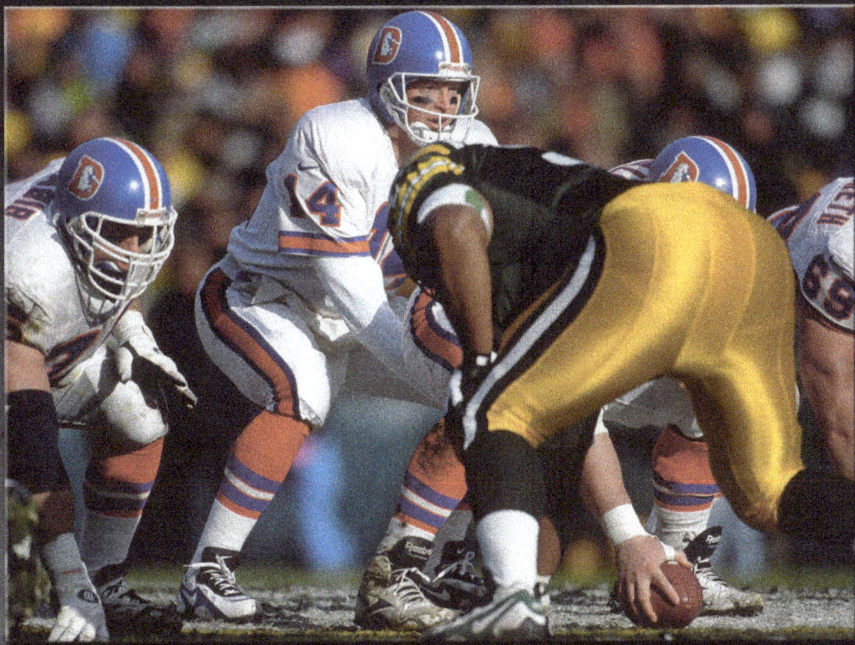

Musgrave wrapped up his collegiate career with quite the resume. He led Oregon to their first ever back-to-back bowl games. He was a four-year starter and three-year team captain who set fifteen school passing records. Musgrave's 8,343 passing yards and 60 touchdowns trailed only Stanford's John Elway for all-time in the Pac-10.

Musgrave was selected in the 4th round of the 1991 NFL Draft by the Dallas Cowboys. After competing for a roster spot against Steve Beuerlein and future Hall of Famer Troy Aikman, Musgrave was released before the season began. He was signed to the San Francisco practice squad a few days later and activated to the team at week eleven. Musgrave made his professional debut in the final game of the season, coming in to relieve Steve Young. In his limited

action, Musgrave completed 4 of 5 passes for a touchdown, which would be the only touchdown of his NFL career.

For the next three seasons, Musgrave would bounce between the practice squad and third-string emergency quarterback on the sidelines. But what he learned playing under coaches George Seifert, Mike Holmgren, and Mike Shanahan would benefit his future in ways he had yet to imagine.

In 1995 Musgrave would reunite with coach Shanahan in Denver as John Elway's backup. He saw action in ten games over the next two seasons, starting one. After being released by the Broncos, he immediately took a quarterback coaching position with the Oakland Raiders. Musgrave would give playing one more shot in 1997 with the Indianapolis Colts, but he was released in training camp. He finished his playing career completing 43 of 69 passes for 402 yards with 1 TD and 2 interceptions.

When you're an understudy of future Hall of Famers like Troy Aikman, Steve Young, and John Elway, you are bound to learn a thing or two about offense. Musgrave quickly became an offensive coordinator for the Eagles in 1998, and his more than two-decade coaching career soared from there.

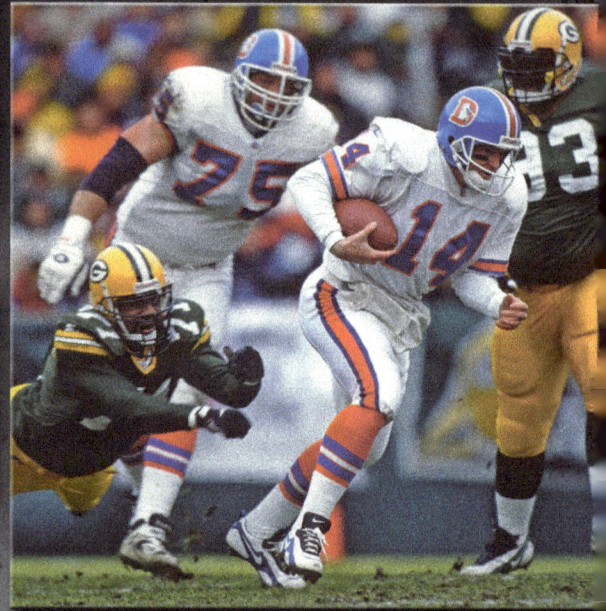

MUSGRAVE'S COACHING HISTORY

- **Oakland Raiders (1997)**
  Quarterbacks
- **Philadelphia Eagles (1998)**
  Offensive assistant/offensive coordinator
- **Carolina Panthers (1999–2000)**
  Offensive coordinator/quarterbacks
- **Virginia (2001–02)**
  Offensive coordinator/quarterbacks/tight ends
- **Jacksonville Jaguars (2003–04)**
  Offensive coordinator
- **Jacksonville Jaguars (2004)**
  Quarterbacks
- **Washington Redskins (2005)**
  Quarterbacks
- **Atlanta Falcons (2006–10)**
  Quarterbacks
- **Atlanta Falcons (2010)**
  Assistant head coach
- **Minnesota Vikings (2011–13)**
  Offensive coordinator
- **Philadelphia Eagles (2014)**
  Quarterbacks
- **Oakland Raiders (2015–16)**
  Offensive coordinator
- **Denver Broncos (2017)**
  Quarterbacks
- **Denver Broncos (2017–18)**
  Offensive coordinator
- **California (2020–22)**
  Offensive coordinator/quarterbacks

Musgrave has coached three different quarterbacks to Pro Bowl seasons: Derek Carr (2015 & 2016), Matt Ryan (2010), and even the player who helped replace him on the Dallas Cowboys his rookie season, Steve Beuerlein (1999).

PHILCOX, TODD

Behind Syracuse starter Don McPherson going 6–2 in 1985, 5–6 in 1986, and 11–0–1 in 1987 and throwing for over 5,600 yards and 46 touchdowns during that stretch, all Todd Philcox could do was watch and wait for his shot. McPherson was drafted by the Philadelphia Eagles in 1987, vacating the starting spot for Philcox to earn.

With only 9 passes to his name, Philcox was little more than a college rookie when starting his senior season in 1988. However, he played like a veteran. With 2,076 yards and 16 touchdowns, Philcox led his Orangemen to a 10-2 record and a 23-10 victory over LSU in the Hall of Fame Bowl. In a game announced by Joe Namath, Philcox completed 16 of 23 passes for 130 yards and a touchdown to complement the dual running threat of two future NFL stars, Robert Drummond (122 yards) and Daryl "Moose" Johnson (74 yards).

Philcox wasn't drafted to the NFL, but

P

he quickly found a job with the Cincinnati Bengals in 1989 as a third-string backup to Boomer Esiason and Turk Schonert. Philcox didn't see any playing time his rookie season but did move up the depth chart in 1990 to play in two games. He was 0–2 passing with an interception and was sacked twice. Not the glamorous beginning Philcox was looking for, but this isn't a story about things coming quickly and easily.

In 1991 Philcox signed with the Cleveland Browns to backup Bernie Kosar. He saw limited action in four games, completing 4 of 8 passes for 49 yards and an interception. The next season finally found Philcox getting his first NFL start between the injured Bernie Kosar and backup Mike Tomczak. After four years of not starting and having never thrown a touchdown in the pros, Philcox won his start and threw 3! Between Bernie Kosar and Vinny Testaverde, Philcox found himself starting four games in 1993, earning a 1–3 record and passing for 699 yards with 4 touchdowns and 7 interceptions. He also scored his first rushing TD.

Over the next couple years, Philcox would become a member of the Buccaneers (1995) and Jaguars (1996) but not see any action on the field. In 1997 Philcox had one last moment in the spotlight, playing in two games for the San Diego Chargers. He completed 16 of 28 passes for 173 yards but couldn't connect on a last touchdown.

In 1998 Philcox finished his career with a brief stint on the Patriots, backing up Drew Bledsoe and Scott Zolak. Not a bad tenure for a guy who didn't start in college until his senior year, wasn't drafted, and didn't start in the NFL until his fourth season.

PICKETT, CODY

Pickett was a national champion at Caldwell High School in Idaho, but not as a football player; he was a rodeo champion, following in his dad's footsteps. His father, Dee Pickett, was not only on the professional rodeo circuit, but a 1984 World Champion cowboy and a member of the Pro Rodeo Hall of Fame. Aside from rodeo, Cody Pickett lettered in football, basketball, and golf. He was highly recruited by the University of Washington, and he accepted a scholarship from the school.

Pickett was granted a medical redshirt after he attempted only 4 passes his freshman year and developed back problems. He backed up Marques Tuiasosopo the following season, attempting just 2 passes, but was part of the 2000 Huskies team that finished 11–1, winning the Rose Bowl and finishing with a no. 3 ranking in the nation.

Pickett took over the starting role for the next three seasons, 2001–03. His breakout year came as a junior in 2002, when he led the Pac-10 in virtually every passing category. Pickett's 612 pass attempts, 365 completions, and 4,458 yards all topped the conference and were within the top three in the nation.

Pickett chose to return for his senior year even after garnering much interest from the NFL. He was off to a hot start and was considered among Heisman candidates by *Sports Illustrated* and other press outlets, but a shoulder

SOUTH LEVEL 3

52	50	DZ	25
TUNNEL	SEC	ROW	SEAT

EST. PR. $30.47 CTY. TX. $1.53 TOTAL $32.00

GAME THREE

W vs. Vandals

SAT., SEPT. 28, 2002
HUSKY STADIUM

P

injury limited some of his productivity. Pickett still completed 257 passes for 3,043 yards and was named the Huskies' Offensive MVP. He finished his college career with 792 completions for 9,916 yards and 53 touchdowns.

A 7th round selection (217th overall) by the San Francisco 49ers in the 2004 NFL Draft, Pickett saw action in only one game his rookie season. He completed 4 passes for 55 yards and threw 2 interceptions. In 2005 Pickett began the season fourth on the quarterback depth chart, but after the 49ers traded starter Tim Rattay and back-ups Alex Smith and Ken Dorsey were injured, Pickett found himself the unlikely starter for two games. He completed 14 of 35 passes for 140 yards with no TDs and 2 interceptions. He also rushed for 42 yards, which was more than he had in his entire collegiate career. With 4 picks and a 40 percent completion ratio in his two seasons by the bay, San Francisco gave up on Pickett, and he was traded to Houston in 2006. The Texans released him early in the season.

Pickett was selected as a free agent by the Rhein Fire of NFL Europe in 2007. He became their starter and completed 132 of 205 passes for a 64.4 completion percentage with 1,373 yards, 6 touchdowns, and 6 picks. Later that year, Pickett was signed by the Oakland Raiders but released before the season started. He then immediately moved north and signed with the Toronto Argonauts of

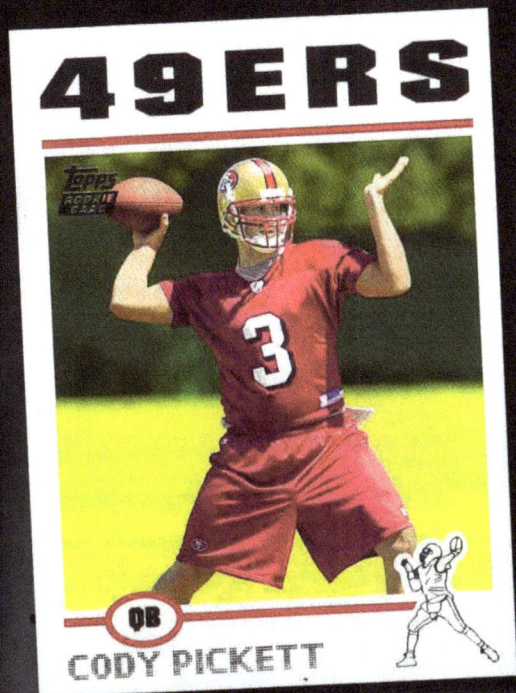

P

the Canadian Football League. Pickett saw relief action that season and made his first start in the next. He would start nine games in his three-year stay with Toronto, completing 208 of 339 passes for 2,163 yards. In 2010 Pickett bounced around the CFL, getting signed and subsequently released by the Montreal Alouettes and Calgary Stampeders.

After 2010 Pickett retired from football, leaving behind his legendary, record-setting college career and seven-year pro career spanning three different professional leagues. He returned to Idaho and coached his younger sister's basketball team and high school boys' basketball.

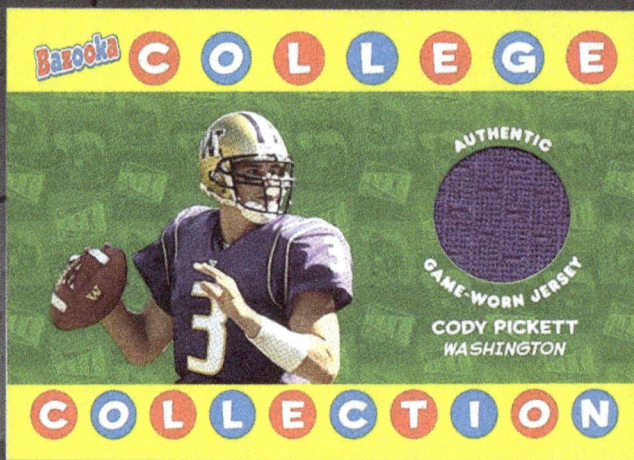

REAVES, JOHN

Reaves was a four-sport star at T. R. Robinson High School in Tampa, Florida. He played baseball, track, football, and basketball. He even scored 52 points in a basketball game once. But football was what put Reaves on the athletic map.

In fact, in 2007 Reaves was named one of the "100 Greatest Players in the First 100 Years" of Florida high school football.

Reaves stayed in Florida to accept a football scholarship at the University of Florida. As a sophomore in 1969, Reaves passed for 2,896 yards on 396 attempts with 24 touchdowns. In a run-heavy era of football, that amount of pass attempts and yards got attention. He led the SEC in pass completions, pass attempts, passing yards, passing touchdowns, total plays, and total

R

yards. His pass attempts and completions were tops in the nation.

Along with fellow sophomores Carlos Alvarez at receiver and Tommy Durrance at running back, the trio led the Gators to a 9–1–1 record, their best season in history. Florida upset Tennessee in the 1969 Gator Bowl, and the star-powered trio became known as the "Super Sophs." Reaves was awarded first-team All-SEC, and the Super Sophs would go on to set every major career passing and receiving record at Florida over the next three years.

With another stellar season, Reaves led the SEC in several passing categories as a junior in 1970, taking the Gators to a 7–4 record. As a senior, Reaves trip-licated his success. He headed the SEC in several categories, was a first-team All-American, and won the Sammy Baugh Trophy for college's best passer. Reaves finished his college career as the NCAA's all-time career leader in passing yards with 7,581 and an SEC career record of 56 touchdowns.

JOHN REAVES   QUARTERBACK
EAGLES

Reaves was selected in the 1st round (14th overall) of the 1972 NFL Draft by the Philadelphia Eagles. He started seven games his rookie season, passing for over 1,500 yards, but lost all seven starts. The Eagles signed veteran Roman Gabriel in 1973, and Reaves would spend most of the next two seasons in a mop-up role. He was

R traded to the Cincinnati Bengals in 1975, but withwith incumbent All-Pro starter Ken Anderson in the lineup, Reaves would take on the backup role, starting just six games in the next four seasons. The Bengals released Reaves in 1979, and he was claimed by the Vikings but not given any playing time. He signed with the Houston Oilers in 1981 and started two games behind veterans Kenny Stabler and Gifford Nielsen.

Like many backups of the time, Reaves jumped to the new USFL league in 1983 with hopes of reviving his career. A revival it indeed was. And it was also a homecoming. Reaves returned to his hometown of Tampa, Florida, to play for the Bandits. Under the pass-oriented coach, Steve Spurrier, Reaves was able to spread his wings and let the ball fly. An injury limited him to only eight games in 1983, but he still completed 139 of 259 passes for 1,276 yards. He returned to form in 1984, completing 313 of 544 passes for 4,092 yards and 28 touchdowns. Keeping up with the expectations he set, he had another banner year in 1985, completing 314 of 561 passes for 4,193 yards

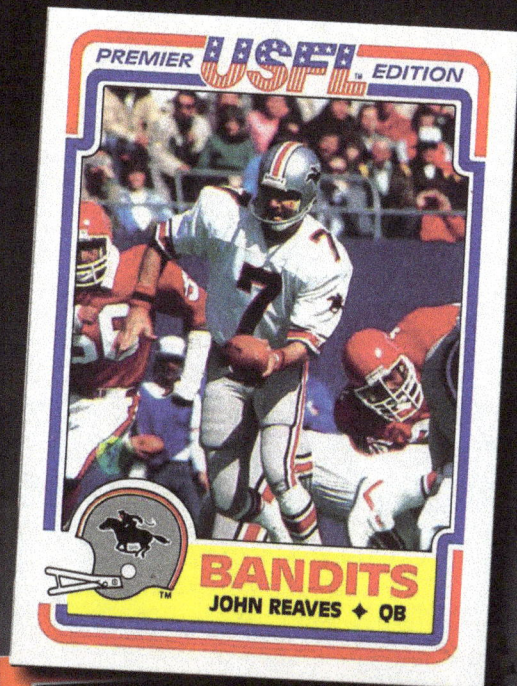

PREMIER USFL EDITION
BANDITS
JOHN REAVES ◆ QB

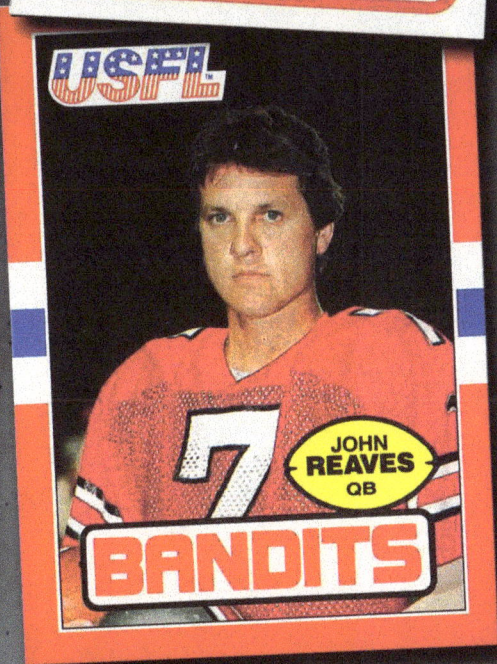

USFL
JOHN REAVES QB
BANDITS

R

and 25 touchdowns. Only future Hall of Famer Jim Kelly threw for more yards than Reaves in the USFL. Reaves had over 4,000 yards in consecutive seasons and finished his USFL career with over 10,000 yards of total offense.

Reaves was set to play for the Orlando Renegades in 1986, but the league went under before the season began. In 1987 Reaves started for his hometown's Tampa Bay Buccaneers as a replacement player during the NFL players' strike. He started two games and had a record of 1–1, throwing for 83 yards and a touchdown to wrap up his sixteen-year professional football career.

Reaves returned to the swamp, where he had set virtually every school passing record, to assist his former USFL coach Steve Spurrier with the Gators. He worked with quarterbacks from 1990 to 1994 and helped Shane Mathews achieve the SEC Player of the Year Award in both 1991 and 1992, before his career in the NFL.

Reaves's son Stephen was a quarterback in the CFL with the Toronto Argonauts. John Reaves died at home in Tampa in 2017. He was sixty-seven years old.

ROBINSON, MATT

"I was standing out front at Hofstra with a cab on the way to take me back to the airport, and John Free, who was the business manager at that time, walked out and said, 'What are you doing?'

I said, 'Well, they cut me. I'm going home.' He said, 'Are you that Robinson kid, the quarterback from Georgia?' I said, 'Yes, sir.' And he said, 'Wait five minutes.'

So, he walked in, and five minutes later he came out and said, 'Get in the locker room.' I have no idea [what occurred during those five minutes,] and I never asked. I just went in and got dressed, kept my mouth shut, walked out onto the field, and never heard another word about it. If it wasn't for that, I probably would have never played for the Jets." —*courtesy "Where Are They Now" on nyjets.com by Jim Gehman*

Robinson started as a sophomore at Georgia in 1974 and led the

R

Bulldogs to a 6–6 record and topped the run-heavy SEC with 1,317 passing yards and 8 touchdowns. Robinson set a school record that still stands today for the average gain per pass completion (season) at an incredible 21.95 yards. That's correct, every time he completed a pass in 1974, it was for over 20 yards. In fact, he still holds the Georgia Bulldogs average gain per completion records for both a season and a career (18.36). Robinson also holds the mark for average gain per pass attempt with 18.88. Aaron Murray came close to it in 2012 with 18.02, but Robinson's mark still stands.

In his junior year on the run-oriented the Bulldogs, Georgia improved to 9–3, and for his senior season, they finished at 10–2 and made a Sugar Bowl appearance. Robinson split time at the helm with Ray Goff, who would go on to become the Georgia head coach from 1989 to 1995.

Robinson was selected in the 9th round (227th overall) of the 1977 NFL Draft by the New York Jets. Richard Todd was groomed to be the Jets' quarterback of the future, so Robinson was an insurance plan and an able body to relieve Todd in practice. With the odds stacked against the 9th round pick from a run-defined college, Robinson made the roster at the third-string slot behind Marty Domres. Robinson even got one start during his rookie season. The next season, Todd suffered a

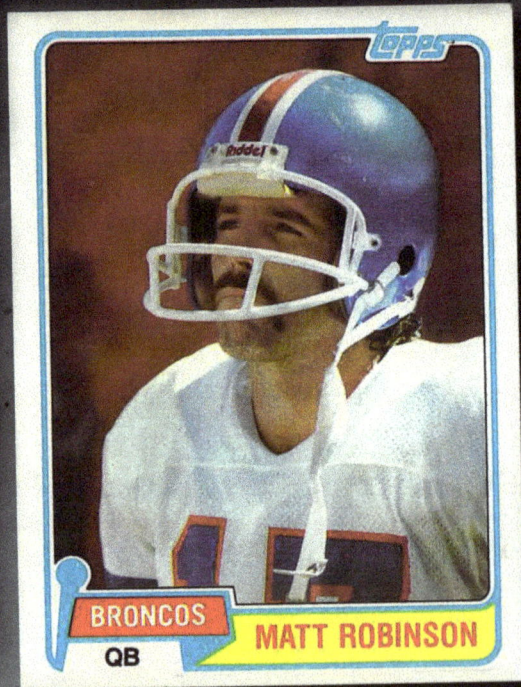

BRONCOS
QB
MATT ROBINSON

R

broken collar bone four games in, and Robinson got the call to become the starter. He lost his first start but then went on a hot streak, winning three in a row. The Jets finished the year with a respectable 8–8 record under Robinson, a huge improvement from their 4–12 mark the previous year. Robinson passed for 2,002 yards with 13 TDs and 16 interceptions. Even with his steady play in 1978, Robinson was relegated back to the bench when Todd returned in 1979.

In 1980 Robinson was traded to the Denver Broncos for 1st and 2nd round picks and backup quarterback Craig Penrose. Robinson beat out veteran Craig Morton to start the first seven games. He was 4–3 in his starts and finished the season with 942 yards passing but only had 2 touchdowns to his 12 interceptions. He did score three more times on the ground, but it wasn't enough for the Broncos to retain him.

1981 would find Matt Robinson with the Buffalo Bills, backing up incumbent starter Joe Ferguson. Robinson would only attempt 10 passes over the next two years with the Bills before finding his way to the newly formed USFL in 1984 to join the Jacksonville Bulls. He split time with Robbie Mahfouz at quarterback, completing 125 of 235 passes for 1,687 yards and 7 touchdowns. The next season (1985), Robinson signed with the Portland Breakers and shared quarterbacking duties with Doug Woodward. Robinson would see the most playing time of his career in his final season as a pro. He completed 156 of 310 passes for 2,182 yards with 15 touchdowns and 20 interceptions.

Robinson has been an important football figure for many years, staying active in the National Football League Players Association (NFLPA) by helping retired players transition from professional athletics to a new life.

ROWE, JEFF

Jeff Rowe didn't become the regular starter at Robert McQueen High School in Reno, Nevada, until his senior year. Then all he did was lead his team to the state title championship game while passing for 2,059 yards and 27 touchdowns in the process.

Rowe's father was a Wolf Pack football season ticket holder for decades, so when Rowe got offers from Nevada and Boise State, it was a point of pride and nostalgia for him to stay near home and play. "We grew up going to those games," said Rowe in a 2022 interview with MSN Daily. Rowe chose the University of Nevada and saw playing time in six games as a true freshman. He was named the team's starter after impressive spring drills but suffered a shoulder injury early in the year that forced him to redshirt. Rowe bounced back to start all fourteen games for the Wolf Pack in 2004, completing 230 of 394 passes for 2,633 yards and 15 touchdowns.

R

In 2005 Rowe started every game again for Nevada. He passed for 2,925 yards and 21 touchdowns and rushed for 6 more, helping lead Nevada to the Sheraton Hawaii Bowl. In the game, Rowe was 22 of 32 passing and scored on a naked bootleg run to beat UCF 49–48 in overtime. In 2006 a hamstring injury kept him out of one game, but he sill managed to pass for nearly 2,000 yards and 17 TDs and was named the team's MVP. Once again, he led the Wolf Pack to a bowl game. Rowe connected on 20 of 31 passes with a touchdown and interception but lost 21–20 to the Miami Hurricanes.

Rowe was a 5th round pick by the Cincinnati Bengals in the 2007 NFL Draft. He had tough competition at the quarterback position and wound up not seeing any playing time at third string behind Carson Palmer and Ryan Fitzpatrick. Rowe began the next season (2008) on the Bengals practice squad and remained there for most of the year until he was signed by the Seattle Seahawks.

The Seahawks waived Rowe during training camp in 2009, and he was picked up by the New England Patriots later in the season. He spent nearly six months with Tom Brady in Patriots camp. He recalls it being an "unbelievable time."

Rowe has since returned home to Nevada and is raising two boys who both play sports. He was inducted into the Nevada Wolf Pack Hall of Fame in 2017, now a legendary, enshrined member of the same team he watched growing up as a child.

RUBBERT, ED

He went undrafted. He was unwanted until a players' strike, and they had no choice but to take him. Then he won every game, turned local hero, and helped inspire Keanu Reaves's character in the movie *The Replacements*. Not a bad football origin story.

The 6'5" Rubbert earned All-County honors for football and basketball in both his junior and senior years at Clarkstown North High School. As a junior in 1981, he led his basketball team to become state champions. In 1982, as a senior, Rubbert was selected as Rockland's Co-Offensive Player of the Year and ended the season with 1,497 yards passing.

Rubbert received a full scholarship to play football at the University of Louisville. He redshirted his freshman year and began his sophomore year (1984) as the starter. In his first start, he broke a school record by completing 29 of 55 passes for 393 yards. He finished his sophomore year ranked fourteenth in the nation with 2,465 total yards.

By the time Rubbert graduated from Louisville, he had broken over ten school records, including some set by the most prolific passer in NFL history, Johnny Unitas.

Rubbert was not selected in the 1987 NFL Draft, but he signed as a free agent with the Washington Redskins. With Doug Williams, Jay Schroeder, and

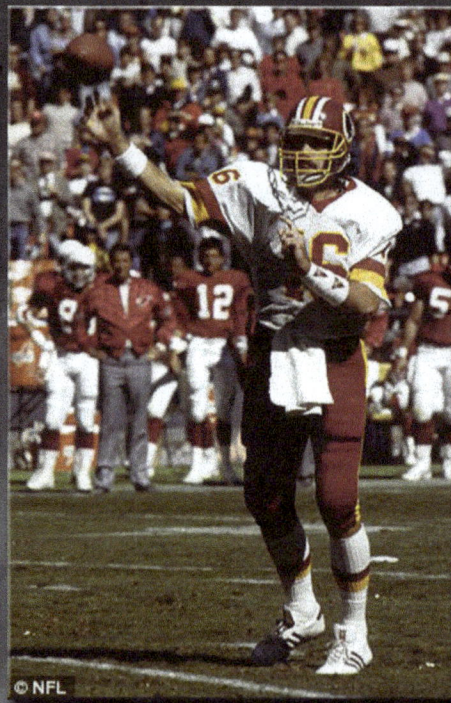

© NFL

R Mark Rypien on the team, there was no room for a fourth quarterback, especially an unproven one, so Rubbert was released in preseason at final cuts. However, Rubbert's name stayed on the radar of Washington's coaches.

A couple months after his release, Rubbert got the call. The NFL players' strike was about to begin, and coach Joe Gibbs enlisted Rubbert to play for the Redskins for the duration of the strike, however long it may last.

In his first NFL game, on a team that consisted entirely of replacement players, Rubbert did the impossible and defeated a St. Louis Cardinals team that had seven non-striking starters playing. He did it in dramatic style, too, leading the league with a 334-yard passing performance and 3 touchdowns. The next week, he led his Redskins to whip the Giants 38–12 in Meadowlands. In his third and final game, Rubbert left early with a shoulder injury, but Washington held on to upset Dallas, who had nearly their entire star lineup back across the picket line. It was one of the greatest upsets in recent NFL history, certainly in the strike era.

The players' strike ended after just three games missed, and just like that, Rubbert's NFL days were over. He would go home on the injured reserve list and in pain, but he could stand tall knowing what he got the chance to do and what he made of the opportunity.

In his short NFL career, Rubbert was a perfect 3–0 with two upset wins. He completed 26 of 49 passes for 532 yards and 4 touchdowns, and his efforts helped Washington make it to the Super Bowl, which they also won in dramatic fashion. Since he was on the injured list, Rubbert received a Super Bowl ring

R

for his contributions.

Rubbert and the 1987 Redskins scab story inspired the hit movie *The Replacements* (2000). Rubbert was fictionalized as Keanu Reaves's character Shane Falco, and the Washington Redskins became the Washington Sentinels.

In The Replacements, Shane Falco was a charismatic college star that never got a chance to prove himself in the pros. When he was called upon as a replacement player, Falco made the most of his opportunity and lead the Sentinels to several wins, keeping them in the playoff hunt and becoming a fan favorite. Much in line with the real life story of Ed Rubbert, Falco returned home after the strike's conclusion and his career was over.

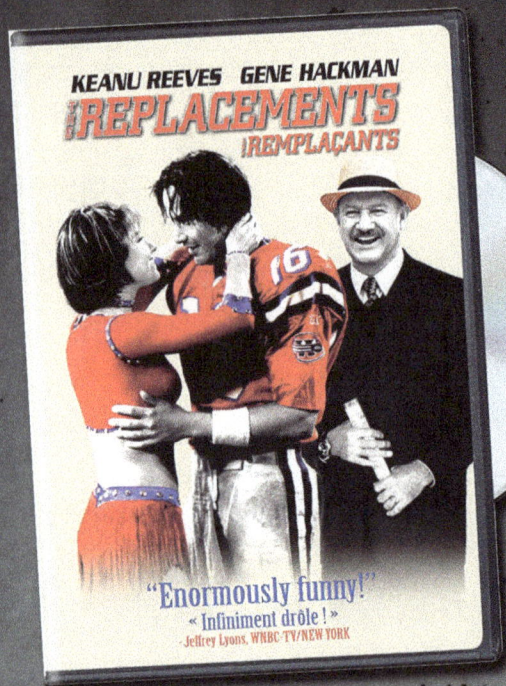

KEANU REEVES   GENE HACKMAN

THE REPLACEMENTS
LES REMPLAÇANTS

"Enormously funny!"
« Infiniment drôle ! »
-Jeffrey Lyons, WNBC-TV/NEW YORK

SALISBURY, SEAN

Who taught Adam Sandler how to be a quarterback for his movie *The Longest Yard*? Salisbury, after his playing career, instructed the movie star on proper footwork, lingo, and mechanics for Sandler's remake of the classic football movie. Sandler later offered Salisbury a role in his 2006 film The Benchwarmers.

Salisbury was a sports star from the get-go. He had such an incredible senior year at Orange Glen High School in Southern California that he had to choose between several Division I football and basketball scholarship offers.

After averaging 26.5 points per game on the court his senior year, the 6'5" Salisbury received scholarship offers from both USC and UCLA. After his senior season on the turf, Salisbury got football offers from USC, UCLA, BYU, Notre Dame, Arizona, ASU, and Cal.

S

Salisbury chose USC and became the starter midway through his sophomore season. He helped lead the Trojans to an 8–3 record, but the team slipped to a 4–6–1 record in 1983, while Salisbury passed for 1,882 yards and 10 TDs. He was on the 1984 Trojan team that beat Ohio State in the Sugar Bowl but did not play due to a season-ending injury suffered very early on. Salisbury's senior effort began strong, but he lost his starting job to Rodney Peete late in the season. Despite not starting as a freshman and for half of his sophomore season, then losing the job during his senior year, Salisbury still finished his USC career as their all-time leader with 346 pass completions and 4,481 yards, beating both marks previously held by Paul McDonald.

Salisbury wasn't drafted and didn't turn many coaches' heads. He auditioned for the Seattle Seahawks in 1986 but didn't make it past their practice squad. In 1987 he got another chance at the NFL and made the Indianapolis Colts during the players' strike season. He saw action in two games, completing 8 of 12 passes but throwing 2 interceptions, while sharing the quarterbacking duties with Jack Trudeau, Gary Hogeboom, and Blair Kiel.

Without further NFL interest, Salisbury moved up north to join the Winnipeg Blue Bombers of the CFL. He earned the starting job partway through the 1988 season and passed for 1,566 yards with 11 TDs and only 5 INTs. His efforts helped lead the Blue Bombers to a Grey Cup Championship, which is equivalent to a Super Bowl Championship in the NFL. In 1989 Salisbury completed the finest season of his entire football career with 4,049 yards and 26 TDs.

S

Salisbury returned to the NFL in 1990 and signed with the Minnesota Vikings. After a couple seasons on their practice squad, he finally saw his first NFL action in nearly five years. Salisbury started four games for the Vikings, winning three of them. He passed for 1,203 yards with 5 TDs and only 2 INTs while filling in for Rich Gannon. Salisbury got the call to start another four games in 1993 behind Jim McMahon and threw for 1,413 yards with 9 touchdowns. The next season, Salisbury would get just one start behind Warren Moon and Brad Johnson and then be released. He caught on with the San Diego Chargers the next season but would not see the field again until 1996. In his final NFL season, Salisbury saw playing time in every game, starting in three.

Salisbury played in forty NFL games over nine seasons and another twenty-four games over two years in the CFL. He won a championship at the top level of professional football and had a career that spanned over a decade. Not bad for a guy who had only one full season of college ball and nobody wanted to draft.

Salisbury entered the entertainment world as a host on Comedy Central's *BattleBots* show. Soon after, he became an analyst for ESPN and a member of Sportscenter and NFL Live.

Salisbury turned down an offer from the Arizona Cardinals in 2004 to become their quarterbacks coach and chose to stay in the entertainment industry, leading to his relationship with Adam Sandler and the movie business.

In 2008 Salisbury left ESPN and has continued to host various sports TV and radio shows.

SCHONERT, TURK

Before coaching and playing in the NFL, before starring at Stanford University, and even before becoming a two-time All-American quarterback at Servite High School, Turk Schonert was a shortstop in the 1968 Little League World Series, and his Garden Grove, California, team finished in third place.

Schonert didn't get much playing time his first three years at Stanford, as he was backing up Guy Benjamin and Steve Dils, both of whom won the Sammy Baugh Trophy for outstanding college quarterback. When they left, Schonert had big shoes to fill, and he did so admirably. He finished as Stanford's third consecutive passing leader, setting a team record with a 67 percent completion percentage. And with a ratio of 19 touchdowns to 6 interceptions, Schonert finished his senior year with an incredible

163.2 passer rating, good for first in the NCAA. Schonert's backup was incoming freshman John Elway.

Schonert was selected in the 9th round of the 1980 NFL Draft by the Chicago Bears, but he never saw Soldier Field as a Bear. He was traded to the Bengals and got his first action a year later. In the 1981 season opener, starter Ken Anderson was having a poor game and was booed off the field at Riverfront Stadium. Schonert and his sunny Californian disposition came in to help his team to a 27–21 win and put a ray of hope on the year. Schonert told Bengals.com in an interview that, when head coach Forrest Greg called out his name to get in the game, he was so anxious that he forgot his helmet and went to the huddle in his ballcap. He then proceeded to fumble his first snap. But Schonert won the game, and the Bengals went on to their first Super Bowl that season.

Schonert played relief roles at quarterback for the Bengals until 1985, then he spent a season doing the same duties for Atlanta in 1986. He started five games for the Falcons, the most he'd ever started in a season, completing 95 of 154 passes for 1,032 yards and 8 touchdowns. He returned to the Bengals the next season and played the following three seasons there, making it to his second Super Bowl in 1988, again, versus the 49ers, and, again, losing the game.

Schonert retired from playing after the 1989 season with 3,788 career passing yards and 11 touchdowns. He was 7–5 as a starting quarterback and loved by his Bengals teammates.

SCHONERT'S COACHING HISTORY

Schonert began coaching in the NFL, under his former Bengals head coachSam Wyche, just a few years later in 1992 as the quarterbacks coach for the Buccaneers. Schonert continued his coaching position with many teams over the next two-and-a-half decades, including stops in the UFL and CFL.

Sadly, Schonert died of a sudden heart attack in 2019. He was coaching right up until his passing.

- Tampa Bay Buccaneers (1992–95)
  Quarterbacks coach
- Buffalo Bills (1998–2000)
  Quarterbacks coach
- Carolina Panthers (2001)
  Quarterbacks coach
- New York Giants (2003)
  Quarterbacks coach
- New Orleans Saints (2005)
  Quarterbacks coach
- Buffalo Bills (2006–07)
  Quarterbacks coach
- Buffalo Bills (2008)
  Offensive coordinator
- Hartford Colonials (2011)
  Quarterbacks coach
- Las Vegas Locomotives (2011)
  Offensive assistant
- Sacramento Mountain Lions (2012)
  Head coach
- Montreal Alouettes (2014–18)
  Receivers coach

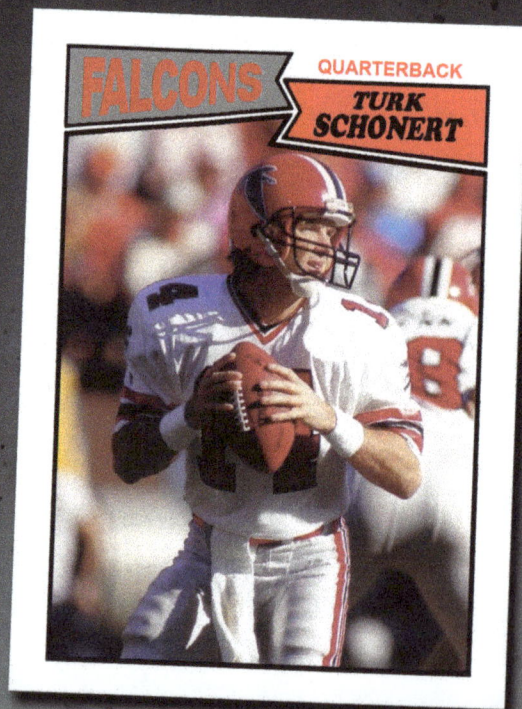

FALCONS QUARTERBACK TURK SCHONERT

SCOTT, BOBBY

Born in Chattanooga, Bobby Scott stayed close to home after high school to attend the University of Tennessee. In his senior year, Scott helped the Volunteers to an 11–1 record and a no. 4 ranking in 1970. Tennessee beat Air Force 34–13 at the Sugar Bowl, and Scott passed for 288 yards and a touchdown, winning the Miller-Digby Award for the game's MVP. Scott had a 385-yard passing game, which set a school record and his career 3,461 yards topped Tennessee's all-time marks.

Scott was selected in the 14th round (340th overall) of the 1971 NFL Draft by the New Orleans Saints. Backing up Archie Manning, Scott didn't see any playing time his first two seasons and saw little field action until 1976,

S

when Archie Manning had surgery on his throwing arm and missed the season. Scott got to start in eight games, which would be the most of his career. However, Scott would miss part of that same season after tripping over a television cable during a televised game and blowing out his knee. He passed for 1,065 yards with 4 TDs and 6 interceptions. Scott would remain with the Saints another five years, completing 237 of 500 passes with 2,781 yards, 15 touchdowns, and 28 interceptions in his eleven years in New Orleans.

After being out of football in 1982, Scott decided to give pro ball one more try. He made his way to the newly formed USFL in 1983, signing with the New Jersey Generals, and partway through the season, he was traded to the Chicago Blitz. Between his two teams, Scott totaled 2,813 yards and 11 touchdowns.

Scott's career came full circle; he got his professional start being drafted by a Chicago team and played his last game with a Chicago pro team thirteen years later.

BOBBY SCOTT

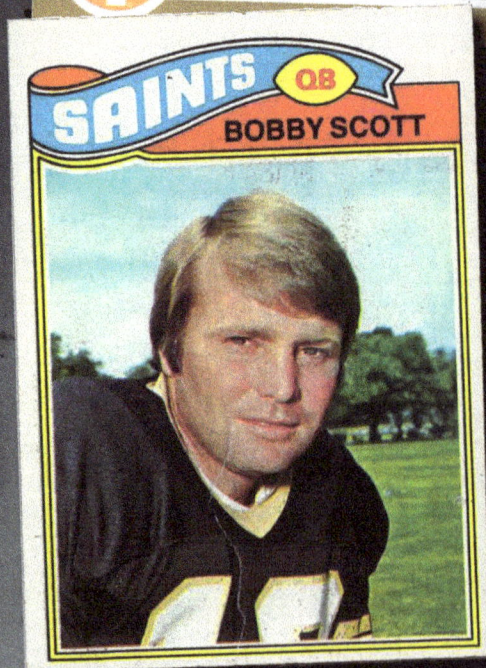

SAINTS QB
BOBBY SCOTT

SORGI, JIM

Jim Sorgi was a basketball, base-ball, and football star in high school. In baseball he recorded a .450 batting average as a senior, but football was his destiny. Sorgi was Fraser High School's MVP for two consecutive years and, as a senior, earned All-League, All-County, and All-State honors and was an Honorable Mention All-*USA Today* selection.

Sorgi attended the University of Wisconsin. As a true freshman in 2000, behind sophomore Brooks Bollinger, Sorgi saw playing time in five games, throwing for 615 yards with 6 TDs and 2 INTs, good for a 164.4 quarterback rating. As a sophomore (2001), Sorgi split the season with junior Brooks Bollinger, seeing much more playing time. He passed for 1,096 yards and 9 TDs. In Sorgi's junior season of 2002, Bollinger had an incredible year that would put him on the road to NFL draftee,

and Sorgi only saw 70 pass attempts for 536 yards. With Bollinger finally gone to the NFL in 2003, Sorgi was freed up to show what he could do as the starter. He led the Badgers to a win over Colorado at the Alamo Bowl, passing for 2,251 yards and 17 TDs on the season. Sorgi tied a school record with 5 passing touchdowns in a single game and his 141.2 career quarterback rating would top Wisconsin's record books.

Sorgi will forever be remembered as the victim in an Ohio State game in which Buckeyes linebacker Robert Reynolds intentionally choked Sorgi after a play. Sorgi's trachea was damaged, leaving him struggling to breathe and unable to to talk, so he couldn't resume the game. Reynolds later made a public apology, and the two players made amends.

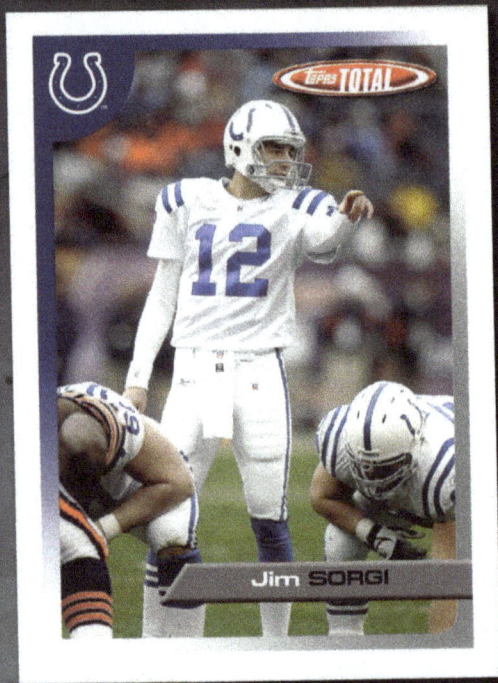

Like his ex-teammate Bollinger the year prior, Sorgi was also a 6th round draft pick. He was selected by the Indianapolis Colts as the 193rd overall pick in the 2004 NFL Draft. Sorgi won the backup quarterback start his rookie season, but it was more of a death sentence since he was playing behind Peyton Manning who was the iron man, perennial All-Pro at the starting position. Sorgi did see a good portion of playing time against the Denver Broncos in his first year, though, throwing for 175 yards and 2 touchdowns.

S

Sorgi saw a little more playing time in five games in 2005, completing 42 of 61 passes for 444 yards and 3 TDs, but he wouldn't throw a single pass the following season. He continued to back up Peyton Manning for a few more years, but then Sorgi was placed on injured reserve with a torn labrum late in the 2009 season. The Colts released him the following season.

Of all the teams to sign Sorgi in 2010, and of all the quarterbacks to back up, it was the New York Giants who contracted him to back up Peyton's brother, Eli Manning. Unfortunately, during a preseason game, Sorgi injured his right shoulder again and was placed on injured reserve, missing the entire season. Sorgi never played in another NFL game. He finished his career completing 63.5 percent of his passes for 929 yards with 6 touchdowns and only 1 interception.

Sorgi never got to start an NFL game, but he did earn a ring for the Colts' win in Super Bowl XLI.

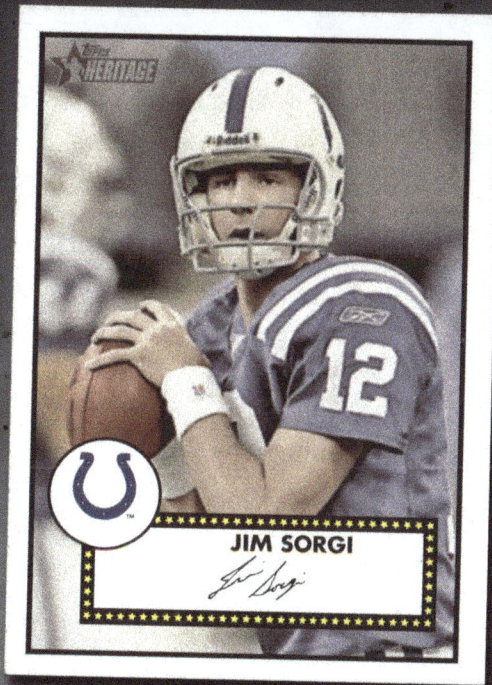

JIM SORGI

STOUDT, CLIFF

At Oberlin High School in Ohio, Cliff Stoudt was not only a top quarterback, he was also one of the top golfers in the state.

Stoudt received a scholarship from Youngstown State University where he started as a true freshman and never relinquished that position. As a sophomore in 1974, he led the Penguins to an 8–1 record and their very first appearance in the NCAA Division II playoffs, against the University of Delaware. Stoudt passed for over 1,000 yards and rushed for over 400 yards in his junior year. As a senior, Stoudt passed for 1,259 yards with 5 TDs and rushed for another 307 yards with 7 TDs. In a run-heavy era of college football, Stoudt's 4,387 passing yards and 5,549 total yards set new school records.

Stoudt was drafted in the 5th

S round of the 1977 NFL Draft by the Pittsburgh Steelers. As a third-string backup to Terry Bradshaw, Stoudt didn't see any playing time his rookie season. Or his second season. Or third. In fact, he set a notorious NFL record for being on an active team roster but not playing in a single regular-season game for his first fifty-six games.

games. In 1983 Stoudt would finally become a regular starter, taking over for the often-injured, aging Terry Bradshaw's last season. Stoudt led the Steelers to nine wins in his fifteen starts, winning the AFC Central Division, and took them to a playoff appearance against the Raiders. He passed for 2,553 yards with 12 touchdowns and 21 interceptions and

S

rushed for another 479 yards and 4 touchdowns.

In 1984 Stoudt signed with the Birmingham Stallions of the new USFL. He started every game, passing for 3,121 yards and 26 TDs while rushing for another 400 yards and 9 scores. Stoudt led the Stallions to the division championship and finished second in passing, behind only future NFL Hall of Famer Jim Kelly.

1985 was almost a repeat of the previous season, had it not been for Stoudt performing even better. Again, he finished second in the league in passing, behind Jim Kelly, throwing for 3,358 yards and 34 touchdowns while using his legs for another 437 yards and 5 touchdowns. And, again, Stoudt led the Stallions to the division championship. No other USFL team won more games (27) than Stoudt's Stallions.

Stoudt returned to the NFL in 1986 after the USFL ceased operations, and he was traded to St. Louis (the Steelers still owned his rights). As Neil Lomax's backup, Stoudt would only

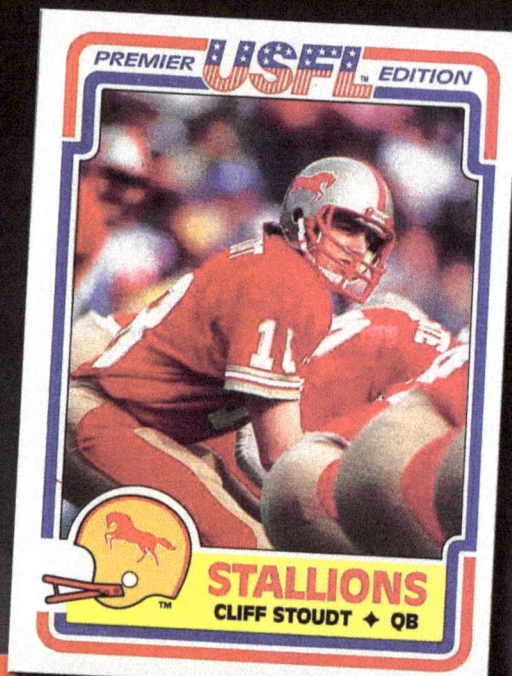

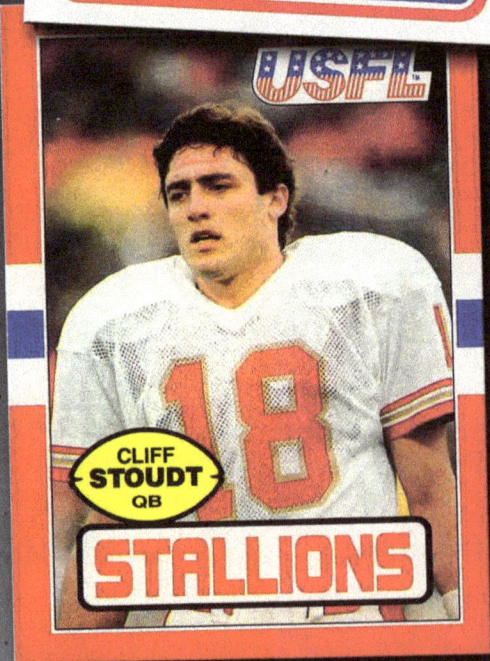

PREMIER **USFL** EDITION

STALLIONS
CLIFF STOUDT ◆ QB

USFL

CLIFF **STOUDT** QB

STALLIONS

S

see two starts during his two years as a Cardinal, although he would see special teams action as the placekick holder. When the Cardinals signed Gary Hogeboom as a backup in in 1989, Stoudt asked for his release and was signed by the Dolphins as a free agent.

Stoudt appeared in three games after Dan Marino bruised his throwing elbow, but never attempted a pass. The Dolphins cut Stoudt in training camp the following season (1990).

On Christmas Eve 1990, Stoudt was signed by the Dallas Cowboys as an emergency backup to Babe Laufenberg for the final game of the year after Troy Aikman injured his shoulder the week prior. He did not get into the game. In 1991 Stoudt competed against Laufenberg and Oregon rookie Bill Musgrave for the third quarterback spot. When the Cowboys traded for Steve Beuerlein to shore up their backup spot with a seasoned veteran, they released Stoudt.

Stoudt retired with three Super Bowl rings earned with the Pittsburgh Steelers and was inducted into Youngstown State University's Hall of Fame.

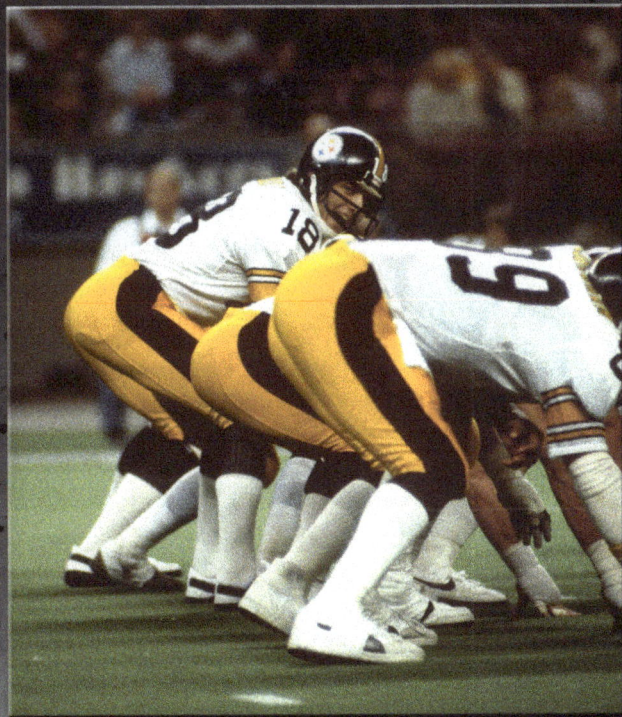

STOUFFER, KELLY

How do you earn the respect of your teammates? Kelly Stouffer learned how when he tripped over his lineman and took an elbow to the face from his running back, Curt Warner, that broke his nose. But he didn't let up, but shook off the blow, and continued searching downfield until he found an open target. He slung the ball to Ray Butler for a 46-yard touchdown. Stouffer may not have been the All-Pro some had predicted, but he was a pro that gave his all.

Stouffer was a complete athlete and excelled at more than just football. Playing basketball at Rushville High School in Nebraska, he averaged over 25 points and 14.8 rebounds per game as a senior. Colleges were interested in Stouffer's football abilities but had some reservations because of the level of competition his smaller high school faced. —*Per the Seattle Times*

Stouffer attended Garden City Junior College in Kansas in 1983. While there, he set a national JUCO record with 74 pass attempts in one game. His season got the attention of more colleges, and Stouffer committed to Colorado State immediately after his campus visit.

Stouffer didn't waste any time in his aerial assault on the Rams' record books.

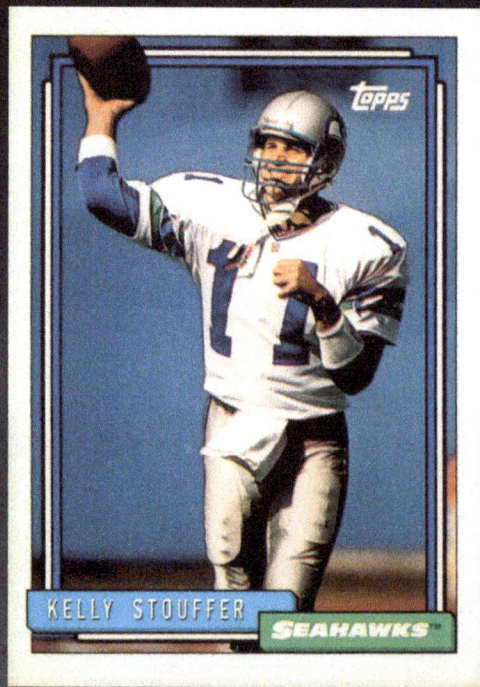

S

.In 1984 he passed for 2,151 yards with 14 TDs, including a 402-yards-passing game against Utah. He followed up with a 2,387-yard and 15-touchdown season in 1985 and a 2,604-yard senior year campaign in 1986. Stouffer's career stats set all-time Colorado State records for 7,141 passing yards, 1,027 pass attempts, 593 completions, and a 57.8 completion percentage. Stouffer was able to accomplish those inflated numbers despite being on only mediocre teams, and the NFL scouts took notice.

Stouffer rose to immediate fame when he became the St. Louis Cardinals' no. 1 pick (6th overall) in the 1987 NFL Draft. However, Stouffer would never play a down in a Cardinals uniform. His agents wanted a four-year deal for $3.2 million, and St. Louis only offered $1.8 million. Stouffer felt that, with the low offer, St. Louis was just using him as a pawn to keep Neil Lomax from being complacent. Stouffer stayed in St. Louis for six weeks, hoping to meet with coaches and learn the team's offense, with every intention of playing, but no coaches sat down with him. He saw no film, no playbook. Stouffer sat out for the season. No contract was settled. —*Details courtesy "The Life and Career of Kelly Stouffer" by Poch de la Roza, 2022*

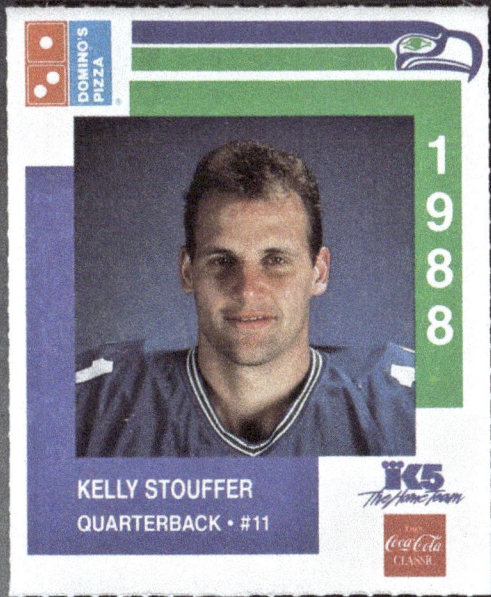

KELLY STOUFFER
QUARTERBACK • #11

1988

In 1988 the Cardinals traded Stouffer to the Seattle Seahawks for three future draft picks. Stouffer would start his Seahawks

S

career at third string behind Dave Krieg and Jeff Kemp. Krieg separated his shoulder in the third game of the season, and Kemp took over, elevating Stouffer to the number two quarterback position. The following week, Kemp was benched at halftime, and Stouffer came in and took the reins.

Stouffer then broke his nose on a play and threw a 46-yard touchdown pass, immediately capturing the fans' hearts. Three games later, Stouffer set a rookie record with 370 yards passing against the Saints. He was beginning to prove why he was a no. 1 draft pick. Stouffer started six games total and passed for 1,106 yards with 4 TDs and 6 INTs, helping the Seahawks to the playoffs. Dave Krieg returned, and the Seahawks finished 9–7 and won the AFC Division. They lost in the divisional round.

With Krieg healthy for most of 1989, Stouffer only got two starts and lost both. He suited up for just five games over the next three seasons and found himself back at third string with the arrival of the new draft pick, Dan McGwire, in 1991.

S

Under new head coach Tom Flores, Stouffer won the starting job in 1992, ahead of McGwire and Stan Gelbaugh. Although the Seahawks began the season 1–4 with Stouffer at the helm, he looked to be returning to form. Then injury struck in week five, and Stouffer was out. His comeback was over. Stouffer regained the starting role upon his return, but he wasn't the same. His injuries took their toll, and he lost the job by year's end. The Seahawks released him the following season.

The Miami Dolphins signed Stouffer in 1994 as a free agent, but he was cut in training camp. Stouffer tried out again two years later with the Carolina Panthers but, as before, was released prior to the season starting. He called it a career afterward. Stouffer completed 225 of 437 passes for 2,333 yards with 7 TDs and 19 INTs in his NFL career.

After his retirement, Stouffer returned to his high school to become their head football coach. Later, he became a college football color analyst for the NFL Network, called games for NFL Europe, and joined ESPN as a college football analyst.

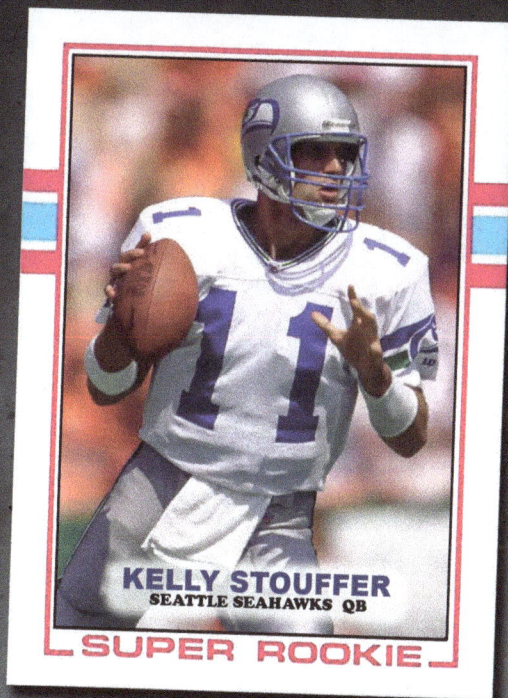

KELLY STOUFFER
SEATTLE SEAHAWKS QB

SUPER ROOKIE

STROCK, DON

Don Strock is one of the most prolific, revered, and respected backup quarterbacks to ever play the game. He may have been lost in time to the passive football fan, but he will never be forgotten by Miami Dolphins fans.

Strock played college football at Virginia Tech where he set countless school records, many of which still stand today, more than fifty years later.

1971 was in an era of college football heavily dominated by the running game. Most of the Heisman candidates were running backs, and the aerial assault was yet to soar. As a junior in 1971, Strock threw for 2,577 yards and 12 touchdowns, formidable numbers for the time and enough to lead his conference in several

S

passing categories. However, it was during his senior season in 1972 that the Strock attack hit the airways.

With future NFL Super Bowl-winning coach Bruce Arians as his backup quarterback, Don Strock had a season that rewrote the record books. He led the nation nation in total passing and total offense with 427 pass attempts, 228 completions, and 3,243 passing yards. Strock didn't win the Heisman Trophy (he finished 9th in voting), which went to one of the aforementioned rushers, but he did capture the Sammy Baugh Trophy for outstanding passer in college.

A 5th round selection (111th overall) by the Dolphins in 1973 NFL Draft, Strock would call Miami home for the next fourteen years. He would learn from the likes of legendary Hall of Famer Bob Griese and veteran Earl Morrall and pass his own knowledge on to a rookie and future Hall of Famer named Dan Marino. Strock didn't see any playing time his rookie year, but he was a member of the

S

team and therefore got a ring for the Dolphins' victory in Super Bowl VIII.

Strock saw his first field action two years after he was drafted, starting three games in 1975 and winning two of them. He would start just one more game until 1978 when he spent half the season filling in for the injured Bob Griese. Strock led the Fins to a 5–2 record during his command and threw 12 touchdowns in his seven games. He started four games the next season (1979) and won three of those, throwing 6 touchdowns in the process. Although he didn't get the call to start games often, he was called upon to finish them. He mopped up messes, filled in for injuries, and was even called on to punt for the injured Reggie Roby once in a game which he ended up finishing at quarterback later.

In his most memorable performance, Strock would be remembered for coming off the bench in 1982 for the AFC Divisional Playoff game against the Chargers. He led the Dolphins from a 0–24 deficit to a tie in the third quarter. San Diego ultimately won in overtime, but Strock completed 29 of 43 passes for 403 yards and four TDs in a game that became part of football lore as one of the greatest in NFL history, dubbed "the Epic in Miami."

Strock was on the losing end of the Dolphins' Super Bowls in 1982 and 1984.

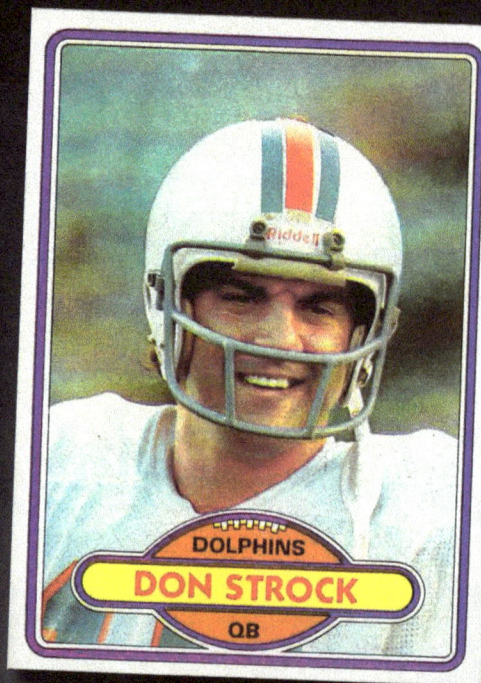

S

After not starting a single game during his last five seasons in Miami, Strock gave another team one more shot. He signed with Cleveland in 1988 and started two games, leading the Browns to win both contests. Strock spent part of the 1989 season with the Indianapolis Colts but didn't see any playing time and called it a career. Over his sixteen seasons in the NFL, Strock completed 443 of 779 passes for 5,349 yards and 45 touchdowns. His career record as a starter was 16–6.

After the NFL, Strock, who was known for his football intelligence, moved to coaching. He was hired as the head coach of the Miami Hooters of the Arena Football League in 1993 and held the same duties for the Massachusetts Marauders the following season. In 1995 he was hired as an assistant coach for the Rhein Fire of the World Football League. In 1996 Strock returned to the NFL as the quarterbacks coach for the Baltimore Ravens for three seasons.

In 2000 Strock was named the first head coach for the new Florida International University and worked as their director of football operations to get the team fielded by 2002. He remained head coach for five seasons.

SULLIVAN, PAT

A three-sport star at Carroll Catholic High School in Birmingham, Alabama, Pat Sullivan chose to pursue football over baseball and basketball. He made the right call, as he would earn the starting quarterback job at Auburn University by 1969.

As a junior in 1970, Sullivan led his Tigers to a 9–2 record, no. 10 national ranking, and victory at the Gator Bowl. Across the field was Archie Manning starting for Ole Miss. But Sullivan got the best of the star quarterback, passing for 351 yards and winning the game's MVP. Sullivan led the entire nation with 2,856 yards of total offense and the SEC with a 59.4 pass completion percentage, 2,586 passing yards, and 17 TDs. He also stood at the head of the NCAA with a 148.2 passer rating and a record-setting 8.57 yards per play. As a result, Sullivan won the 1970 SEC Player of the Year and the Sammy Baugh Trophy for most outstanding passer

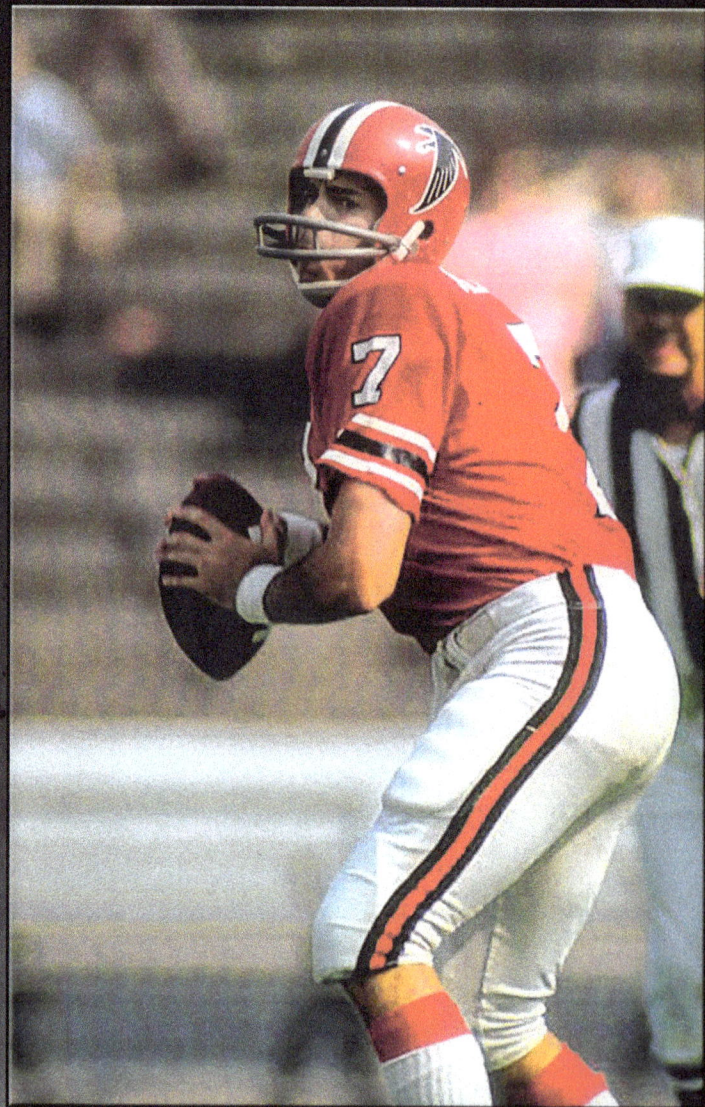

in college football. Sullivan finished sixth in Heisman Trophy voting with 180 votes.

Teammates, coaches, and fans hoped Sullivan could repeat the feats in his cleats from his 1970 junior season, and in 1971 he didn't just duplicate his prior achievements, he built upon them. His touchdowns climbed from an SEC-leading 17 the previous season to an NCAA-leading 21. Once again, Sullivan topped the SEC in passing yards (2,262), pass completion percentage (56 percent), total yards (2,328), and passer rating (127.8). He was a consensus All-American and won the Walter Camp Award along with a little award called the Heisman Trophy. The Academic All-American, Sullivan, was also selected to play in the Senior Bowl and led the South team to victory, earning the game's MVP award. He finished his college career with 472 completions for 6,534 yards and 54 touchdowns, setting new school records that would eventually get his number 7 retired by Auburn.

Sullivan was selected in the 2nd round (40th overall) of the 1972 NFL Draft by the Atlanta Falcons. He wouldn't, however, have the same success in the pro ranks as he had in college. In his first two seasons, Sullivan was a backup, primarily getting into games late for mop-up work. In 1974 he backed up Bob Lee and started three games, but throwing 1 touchdown and 8 interceptions didn't help his cause, and he lost all three starts. Sullivan got one more chance to start in 1975 behind the no. 1 pick in the country, rookie Steve Bartkowski, but he lost that contest as well. That would be the last time Sullivan saw field action in the NFL.

S

Sullivan signed with the Washington Redskins in 1976 as a free agent but was cut in preseason. In 1977 he was signed by the Chicago Bears then sold to the San Francisco 49ers but was cut again before the season started. Pat Sullivan retired with 70 completions for 1,155 yards and 5 touchdowns. He may have been done playing football, but football wasn't done with him, not by a long shot.

Sullivan was the radio color commentator for Auburn football for five years before joining the staff as their quarterbacks coach in 1986, and he remained there another six years. In 1992 he was hired as the head coach for TCU, where he would produce winning seasons, a Southwest conference title, and SoCon Coach of the Year (1994) honors even though he inherited Texas Christian University's past probation that limited the number of scholarships they could offer.

In 1999 Sullivan took an offensive coordinator position at UAB, where he would remain for the next eight years. 2007 brought another move for Sullivan when he took the head coaching position at Samford University. He would win his second SoCon Coach of the Year award in 2012 and lead the Bulldogs to becoming Southern Conference champions in 2013.

Pat Sullivan died after a long battle with cancer on December 1, 2019. Exactly one month later, on New Year's Day 2020, Auburn players wore number 7 decals on their helmets to commemorate Sullivan during their Outback Bowl game.

TOLZIEN, SCOTT

As a two-star recruit, Tolzien did not attract many offers. The Palatine, Illinois, native Tolzien chose to attend the University of Wisconsin and had a long climb ahead of him.

Tolzien redshirted his freshman year of 2006, and, behind a slew of good quarterbacks, he did not play in a single game in 2007. Finally in 2008, when the starter Allan Evridge was benched following a few poor performances, Tolzien saw his first real game action. He completed 5 of 8 passes for 107 yards but threw a red-zone interception and was eventually replaced by Dustin Sherer.

Tolzien beat out Sherer for the starting spot in 2009,

and the rest is Badgers history. He led Wisconsin to a 9–3 record and a win over Miami in the Champs Sports Bowl. Although Tolzien had a couple multi-interception games, he bounced back to earn Big 10 Offensive Player of the Week honors against Michigan State. He finished his junior season with a 64.3 percent completion ratio, connecting 211 of 328 passes for 2,705 yards with 16 TDs and 11 interceptions. Tolzien's 143 quarterback rating was tops in the conference.

As a senior, Tolzien led Wisconsin to an 11–1 record and a Rose Bowl appearance. The Badgers lost to TCU's Horned Frogs 21–19, but that didn't diminish what Tolzien accomplished in 2010. He passed for 2,459 yards with 16 TDs and only 6 interceptions, and his 165.9 quarterback rating led the nation once again. Tolzien completed 194 of 266 passes for an incredible 72.9 percent completion ratio, good for second in the NCAA and a new Wisconsin school record. Tolzien beat out Andy Dalton, Christian Ponder, and Colin Kaepernick to win the Johnny Unitas Golden Arm Award.

Tolzien went undrafted in the 2011 NFL Draft and signed with the San Diego Chargers as an undrafted free agent. He passed for 302 yards, 1 TD, and 1 interception in the preseason and was released before the season started. Tolzien was picked up off waivers the very next day by San Francisco. He was third on the quarterback depth chart behind starter Alex Smith and backup Colin Kaepernick. Tolzien remained with the 49ers from 2011 to 2012 but never saw any game time and was waived during the 2013 preseason.

Green Bay signed Tolzien to their practice squad days after San Francisco released him. After Aaron Rogers suffered an injury, Tolzien was called up to the active roster. Tolzien made his first NFL appearance when Rogers's backup, Seneca Wallace, was injured in a game on November 10, 2013. In his start, Tolzien completed 24 of 39 passes for 280 yards with 1 TD and 2 picks in a losing effort against the Eagles. It was a good enough effort to earn him a start the next week against the Giants, in which he completed 24 of 34 passes for 339 yards but threw 3 interceptions. He had a touchdown run the next game and was eventually replaced by Matt Flynn. Tolzien fell back to third in quarterback depth and didn't see any playing time in 2014. In 2015 he got into three games, throwing just one pass and completing it.

Tolzien signed as a backup with Indianapolis in 2016. When starter Andrew Luck suffered a concussion, Tolzien was called up to start on Thanksgiving in a losing game against the Pittsburgh Steelers. He saw mop-up action in two other games afterward. In 2017 Tolzien would play in his last NFL game, starting as the season opener since Andrew Luck was sidelined with a shoulder injury. He completed 9 of 18 passes for 128 yards and had 2 pick-sixes scored on him. He was later benched in favor of Jacoby Brissett.

Tolzien retired after seven years in the NFL, not bad for a two-star recruit that nobody wanted.

Tolzien remains in football. In 2019 Tolzien's alma mater, Wisconsin, hired him as a scouting analyst. In 2020 Tolzien's former head coach Mike McCarthy, now the Dallas Cowboys head coach, hired him as an assistant coach.

TROUP, BILL

Pittsburgh native Bill Troup was about as unlikely as anyone to make it to the NFL, let alone play seven years of professional football. He was a lanky 6'5" and looked more like Magnum, P.I., than a professional athlete.

Troup didn't wow many scouts in college. In 1970 he played for Virginia, barely completing 50 percent of his passes and throwing 50 percent more interceptions than touchdowns. After not seeing the field in 1971, he transferred to South Carolina in 1972, where he completed only 43.4 percent of his passes for 758 yards, platooning with Bobby Grossman. Troup had over twice as many interceptions (9) as touchdowns (4), his team had a losing record, and he didn't win any awards or bowl games. His immobility allowed for opponent sacks, and he racked up −126 yards rushing. However, Troup's lack of speed didn't slow him down.

This is a story of triumph and overcoming obstacles, and Troup triumphed. He was not drafted to the NFL in 1972. He was not drafted to the NFL in 1973. But he tried out for the Baltimore Colts in 1974 and made the team . Although he didn't see any action on the field, Troup persevered. In 1975 he made the Eagles practice squad and was back in Colt blue in 1976, where he finally saw his first NFL action. He completed 8 of 18 passes for 117 yards with an interception and rushed for a TD. In 1977 Troup got action in two games, throwing 2 passes that only connected for another interception. He persevered. With an injury to starter Bert Jones in 1978, almost five years after Troup first made the Colts roster, he got his first start. He got eleven of them in fact. Troup had his most productive season ever and passed for more yards (1,882) and at a higher completion percentage (52 percent) than he ever did in college. He completed 154 of 296 passes, throwing 10 TDs and 21 interceptions. Troup was released after the season.

Troup headed north in 1979 to play in Winnipeg for the Canadian Football League. Backing up CFL legend Dieter Brock, he wasn't expected to get any playing time, but with an injury to Brock, he did see substantial action. Troup competed 81 of 148 passes for 963 yards with 3 TDs and 8 interceptions.

In 1980 Bart Starr signed Troup to back up Lynn Dickey. He saw playing time in two games, completing 4 of 12 passes to his own players and 3 to the opposing team. Unfortunately, not long into the season, Troup suffered a severe concussion and would never play another NFL game. He was replaced by Steve Pisarkiewicz and released.

Troup wasn't fast or flashy; he didn't set records or win championships. But when no team wanted him, he kept pushing. When nobody wanted him again, he pushed harder. He turned a nothing college career into a seven-year professional football career. He did more in the NFL and earned more playing time than hundreds, maybe thousands, of quarterbacks before and after him with less natural talent and hype, fewer accolades, and with more doubters.

After life in football, everything changed for Troup.

From the article "Head in the Game" by Ron Cassie:
Backup quarterback Bill Troup suffered from memory loss, depression, and substance abuse before his death at 62 in 2013. It was only at the time of his passing that his adult daughters learned he'd joined a concussion lawsuit against the NFL. "We realized he must've known his problems were related to football. That's when my sister and I decided to donate his brain and learned he had CTE."

"Our parents got divorced after he retired," says Laurin Garcia, one of Troup's daughters. "I was in high school by then. My mother knew something was happening to him, but you also don't know [what it is]. His symptoms ran the gamut. They just change. Unfortunately, Dad ended up by himself, isolated," she says, choking up. "We couldn't help him."

VAN GLADER, TIM

Van Galder has a quiet story of remarkably loud accomplishments throughout college and pro ball, on the field and on the mound.

After a year at New Mexico Military Academy, Van Galder enrolled at Iowa State in 1963. Nicknamed Spider by his teammates, Van Galder had a rifle arm that unfortunately went underutilized during his first season in 1964. Like the entire Big East conference, Iowa State was a running team, sometimes even featuring four running backs in a single-wing scheme, so Van Galder didn't get to throw much. In fact, he didn't get to drop back and pass; he was relegated to rollouts and threw an average of 2–4 passes per game.

Luckily, his sophomore

year saw a new coach who recognized the strong-armed talent he had in Van Galder and changed the offensive scheme to better utilize his skills. In 1965 Van Galder was throwing 15–20 passes per game instead of 2–4, and he led the Big 8 in pass attempts, pass completions, passing yards, touchdowns, total plays, total yards, and quarterback rating. In his senior year (1966), Van Galder rewrote the ISU record books. His 1,645 passing yards and 1,749 total yards set new marks, and he recorded the first 300+ yard passing game (335) in school history. Again, Van Galder led the Big 8 in virtually every passing category.

But it wasn't just football that had Cyclones fans talking about Van Galder. During his junior year, he injured his arm in football and couldn't play on the freshman team, but in 1965 he was named All-Big 8 as a pitcher with a 1.57 ERA and six complete games.

Van Galder would practice spring football Monday through Thursday and play a double-header on Fridays, pitching the first game and playing in the field for the second game. Then he would return to football practice Saturday mornings. During the summer of his 1966 senior season in baseball, before annihilating the football record books in the fall, Van Galder pitched a no-hitter—a feat that has yet to be matched in ISU baseball history.

Van Galder was drafted by both the St. Louis Cardinals in the 1966 NFL Draft and the Houston Oilers in the 1966 AFL Draft. After signing with St. Louis, he spent his first couple seasons on the Cardinals taxi squad. He was briefly activated in 1967 but didn't see any action in a game. Van Galder then had to fulfill his Army ROTC obligations and spent two years in the military, serving in Korea. He returned to the Cardinals practice team for another season in 1971. Finally in 1972 he not only saw his first field action, but he also got the call to start the first NFL game he would ever play. As a twenty-eight-year-old rookie, he would quarterback across from his childhood hero, the world's greatest quarterback Johnny Unitas. Completing 10 of 15 passes for 110 yards, Van Galder upset the Colts at their own home, Memorial Stadium in Baltimore.

Van Galder started four more games that season but lost them all and missed several games due to a concussion. He completed 40 of 79 passes for 434 yards with 1 touchdown and 7 interceptions. It would be the last time he ever saw action on an NFL field.

Van Galder was cut by the Cardinals the following year. He was quoted as saying, "It was my own fault. I didn't say the right things. They were deciding to keep me as a backup, and I didn't give them what they wanted to hear. I should have told them that I'll be the best backup quarterback in the league. I wasn't smart enough." —As quoted in an interview from "The Life and Times of Tim Van Galder" by Mike Green

Van Galder signed with the Cincinnati Bengals to replace Virgil Carter as Ken Anderson's backup in 1973 but was released after their first game, in which he did not play. The New York Jets then signed him to back up the injured Joe Namath and Al Woodall but released him after two games, in which he also didn't play.

Van Galder returned to St. Louis to become a sportscaster for thirteen years. He passed away from cancer at age seventy-seven in 2022.

Although he only had five games of playing time in the NFL, Van Galder was a legend on the football field, baseball field and battlefield. He was a professional quarterback for five years, set virtually every football passing record in college, pitched a no-hitter, and served his country.

TIM VAN GALDER, Iowa State, led Big 8 quarterbacks with 100...

A Real Pro

Tim Van Galder—Professional athletic experience gives this Sports Director the inside track when it comes to television sports. Tim Van Galder, one of the NEWSROOM PEOPLE WORKING FOR YOU!

5, 6 & 10 PM
NEWSROOM GETS IT ON!
KMOX-TV 4 CBS

WEESE, NORRIS

How does one follow in the cleat prints left by Archie Manning? Well, you run your butt off. And that is exactly what Norris Weese did at Ole Miss in 1971. After his predecessor, Manning, left for the NFL draft, Weese became the start-er, and his quick legs rushed for 520 yards with 6 TDs in addition to his 766 passing yards with 6 TDs. He ran the Rebels to a 10–2 record and a 41–18 win over Georgia Tech in the Peach Bowl.

Weese had another 500-yard rushing season his junior year (1972) and scored 5 times on the ground to accompany his 917 yards and 11 touchdowns in the air. His 178 rushing yards against Mississippi State set a school record for quar-terbacks.

As a senior in 1973, Weese was awarded the

Hula Bowl game Offensive MVP and was selected to play in the East-West Shrine game. Weese finished his Ole Miss career with 3,327 yards of total offense and 35 total touchdowns. He was a two-time Academic All-SEC selection.

Weese was selected in the 4th round (99th overall) by the LA Rams in the 1974 NFL Draft but elected to sign with the Hawaiians of the newly formed World Football League instead. In his rookie season, Weese completed 142 of 280 passes for 1,847 yards and 15 touchdowns and rushed for another 240 yards and 3 scores.

Weese joined the Denver Broncos in 1976 as a backup to Steve Ramsey. He only passed for 314 yards in relief duty but set a Broncos team record for 120 yards rushing on 12 carries against the Chicago Bears. He would assume the same role in 1977, backing up Craig Morton. The highlight of Weese's career came in the form of Super Bowl XIII against the Dallas Cowboys at the conclusion of the season.

All the hype and storylines around the Super Bowl were built upon the rivalry between former Dallas Cowboys teammates Roger Staubach and Craig Morton, now facing off against each other in the biggest game of their careers. However, Morton performed so poorly in the game that he was pulled in favor of Weese in the third quarter. The Broncos ultimately lost, but Weese recorded 22 yards passing and 26 yards rushing while playing the second half in front of the nation.

The next season (1978), Weese finally got and won his first NFL start. Weese was named the Broncos starter for the 1979 season, in which he started six games, winning four of them, but a sever knee injury later in the year would abruptly end his career. In four NFL seasons, Weese completed 143 of 251 passes for 1,887 yards and 7 touchdowns. He also rushed for 362 yards on 69 carries with 5 touchdowns.

Weese remained in Denver and became an accountant. Sadly, Weese died at the age of forty-four in 1995 after a battle with bone cancer.

WILHELM, ERIK

He set Beavers records. He set Prowlers records. He played for the Bengals, Cardinals, Bengals again, Jets, Bengals again, and Avengers. He was Erik Wilhelm, and his story is one of true passion and the refusal to give up.

Wilhelm began his high school career at Gladstone High School outside Portland, Oregon. As a junior in 1982, he earned Class AA Oregon All-State team. After moving across town to Lakeridge High School in 1983, Wilhelm had another great year his senior season, worthy of a scholarship offer from nearby Oregon State.

Wilhelm won the starting job as a freshman and started off hot with a couple wins. While completing almost 60 percent of his passes, Wilhelm had 890 yards and 9 TDs. After leading the Beavers to their best start in eighteen years,

Wilhelm suffered a season-ending injury, and the team won only one more game. In his sophomore season, Wilhelm would lead the country with 470 pass attempts and 283 completions and the Pac-10 conference with 2,871 yards. Unfortunately, with his gunslinging ways, he led the conference with 17 interceptions as well. However, he was a bright star in an otherwise dismal OSU football program.

In his junior season, Wilhelm more than doubled his touchdown output from the year prior, throwing 17 scores. Again, he lead the Pac-10 conference with 423 pass attempts, 226 completions, and 2,736 yards. The Beavers team, however, didn't lead the conference in anything but losses and standings. In his 1988 senior season, Wilhelm proved he could thrive in the West Coast offense. His 442 pass attempts and 275 completions led the Pac-10 for the third consecutive year. He finished second in the conference with 2,896 yards passing and completed a personal best, 62.2 percent of his passes. Wilhelm led the Beavers to a 4–6–1 record, the school's best win ratio since 1971.

Wilhelm set numerous passing records at Oregon State and finished his college career at 870 completions for 9,393 yards with 52 TDs and a Pac-10-record 61 interceptions. Aside from the picks, his numbers and arm strength were plenty to get noticed by NFL scouts.

Wilhelm was drafted in the 3rd round of the 1989 NFL Draft by the Cincinnati Bengals. With the recent success of the West Coast offense, many teams were now looking for pro-style quarterbacks who could manage those offensive systems, especially quarterbacks with accuracy and arm strength. Wilhelm fit that mold perfectly and was slated to be a skilled and proficient backup to Boomer Esiason, who was the previous season's league MVP (1988). Like Esiason, Wilhelm was left handed and so would be an easier adjustment for receivers and linemen, had he been needed. Unfortunately for Wilhelm, Esiason was very durable, and Wilhelm would see limited playing time in his rookie season. In fact, Wilhelm wouldn't get the call for his first start until his third season in 1991. In his first three years, Wilhelm saw action in seventeen games, passing for 759 yards with 4 TDs and 4 INTs.

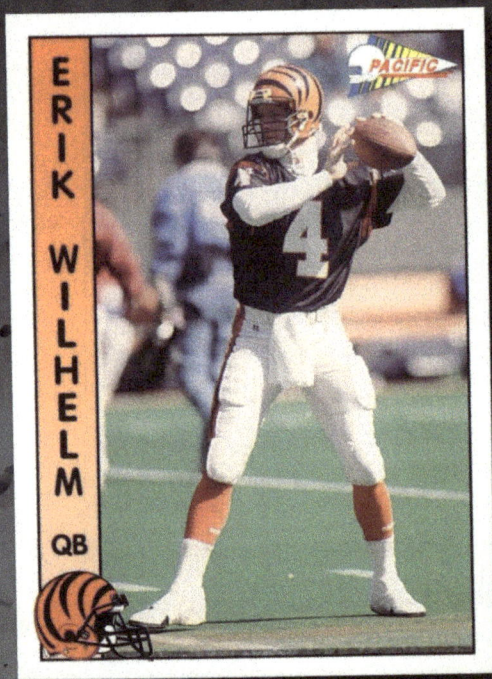

ERIK WILHELM QB

Wilhelm was released in 1992 and signed with the Phoenix Cardinals. He would be relegated to third string behind starter Chris Chandler and backup Timm Rosenbach, a fellow Pac-10 star he played against in college. Wilhelm did not see the field in 1992 and re-signed with the Bengals in 1993.

Starting stalwart Boomer was no longer a Bengal, but Wilhelm would find himself third on the depth chart behind David Klingler and veteran Jay Schroeder. Wilhelm only got into one game, completing 4 of 6 passes for 63 yards. With the arrival of Jeff Blake the following season, Wilhelm would, again, be third on the quarterback chart behind Blake and Klingler. The Bengals released Wilhelm in 1995.

Wilhelm would back up none other than Boomer Esiason with the Jets and not see any playing time. In 1996 the Bengals signed Wilhelm for a third time. Jeff Blake started all sixteen games, and Wilhelm only saw action in three, completing 7 of 13 passes for 90 yards with a touchdown and 2 interceptions. Wilhelm would never play in the NFL again, but his professional football career was far from over.

Wilhelm worked out hard. He knew he could play at a professional level and refused to give up his dream, so he worked out for three years. He played flag football and threw to his receiver friend, Chad Carlson, who formerly played in the CFL. Carlson convinced Wilhelm to try out with him for the Portland Prowlers of the new Indoor Professional Football League (IPFL). In 2000 Wilhelm joined the Prowlers and immediately won the starting quarterback spot.

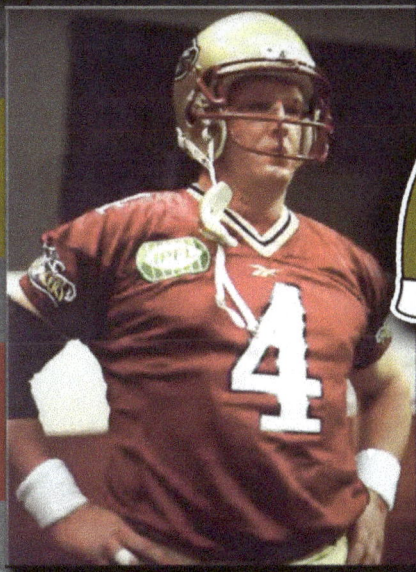

Wilhelm threw 62 touchdowns and led Portland to an 11–5 record and the IPFL Championship game. Portland lost the game to another former NFL quarterback, John Fourcade, and his Mississippi Fire Dogs. About his time in the IPFL, Wilhelm stated, "I'm enjoying it tremendously because it's guys coming together, bonding, and going for a common goal to win games and to learn an offense together, to practice together, to get beat up by the other team. Whether you have success or fail, you do it together. There's nothing that can really replace something like that. It's why guys play football. No matter if it's the NFL and you're getting paid a whole bunch of money or this league where you're getting beer and pizza money." *—interview from the article "One More Shot At Glory" in the Albany Democrat-Herald.*

Wilhelm moved to the Arena Football League (AFL) in 2001 and signed with the Los Angeles Avengers. He beat out former NFL alumni Todd Marinovich, Tony Graziani, and Jim Druckenmiller to become the starter. Wilhelm completed 142 of 269 passes for 1,687 yards with 23 TDs and 8 INTs. That would be Wilhelm's last season as a professional football player.

Wilhelm played professional football for a decade: eight seasons in the NFL, one year in the IPFL, and another in the AFL. After retiring from the game, he returned home to the Portland, Oregon, area to be near his family.

WILLIS, PETER TOM

Willis, the decade-long radio color analyst for Florida State University, was fired for being too truthfully analytical about the Seminoles' offensive woes. A rift developed between Willis and head coach Bobby Bowden when Willis said that Bobby's son, offensive coordinator Jeff Bowden, ran "a high school offense." Willis continued, telling the Tallahassee Democrat, "I don't know how you say things are going good (on offense) when they are not."

Willis attended Florida State but did not start until his senior season. When Willis was a sophomore, Danny McManus took the Seminoles to within a field goal of the National Championship, and in Willis's junior season, Chip Ferguson led them to an 11–1 record and a top-five finish. With both competitors

gone for his senior year, Willis earned the starting spot and had to perform well because his underclassmen were also brimming with talent. Charlie Ward and Casey Weldon were both chomping at the bit to get some playing time. Willis did not disappoint and led the Seminoles to a no. 3 national ranking and a 41–17 victory over Nebraska in the Fiesta Bowl. Racking up one of the Seminoles' best quarterback seasons in history, Willis set fifteen school records in 1989. His 3,124 yards passing surpassed **Gary Huff** for most in a single season, and his 211 completions and six 300-yard games both set new single-season marks. Willis's 148.5 career passer rating set a new Florida State lifetime record as well.

Willis was drafted in the 3rd round of the 1990 NFL Draft by the Chicago Bears. He saw limited playing time in his first two seasons backing up starter Jim Harbaugh, attempting only 31 passes. With an injury to Harbaugh, Willis got his first two starts in 1992. After losing both and throwing twice as many interceptions as touchdowns, third-stringer **Will Furrer** got the remaining start. Willis saw action in five games in 1993, getting one more start. Sadly, he lost that decision, too, and threw 5 interceptions to 0 TDs. Willis was cut following the season, ending his NFL career with 1,261 yards and 6 touchdowns.

But Willis wasn't yet finished with professional football and decided to give it another shot a couple years later when he signed with the Tampa Bay Storm of the Arena Football League in 1997. Willis's 2,846 yards passing with 41 touchdowns helped lead the Storm to the semifinals where they would lose to the Arizona Rattlers by a field goal. The Rattlers then proceeded to beat Kurt Warner and his Barnstormers in ArenaBowl XI. The following season, Willis wouldn't stop at the playoff semifinals. He led the Storm to ArenaBowl XII where they lost to the Orlando Predators. Willis completed 255 of 425 passes for 3,411 yards and 70 TDs to earn second-team All-Arena for his efforts on the season. Willis triplicated his success in 1999 by leading the Storm to another playoff berth. He completed 238 of 417 passes for 3,233 yards and 65 TDs. After three incredible years in the AFL, Willis called it a playing career. He amassed 9,490 yards with 176 touchdowns and only 37 interceptions, taking Tampa by storm.

Directly after his playing career, Willis began a broadcast career back at his alma mater in 1998 that would span the next decade. He was also inducted into the Florida State University Sports Hall of Fame the same year.

Florida State

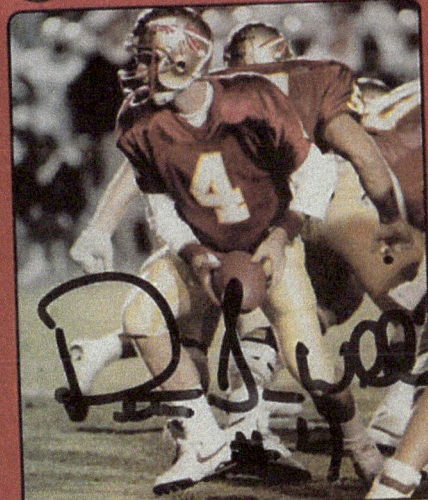

PETER TOM WILLIS

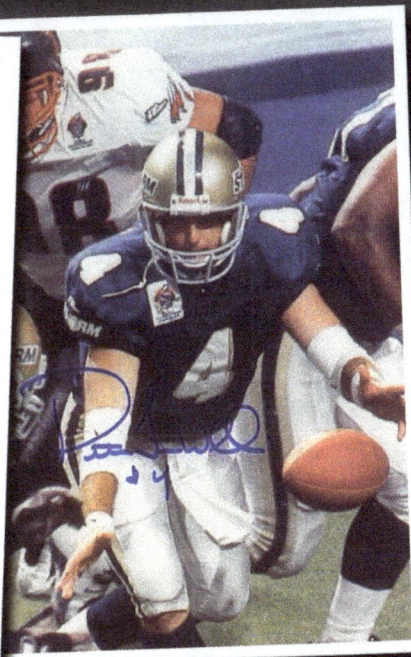

PETER TOM WILLIS

WOODLEY, DAVID

Woodley's tale is the juxtaposition of glorious tragedy. He made it to the elite level of professional football but burned out hard when it was over.

Born in Shreveport, Louisiana, David was the fifth of seven Woodley children. David's father, John, was an alcoholic, which caused David to become introverted. David fought through daily struggles to become a three-year starting quarterback at Byrd High School in Shreveport, earning All-State honors.

Woodley stayed in Louisiana to attend LSU. He shared time platooning as starter with Steve Ensminger. Being from LSU's home in Baton Rouge, Ensminger was the fan favorite, and fuel, but it would eventually eat away at him.

Woodley and Ensminger both

had good arms, but it was Woodley's legs that set him apart. As a junior, Woodley rushed for 398 yards and 5 touchdowns and ran for another 7 as a senior. He actually finished his college career with more rushing TDs (15) than passing (8). Woodley passed for 2,081 yards during his three years at LSU.

One of Woodley's brightest college highlights was leading the Tigers to the 1979 Tangerine Bowl, defeating Wake Forest 34–10 and earning the game's MVP honors.

As described in a wonderful article by Robert Marvi on profootballhistory.com, the pressure and expectations from competing at quarterback at a prominent football school, coupled with the boos and stress, caused Woodley to turn inward. He started drinking to numb the pain and deal with depression.

Nonetheless, Woodley's legs, quick release, and intelligence at the position attracted several NFL teams, and he was selected deep in the draft. With their perennial star, Bob Griese, aging and hobbling, the Miami Dolphins took Woodley as the 214th overall pick in the 18th round of the 1980 NFL Draft.

Woodley got his first start on week four of his rookie season but didn't do too well, completing only 4 of 15 passes and throwing 3 interceptions. Local newspapers chastised Woodley, and it affected him deeply. Griese would start again but soon injure his shoulder, making Woodley the regular starter thereafter. He had his ups and downs but was improving. During the week ten contest against the Rams, Woodley threw 3 passing TDs and scored another 2 on the ground. Woodley salvaged his rookie campaign enough to become the first

Dolphins rookie since his counterpart, Griese, to win the team's MVP. He finished the season with 14 touchdowns and was named to the NFL All-Rookie team.

Bob Griese retired the next season, and Woodley would start most of the games but split a lot of playing time with veteran backup Don Strock in a duo that would be known as "WoodStrock." Woodley passed for 2,470 yards with 12 TDs and 13 Interceptions in 1981, rushing for another 4 scores. Miami finished 11–4–1, but Woodley wasn't winning in his own mind. It was more like a repeat of his college days, and with his quiet, stand-offish demeanor, the outgoing Strock became the fan favorite.

In the 1982 season, shortened by the players' strike, Woodley fared well and made NFL history when he caught a TD pass against the Jets. Not many players have caught, thrown, and run for a touchdown all in the same season, making Woodley's a truly rare feat. The Dolphins would make it to the Super Bowl that season to face the Redskins, and what should have been a life-altering and exciting time in a player's career was

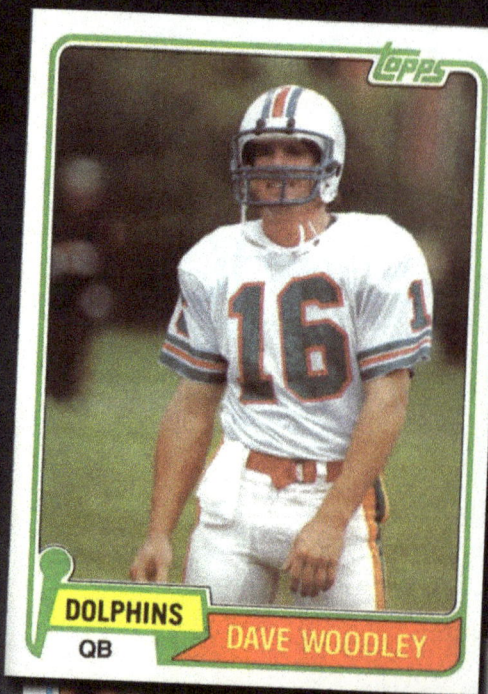

nothing but more stress for Woodley. At twenty-four years old, he was the youngest quarterback to ever start a Super Bowl. When the players went out the night before, he stayed in his hotel room smoking cigarettes. Woodley came into the game sharp, throwing a 76-yard TD to Jimmy Cefalo, but the second half was a different story. Woodley went into arguably the worst slump of his life and didn't complete a single pass. Maimi's offense subsequently fell apart, and they lost the championship.

The Super Bowl loss would start Woodley on a downward spiral, and he was soon benched in 1983 in favor of rookie Dan Marino. Dan the Man's legend was born, and Woodley didn't see the field again. Miami traded Woodley the next season to Pittsburgh, where he would be replacing a fellow Shreveport native and legend Terry Bradshaw.

Bradshaw's shoes proved very big and hard to fill. Woodley would start but also end up splitting time with backup Mark Malone. With poor performances and several concussions, Woodley again found himself on the bench and forgotten. Malone would start the 1985 season as well, and the negativity, bad press, and feeling of not living up to expectations continued to take their toll on Woodley's psyche.

Woodley was going to quit before the start of a game in 1985, but his wife talked him out of it over the phone just before kickoff. He ended up having one of the best games of his career, throwing 3 touchdowns and rushing for one more. In 1986 coach Chuck Noll informed Woodley that he would not be starting once again. Woodley couldn't take the weight of it anymore and decided to retire instead, giving up hundreds of thousands of dollars. He was only twenty-seven. Woodley completed 687 of 1,300 passes for 8,558 yards with 48 passing and 11 rushing touchdowns in his NFL career.

Football was Woodley's one joy that brought him meaning and happiness. Without it he went downhill quickly. His drinking worsened, and it caused a divorce. Former teammates tried to reach out to him to no avail.

For a brief time, Woodley pulled himself together to get a degree, and he did color commentary on the radio for his old high school. But his drinking got so bad that Woodley needed a liver transplant in 1992, which inevitably put him in financial ruin.

Perhaps knowing his end was near in 2002, Woodley began to reconnect with some old teammates and even apologized to his ex-wife for the pain he caused her. Woodley battled the demons of addiction and depression, and the demons got the best of him. Woodley died in 2003 from alcohol-related complications.

Woodley's life was a tale of triumph and tragedy.

ZOLAK, SCOTT

Zolak had early motivation to be a quarterback. As a child, he was the water-boy for Ringgold High School where his father coached, and the quarterback gave him a football, which he cherished and rubbed for luck before every game. That quarterback at the time was a guy named Joe Montana. Zolak followed in Montana's steps to become the starting quarterback for Ringgold High and lettered four times.

Zolak enrolled at the University of Maryland. He sat out his freshman season and would wind up at third string behind Dan Lanning and future NFL mainstay Neil O'Donnell the next season. Zolak challenged O'Donnell for the starting job his

Z

job his junior season, but the senior O'Donnell won out, and Zolak just saw relief action in eight games. 1990 rolled around, and Zolak was finally starting as a senior. In his first start, Zolak completed 28 of 46 passes for 303 yards and 2 TDs. Although he was sacked twenty-three times in a four-game stretch, Zolak won the Atlantic Coast Offensive Player of the Week four times. He led his Terrapins to a tie in the Independence Bowl.

Zolak was selected in the 4th round (84th overall) of the 1991 NFL Draft by the New England Patriots. He spent his rookie year as the third-string quarterback behind Hugh Millen and Tommy Hodson and did not see any playing time. 1992 started out with the same quarterback trio lineup, but when starter Hugh Millen was injured, Zolak became the primary backup to Hodson. With a 0–9 start, the Patriots looked to shake things up and gave Zolak his first start later in the season. He completed 20 of 29 passes for 261 yards and 2 touchdowns, leading New England to their first win of the year and earning himself AFC Player of the Week. Zolak led the Patriots to another victory the following week but struggled after that and lost the starting job. He finished with a 2–2 record and was responsible for the Patriots' only wins as they finished 2–14.

With the arrival of new head coach Bill Parcels in 1993, the Patriots rearranged their quarterback lineup and drafted Drew Bledsoe. Zolak was back to third string and saw brief playing time in three games, attempting only 2 passes. 1994 was much of the same. Zolak only attempted 8 passes while backing up Drew Bledsoe, who started every game once again. When Bledsoe separated his shoulder in 1995, Zolak got the call to start and passed for 252 yards and a TD but lost the game, then he was relegated to backing up when Bledsoe returned the next game. In 1996 Zolak beat out Jay Barker for the

Z

backup spot and saw action in three games, completing the only pass he threw. Although he tasted action in the playoffs, Zolak did not play in the Super Bowl XXXI loss to Green Bay. In 1998 Bledsoe was sidelined with an injury for a few games and Zolak made two starts, winning one and losing the other. He saw more playing time in relief work and in the playoffs, but his time as a Patriot would end after the season.

Zolak signed with the New York Jets in 1999 to compete with Ray Lucas as Vinny Testaverde's backup, but when veteran Rick Mirer was added to the roster, Zolak became expendable. He then signed with the Miami Dolphins as an emergency backup behind Damon Huard. Zolak saw the field one time and passed 0 for 4 in what would be his last NFL game.

Zolak worked out with the Detroit Lions in 2000 but called it a career after nine seasons in professional football. He began a broadcasting career as a host for *Patriots Gameday*. Zolak later became an analyst for CBS College Sports and radio broadcaster for the Patriots.

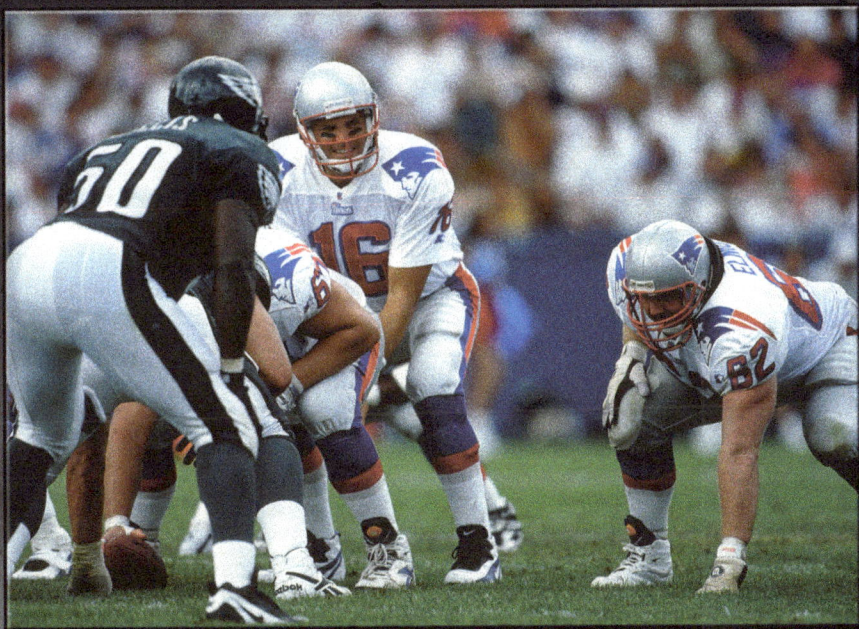

TO ALL THE QUARTERBACKS THAT GAVE
THEIR ALL TO THE GAME,

THANK YOU

www.ingramcontent.com/pod-product-compliance
Lightning Source LLC
Chambersburg PA
CBHW040246100426
42811CB00011B/1166